Ethnic Studies

Ethnic Studies

ISSUES
AND
APPROACHES

Philip Q. Yang

STATE UNIVERSITY OF NEW YORK PRESS

Published by
State University of New York Press

© 2000 State University of New York

For information, address the State University of New York Press,
State University Plaza, Albany, NY 12246

Marketing by Anne M. Valentine • Production by Bernadine Dawes

Library of Congress Cataloging-in-Publication Data

Yang, Philip Q.
    Ethnic studies : issues and approaches / Philip Q. Yang.
        p. cm.
    Includes bibliographical references and index.
    ISBN 0-7914-4479-1 (HC : alk. paper)—ISBN 0-7914-4480-5 (PB : alk. paper)
        1. United States—Ethnic relations—Study and teaching. 2. United States—Race
relations—Study and teaching. 3. Minorities—United States—Study and teaching.
4. Ethnology—United States—Study and teaching. 5. Ethnicity—United States—Study and
teaching. I. Title.

E184.A1 E845 2000
305.8'00973—dc21

                                                                                        99-047239

1   2   3   4   5   6   7   8   9   10

For my wife
Jianling Li
and my daughter
Ming Yang

BRIEF CONTENTS

DETAILED CONTENTS

FIGURES AND TABLES

FIGURES

TABLES

PREFACE

As race and ethnicity move to the center of scholarship and national dialogue, the literature in ethnic studies is growing on a daily basis. A preponderance of volumes that highlight the experiences of particular ethnic or racial groups already exists. Unparalleled by any that precedes it, this book focuses on major issues and social science approaches in ethnic studies.

As a multidisciplinary and interdisciplinary field, ethnic studies includes the approaches of the social sciences and the humanities, as well as other disciplines. Space limitations and the requisite sophisticated knowledge of all major fields preclude an encyclopedic coverage of all the approaches in this small volume. Hence, the focus here is on those social science approaches that best address the developing field of ethnic studies as a whole. Topics for this book were chosen for their centrality and for their currency in ethnic studies.

This book grew out of my experience of teaching Introduction to Ethnic Studies at California Polytechnic State University (Cal Poly), San Luis Obispo. When I started preparation for this course, I could not find an appropriate textbook, even after a thorough library search. I was forced to compile a reader for my students. Since most readings were not initially written for this course and were drawn from different sources and styles of publication, students often had difficulties with the readings, found the content inadequate, or complained about the repetition and inconsistency across readings. Compounding the problem were high copyright permission fees, which translated into a higher cost to the student. Sharing my frustration were my many colleagues who teach similar courses. Our common belief is that students of ethnic studies deserve a well organized, readable, and affordable text.

The academization and advancement of ethnic studies as a discipline also call for a book that addresses its important issues and approaches. While the past three decades have witnessed a tremendous growth in ethnic studies, ensuring its essential place in the academy, the scholarly merits of ethnic studies have largely been ignored. The lack of texts that systematically organize research issues and approaches in the field is one important reason. Although numerous volumes on particular ethnic or racial groups have been produced, we have not yet seen a major work that coherently threads together issues and perspectives in ethnic studies. Moreover, a recent move of the discipline toward a comparative emphasis gives prominence to its key issues. Thus, the further advancement of ethnic studies demands a work that systemizes its major issues as well as its theoretical and methodological approaches. This book seeks to answer that demand.

This book best serves as a convenient reference for researchers, teachers, and other professionals in ethnic studies and as a main or supplemental text for such courses as Introduction to Ethnic Studies, Theories and Methodologies of Ethnic Studies, Racial and Ethnic Relations, and the like. From the very beginning, I have envisioned a text with the following characteristics: First, distinguishing it from existing works on ethnic studies, this book is issue-oriented rather than group-oriented, though group experiences are used as examples to illustrate or assess theories. Second, rather than investigating issues in depth from a unidimensional approach, I have chosen to take a bird's-eye view of different approaches to the major issues discussed. Ethnic phenomena must be understood from different dimensions of human existence such as economic, political, social, psychological, historical, and so on. Third, more than a mere synopsis of the literature, this book also attempts, whenever possible, to shed light on integrated approaches. Finally, I have designed the book to be brief. Instructors then have the flexibility to use it as part of a course or in combination with other readings, and the cost to students is also minimized. Because of the space constraints, I have confined this work mainly to the context of the United States. Nevertheless, readers will find much broader global applications of the many issues and approaches discussed in this book.

I am grateful to the many people who have helped with the production of this book: To Robert Gish, Director of the Ethnic Studies Department at Cal Poly, who encouraged me to work on the project, read through the first draft of the manuscript, and provided valuable and constructive comments. To former students enrolled in my Introduction to Ethnic Studies course, who listened and reacted to many of the ideas in this book as they were formulated and refined. The suggestions and comments on the first draft of the manuscript from students in my Winter 1998 classes have especially enhanced the quality of the work. To the three anonymous reviewers who carefully read the manuscript and offered tremendous encouragement and precious comments. However, any errors in the contents remain with my own responsibility.

Thanks are also due to Tammy Mar, who helped prepare some tables and figures, and to Susan Stewart who assisted editorial fine-tuning. I acknowledge the Cal Poly Faculty Development Grant Program for the provision of release time and a grant, which facilitated the completion of this project.

At SUNY Press, I am indebted to Zina Lawrence, acquisition editor, for her enthusiasm for this project and her perseverance; to Nancy Ellegate, acquisition editor at SUNY Press, for her professionalism and great assistance during the critical stage of this project; to Alan Hewat for his fine editorial assistance; to Bernadine Dawes, production editor, for ensuring the quality of the book; and to Anne Valentine, marketing manager, for her meticulous work.

Finally, the support of my family has been indispensable. During the year of intensive manuscript writing, my mother-in-law, Wanlin Chen, took care of the bulk of the family chores and my daughter, Ming Yang, while my wife spent most of her time at UC Berkeley. My mother, Xuan Ma, has been a constant source of inspiration and support. This book is dedicated to my wife, Jianling Li, and to my daughter, Ming Yang, for their love and support.

CREDITS

Grateful acknowledgment is made to the following for the use of figures and tables:

Figures 5.1 and 5.2 are from Andrew Greeley's *Ethnicity in the United States: A Preliminary Reconnaissance*, and have been reprinted and/or adapted with permission from John Wiley and Sons, Inc., copyright © 1974.

Table 7.2 is reprinted with permission from *Sociology and Social Research* 66, no. 1, 1981, "A Half-Century of Social Distance Research: National Replication of the Bogardus' Studies" by Carolyn Owen, Howard Eisner, and Thomas McFaul.

Table 7.1 is reprinted with permission from *Sociology and Social Research* 70, no. 3, 1986, "College Student Stereotypes of Blacks and Jews on Two Campuses: Four Studies Spanning 50 Years" by Leonard Gordon.

PART I
BASICS OF ETHNIC STUDIES

CHAPTER 1

INTRODUCTION

Newcomers to the discipline of ethnic studies often ask, "What is ethnic studies?" Even for ethnic studies specialists, this question demands constant rethinking and reformulation because of the emerging nature of the discipline. This introductory chapter attempts to define ethnic studies and to describe its basics and essentials. A brief history of ethnic studies in the United States at the outset serves to provide the historical context for understanding and configuring the discipline. At the core of this chapter are a formal definition of ethnic studies, a description of its subfields, and a demarcation of the discipline in comparison with its neighboring fields. The final section of the chapter outlines the structure of the book.

BRIEF HISTORY OF ETHNIC STUDIES IN AMERICA

Although American scholars embarked on the study of ethnic groups and their interrelations a long time ago, ethnic studies as a discipline did not emerge until the late 1960s (Gutierrez 1994; Hu-DeHart 1993). Before then, there existed no ethnic studies programs and no ethnic studies faculty, and almost no ethnic studies courses were offered at universities and colleges. School curricula had remained unchanged since the beginning of the century and primarily reflected Eurocentric histories and views; they largely overlooked the histories, cultures, and perspectives of minority groups. Faculty and administrators of higher education were predominantly white males. Ethnic studies was not a concern of American society; ethnicity was viewed by the then-dominant paradigm of ethnic relations—assimilation theory—as a social problem that prevents the full assimilation of ethnic groups into the mainstream of society. The emphasis of American society at that time was on Americanization or assimilation into white Anglo-Saxon Protestant culture.

The turbulent 1960s witnessed waves of social movements and social unrest. The Civil Rights movement, which began in the 1950s, culminated in the mid-1960s, resulting in the enactment of the Civil Rights Act of 1964. More and more American people came to agree with the principle that all Americans, regardless of their race or ethnicity, should be treated equally, should have equal access to higher education, and should have their voices heard and their perspectives reflected in higher education. The women's movement arose in about the same period, adding its demand for equal rights and an equal voice to the foray. Anti-Vietnam War demonstrations erupted across the nation. Outside the United States, especially in Africa, Third World people were rising up against colonialism.

These movements inspired student activism on university campuses. In 1968, students at San Francisco State College (now San Francisco State University) formed a coalition of separate ethnic action groups known as the Third World Liberation Front. Students at UC Berkeley rallied for the creation of a Third World College. They rebelled against the status quo and denounced racism, sexism, and elitism. These events culminated in students' occupation of the administrative offices at both campuses, with a demand for fundamental changes in higher education (Hu-DeHart 1993). The movement soon spread to many other campuses throughout the country. Students of color, as well as their white supporters, demanded better access to higher education, changes in curricula to reflect their ethnic cultures and perspectives, recruitment of minority faculty, and establishment of ethnic studies programs.

As a result, ethnic studies programs were created in the late 1960s and the early 1970s as "fire insurance" to appease militant students (Hu-DeHart 1995). Among the pioneers were the School of Ethnic Studies at San Francisco State University and the Ethnic Studies Department at UC Berkeley. Following their lead, black, Asian American, Chicano/Chicana, and Native American studies programs mushroomed across the nation. Scholars began to pay greater attention to ethnic issues. Ethnic groups, especially minority groups, started to emphasize ethnic consciousness, ethnic identity, and ethnic pride. Slogans such as "Black is beautiful" and "Yellow is mellow" partly reflected this shift. Hyphenated terms indicating ethnic identities, such as African-American, Japanese-American, Mexican-American, and Jewish-American became buzzwords. Societal emphasis gradually shifted from assimilation toward ethnic distinctiveness. Ethnic studies as a discipline grew out of this historical context.

Joining this emerging discipline was a renewed interest in the study of white ethnic groups, especially Catholic groups (e.g., the Italians, the Irish), Jews, and Easter European groups (e.g., the Polish). Researchers who have written about this so-called "ethnic revival" (e.g., Alba 1990; Gans 1979; Kivisto 1989; Novak 1973; Waters 1990) found that even among white ethnic groups, ethnic identities and ethnic cultures did not die out, as evidenced by ethnic awareness, ethnic foods, ethnic languages, ethnic literatures, ethnic festivals, ethnic holidays, and ethnic customs, although they disagreed on the meanings and causes of this ethnic revival. By the late 1970s, a significant number of ethnic studies programs on European groups such as Armenians, Germans, Italians, Polish, Jewish, English, Welsh, Canadians, Czechs, Slavics, Ukrainians, Amish had appeared on the scene (see Washburn 1979). Hence, ethnic studies was not limited to the study of minority groups.

During the latter half of the 1970s, the demand for social justice that bred the Civil Rights movement waned significantly. Budgetary crises in the 1970s forced severe cutbacks in, and consolidation of, ethnic studies programs, and less than half of the existing programs survived into the 1980s. Furthermore, the politically inhospitable climate in the 1980s instigated a backlash against ethnic minority communities and a degradation of their concerns. On college and university campuses, racism was resurrected and racial tension intensified. Ethnic studies was at a low ebb.

Despite setbacks, the reorganization, reconceptualization, and redesign of ethnic studies programs revitalized the field. By the 1990s, ethnic studies as an academic discipline had grown stronger than ever before. One salient feature of this maturation has been the growing institutionalization of ethnic studies programs. Today, there are more than eight hundred ethnic studies programs and departments in the nation (Bataille, Carranza, and Lisa 1996, xiii). Several of the strongest comprehensive ethnic studies programs are housed in public research universities, especially in the West. The Comparative Ethnic Studies Department at UC Berkeley includes programs in Asian American studies, Chicano studies, and Native American studies and houses the first Ph.D. program in ethnic studies in the United States. Founded in 1990, the Department of Ethnic Studies at UC San Diego takes a comparative approach with no ethnic-specific programs and started its Ph.D. program in ethnic studies in academic year 1996–97. The Department of Ethnic Studies at UC Riverside offers a bachelor's degree in ethnic studies. The Department of American Ethnic Studies at the University of Washington, Seattle, was launched in 1985 by consolidating the existing programs in African American, Asian American, and Chicano studies. In a similar vein, the University of Colorado at Boulder created its Center for Studies of Ethnicity and Race in America (CSERA) in 1987 by merging the black studies and Chicano studies programs and adding new ones in Asian American and American Indian studies. In 1996 the Department of Ethnic Studies took the place of CSERA. Bowling Green State University has one of the oldest ethnic studies departments, founded in 1979 with a comprehensive and comparative orientation (Perry and Pauly 1988).

Many other research universities have departments, programs, or centers in one or more ethnic studies subfields. Examples include Harvard University, Brown University, Cornell University, the University of Pennsylvania, the University of Michigan, the University of Southern California, UCLA, and other UC campuses. In recent years, an increasing number of research universities outside the West have been making genuine efforts to establish ethnic studies programs, partly as a response to student demonstrations or demands. Many teaching universities have also installed ethnic studies departments or programs. Most notable is the twenty-three-campus California State University system. Almost all the Cal State campuses have either a comprehensive ethnic studies department or ethnic-specific departments or programs. Particularly, San Francisco State University houses the only College of Ethnic Studies in the country.

The institutionalization of ethnic studies programs has been accompanied by a growing number of faculty engaged in ethnic studies teaching and research. They are represented by several professional associations: The National Association for Ethnic Studies, the American Indian Studies Association, the National Association of African American Studies, the National Council for Black Studies, the Association for Asian American Studies, the National Association of Hispanic and Latin Studies, the National Association of Chicano Studies, and the Puerto Rican Studies Association.

The establishment of ethnic studies departments or programs and the recruitment of full-time faculty in ethnic studies have resulted in a prodigious amount of scholarship. Exemplary works encompass not only the well-known writings of Cornel West, Henry Louis Gates, and bell hooks, but also Ramon Guitierrez's highly original study of power and sexuality in colonial New Mexico; Michael Omi and Howard Winant's acclaimed book on racial formation; Ronald Takaki's and Sucheng Chan's outstanding narratives of Asian American history; and Ward Churchill's powerful defense of Native American sovereignty (Hu-DeHart 1993).

Increasingly, ethnic studies courses have become part of requirements for degree programs or an important portion of the curriculum. For example, successful completion of a number of ethnic studies courses is a graduation requirement for all undergraduate students at many UC and Cal State campuses, the University of Colorado at Boulder, Washington State University, etc. Enrollments in ethnic studies programs or courses have increased substantially. At UC Berkeley, the Ethnic Studies Department enrolls more than eight thousand students each year, and there are still about two thousand students on the waiting list (Hu-DeHart 1995).

Ethnic studies is gaining importance. This trend is likely to continue in the near future as American society becomes increasingly multiethnic and the ethnic composition of the college student population continues to diversify.

WHAT IS ETHNIC STUDIES?

Defining Ethnic Studies

Unlike well-established disciplines, there is a lack of consensus among ethnic studies scholars as to what ethnic studies is, or what constitutes the domain of ethnic studies. The National Association for Ethnic Studies defines ethnic studies as "an interdisciplinary voice for the continuing focused study of race and ethnicity," while others consider ethnic studies as the study of minority groups. Still others maintain that ethnic studies should focus on the intersection among race, ethnicity, gender, and class (Butler 1991).

In this book, I define *ethnic studies* as an interdisciplinary, multidisciplinary, and comparative study of ethnic groups and their interrelations, with an emphasis on groups that have historically been neglected. Elaboration of this definition is in order.

One important component of ethnic studies is the study of ethnic groups (defined in this chapter). Ethnic studies has profound interests in all social aspects of ethnic groups including their histories (e.g., origin, immigration, settlement, population changes, and socioeconomic transformations); cultures (e.g., languages, religions, customs, and popular cultures); institutions and organizations (e.g., family, school, economic institutions, political, social, and religious organizations); identities; experiences; and contributions to American culture and society.

Another vital component of ethnic studies is the study of intergroup relations, which include ethnic stratification; social, economic, and spatial interactions among ethnic groups; political power relations; cooperation and conflict between groups; ethnic prejudice and stereotype; ethnic discrimination; and so on. Individual ethnic groups may be better understood in comparison with and relationship to other ethnic groups. Ethnic studies seeks to capture the social, economic, cultural, and historical forces that shape the development of diverse ethnic groups and their interrelations.

Ethnic studies adopts interdisciplinary, multidisciplinary, and comparative approaches to knowledge. Ethnic studies scholars study ethnic groups and their interrelations through the combination and integration of perspectives of various disciplines, including anthropology, economics, history, political science, psychology, sociology, and humanities (e.g., philosophy, literature, linguistics, arts). That is why ethnic studies scholars are of very diverse backgrounds, including social scientists and humanities specialists. Furthermore, ethnic studies emphasizes a comparative approach in order to understand the history, culture, and institutions of ethnic groups in comparison with others. It focuses on common trends and experiences of different ethnic groups. In addition, ethnic studies uses some discipline-based methodologies of the social sciences and humanities. The methodologies of ethnic studies will be discussed in greater detail in chapter 2.

Currently, the emphasis of ethnic studies is on those ethnic groups that have been neglected in the past. Ethnic studies is concerned about all ethnic groups but focuses on minority groups such as African Americans, Asian Americans, Latinos, and Native Americans. A prime reason is that traditional disciplines have largely omitted the history, culture, and experience of minority groups and their contributions to the shaping of U.S. culture and society. This partly explains why ethnic studies departments or programs are normally staffed with specialists in specific minority groups or in comparative studies of ethnic groups. Ethnic studies seeks to recover and reconstruct the history of minority groups, to identify and credit their contribution to American culture and institutions, to chronicle their protest and resistance, and to establish alternative values and visions, cultures and institutions (Hu-Dehart 1993, 52).

Ethnic Group

Since ethnic group comprises an important constituent of ethnic studies, an accurate grasp of this concept is a prerequisite for further discussions. Scholars have not yet reached an agreement on how to define this seemingly straightforward concept. Two definitions are often used: a narrow definition and a broad definition. In terms of the narrow definition, an *ethnic group* is a group socially distinguished, by others or by itself, on the basis of its unique culture or national origin (see, for example, Feagin and Feagin 1993).

According to this definition, ethnic group is defined by cultural characteristics (e.g., language, religion, customs) or by national origin. Note that one of the two conditions—a unique culture *or* a unique national origin—suffices to define an ethnic group. For example, Italians are an ethnic group because they have a distinctive culture (e.g., the Italian language and Catholicism) or a unique national origin (i.e., Italy). Similarly, Germans, the Irish, the English, and the Polish are ethnic groups since each group has a unique national origin and/or culture. This determination can be made by others or by the group itself.

However, according to this definition, whites are not an ethnic group, because they lack a distinctive national origin and do not have a uniform culture. Whites consist of many nationality and cultural groups. You may wonder, if whites are not an ethnic group, what are they? The answer is that whites are a racial group. A *racial group* is a group socially distinguished, by others or by itself, on the basis of its unique physical characteristics such as skin color, eye color, hair color, facial structure, etc. Based on this definition, racial groups are defined physically *and* socially. Physical characteristics are the basis, but social determination is also important.

It should be emphasized that racial group categorization is mainly determined by the larger society and by the group itself rather than determined by purely biological factors. The change of racial identity of Asian Indians (not to be confused with American Indians) provides a good example. In the 1950 to 1970 U.S. censuses, Asian Indians were classified as whites. The primary reason was that the bulk of their ancestors were Caucasians (Aryans) who migrated about four thousand years ago from Europe to India where they subdued and intermarried with the natives of the India subcontinent—the Dravidians. As a result of the intermarriage between the tall, light-skinned Caucasians and the short, darker-skinned Dravidians as well as India's close location to the Equator, their descendants today have Caucasian features but darker skin. However, Asian Indians did not like to be classified as whites partly because this classification would not enable them to obtain an accurate count of their group population and to receive benefits entitled to minority groups. During the 1970s, the Association of Indians in America (AIA) intensively lobbied Congress, pressing for their reclassification (Sheth 1995). They argued that their ancestors came from Asia rather than from Europe. The Census Bureau held many hearings. Finally, starting in the 1980 U.S. census Asian Indians were reclassified as Asian Americans (Sheth 1995). The social construction of race or ethnicity will be further elaborated in chapter 3.

Currently, the U.S. government defines white Americans, black or African Americans, Asian Americans, and Native Americans as racial groups. However, the government does not define Hispanic Americans or Latinos as a racial group. Hispanics are defined solely in terms of the Spanish language rather than in terms of physical characteristics. Latinos are defined in terms of geographical origin—Latin America—rather than physical traits. In the 1980 and 1990 U.S. censuses, Hispanics were classified as culturally defined ethnic groups. As a result, they overlapped with whites, blacks, or Asians. For instance, some Cubans and Mexicans were also classified as whites, just as some Puerto Ricans were pigeonholed as blacks. Moreover, many people, as well as the federal government, use the terms *Latino* and *Hispanic* interchangeably.[1] A scrutiny of some basic facts reveals their nuance. Hispanics are to Americans who speak Spanish while Latinos refer to Americans whose origins can be traced back to Latin America. Note that not all people from Latin America speak Spanish; rather, a significant proportion of them speak English (e.g., those from Jamaica, Trinidad and Tobago, Guyana, the Bahamas, and Grenada),

---

1. Since Latino is a more popular term in the western United States, the Clinton administration decided in October 1997 that, in lieu of the term "Hispanic," "Hispanic or Latino" will be used for the Hispanic origin question on the 2000 census.

French (e.g., Haitians), Portuguese (e.g., Brazilians), and Dutch (e.g., Surinamese). Hence, Hispanics and Latinos are not synonymous. They do overlap to a great extent though. For example, Mexicans, Puerto Ricans, and Cubans—the three largest Latino groups—are all Hispanics. In this book the term Latino is preferred over the term Hispanics. Neither, however, may fit the definition of racial group.

The *broad* definition of *ethnic group* defines ethnic group as a group socially distinguished, by others or by itself, on the basis of its unique culture, national origin, or racial characteristics.

The only difference between the broad definition and the narrow definition lies in that the broad definition includes racial or physical characteristics as a determining factor. In light of the broad definition, ethnic groups include racial groups. Not all the three conditions (culture, national origin, or race) are required, and an ethnic group can be identified as long as one of the conditions is met. Hence, Italians, Germans, Jewish, Irish, English, Polish, and other European groups are ethnic groups; whites are also an ethnic group because they can be defined in terms of their racial characteristics. To distinguish between the two categories of ethnic groups, one may consider white Americans, black Americans, Latinos, Asian Americans, and Native Americans as *broad ethnic groups*, while Irish Americans, Chinese Americans, Mexican Americans, and so forth may be labeled *specific ethnic groups*.

Unless specified otherwise, this book uses the broad definition of ethnic group. The broad definition enables us to include both racial groups and culturally defined ethnic groups in our studies. Both racially defined ethnic groups and culturally defined ethnic groups are within the domain of ethnic studies. The broad definition can also help us understand the process of ethnic formation and thus avoid unnecessary altercation over the complex and sometimes overlapping boundaries between a culturally defined ethnic group and a racial group. For instance, African Americans are a racial group, but it can be argued that African Americans have also *become* an ethnic group through the creation of new African American culture, institutions, identity, and sense of peoplehood (Pitts 1982). Using the broad definition of ethnic group avoids the unneeded dispute over whether African Americans should be treated as a racial group or as an ethnic group. Furthermore, the broad definition is increasingly being used by scholars and the public. Although some researchers sense political overtones here, scholarly coherence and practical consideration probably overshadow the political tinge (see, for instance, Essed 1991, 28). Finally, the use of the broad definition of ethnic group can be traced back to the writings of such important scholars as Max Weber (1961), Milton Gordon (1964, 27), Nathan Glazer (1971), and Thomas Sowell (1981), to name just a few. Despite the embrace of the broad definition of ethnic group in this book, the term racial group is. also used from time to time in a context strictly related to racially defined ethnic groups.

SUBFIELDS OF ETHNIC STUDIES

In the United States, ethnic studies currently consists of several subfields: African American studies or black studies, Asian American studies, Hispanic and/or Latino studies, and Native American studies. All of these subfields share some common concerns, assumptions, and principles, but each subfield has its special interest in a particular minority group. African American studies, for instance, focuses on the experience of African Americans and their relations with other groups. The most organized fields within Latino studies are Chicano/a studies and Puerto Rican studies, the former having an emphasis on Americans of Mexican descent. There are further divisions within some of these subfields. Chinese American studies, Japanese American studies, Filipino American studies, and Korean American studies are some examples of such divisions within Asian American studies.

These subfields are relatively autonomous. Each has its own constituency. Each is represented by at least one national professional association, such as the American Indian Studies Association, the National Association of African American Studies, the National Council for Black Studies, the Association for Asian American Studies, and the National Association of Hispanic and Latin Studies.[2] Each organization convenes an annual meeting. All organizations have their own publications.

In the past three decades, the combination of the subfields has generated numerous volumes of commendable caliber on particular ethnic groups. The present book does not seek to duplicate this endeavor and therefore devotes no special chapters to particular ethnic groups. It does, however, use the experience of particular ethnic groups as illustrations. The reader interested in specific groups is referred to the following texts: John Franklin and Alfred Moss Jr.'s *From Slavery to Freedom*, and Alphonso Pinkney's *Black Americans* on African Americans; Ronald

2. These associations often proclaim their domains to be independent disciplines.

Takaki's *From a Different Shore* and Sucheng Chan's *Asian Americans: An Interpretive History* on Asian Americans; Joan Moore and Harry Pachon's *Hispanics in the United States*, Rodolf Acuna's *Occupied America: A History of Chicanos*, Clara Rodriguez's *Puerto Ricans: Born in the U.S.A.*, and Jose Llanes's *Cuban Americans: Masters of Survival* on Latinos; and Annette Jaimes's *The State of Native America* and Matthew Snipp's *American Indians: The First of This Land* on Native Americans.

WHAT ETHNIC STUDIES IS NOT

Increasingly, traditional boundaries of disciplines are blurred. Nevertheless, certain confines do exist in order to define a discipline, at least until a greater integration of disciplines arrives. This section seeks to briefly demarcate ethnic studies from other disciplines where confusion about its boundaries often arises.

Ethnic studies is not international area studies. Often students and laymen mistake international area studies for ethnic studies. For instance, "Asian American studies" is often mixed up with "Asian studies." The Asian American Studies program at UC Berkeley had to post a note outside its office, proclaiming that "This is Asian American Studies Program, NOT Asian Studies Program." Similarly, distinctions between African American studies and African studies and between Latino studies and Latin America studies seem less palpable to outsiders. In general, area studies focuses on a particular region or country outside the United States and its relations with the United States, while ethnic studies centers on a particular group in America that originates from a region or country. The former is internationally oriented whereas the latter is domestic in orientation. Sharp distinctions notwithstanding, linkages and overlapping between the two fields do exist. For instance, ethnic studies pays attention to how conditions in the country of origin and its relations with the U.S. affect the status and experience of the ethnic group in America from that area, and area studies is also interested in the impact of the ethnic group in the U.S. on its country of origin. Because of the connections between countries of origin and experiences of ethnic groups in America as well as the need for cross-national comparison of ethnic relations, ethnic studies also demands an international component to its curriculum.

Ethnic studies does not equate with cultural studies, though the two disciplines do overlap to some extent. Emerging in the 1950s in Great

Britain, cultural studies is a field that has continuously shifted its interests and focus (During 1993, 1–25). A main difference is that cultural studies emphasizes the culture of a society, which may include ways of life, cultural forms, cultural industries, cultural markets, cultural products, cultural policies, and subcultures, whereas ethnic studies focuses on ethnic groups (including their cultures as well as their histories and social institutions) and intergroup relations.

Ethnic studies and women's studies should have different emphases. Both ethnic studies and women's studies grew out of the 1960s and share similar concerns of achieving equality between the sexes or among ethnic groups. Some ethnic studies scholars underscore the importance of researching the intersection of race, ethnicity, gender, and class. While this is legitimate, women's studies also places a great emphasis on the intersection among race, ethnicity, gender, and class. In spite of common interests, a division of labor between the two disciplines ought to be made. Naturally, ethnic studies should focus on the ethnic dimension while women's studies should devote more effort to the gender dimension, even when both deal with the junction of the multiple dimensions.

Ethnic studies differs from other disciplines of social sciences and humanities in its basic methodologies. Other disciplines of social sciences and humanities study issues that concern ethnic studies scholars, such as ethnic stratification, ethnic interactions, ethnic prejudice and discrimination, etc. However, ethnic studies differs from those disciplines in that it uses interdisciplinary, multidisciplinary, and comparative approaches while those disciplines mainly rely on discipline-bound methodologies.

Some people outside ethnic studies tend to equate ethnic studies with political activism. Undeniably, ethnic studies originated from student political movement. Nevertheless, as it has evolved, ethnic studies cannot and should not be characterized as political activism, demonstration, protest, or the like. Ethnic studies is a scientific inquiry of ethnic groups and their interrelations. It pursues knowledge that will advance the interests of traditionally underprivileged ethnic groups and will help achieve eventual equality among all ethnic groups.

STRUCTURE OF THE BOOK

Ethnic Studies: Issues and Approaches consists of three parts and fifteen chapters. Part I, Basics of Ethnic Studies, includes two chapters. Following the current introductory chapter, chapter 2 acquaints the reader with methodologies of ethnic studies. To lay a foundation for the basic methodologies of ethnic studies, this chapter first introduces a number of important disciplinary methods used by ethnic studies researchers, such as field research, survey research, experiment, and content analysis. It then focuses on the overarching methodologies of ethnic studies— interdisciplinarity, multidisciplinarity, and comparativeness—with an emphasis on their characteristics, advantages, and disadvantages in comparison to traditional disciplinary methodologies. The chapter also briefly discusses discourse analysis, which is gaining recognition in ethnic studies.

Part II, Major Issues in Ethnic Studies, comprises eleven chapters. Chapter 3 focuses on competing theoretical perspectives on the nature and basis of ethnicity. These theories are categorized into three schools of thought: the primordialist school, the constructionist school, and the instrumentalist school. Specific theories within each school are analyzed and evaluated. The emphasis of this chapter is the presentation of my own approach, which integrates the contesting theories of ethnicity.

Chapter 4 considers ethnic stratification, a very common phenomenon in societies consisting of different ethnic groups and a central issue in ethnic studies. This chapter defines some basic concepts relating to ethnic stratification, describes ethnic stratification among human societies, outlines preconditions for its emergence, and delves into its origins. Several theoretical perspectives on ethnic stratification including the social-Darwinian approach, the social-psychological approach, the functionalist approach, the conflict approach, and the Donald Noel hypothesis are reviewed. It also examines the genesis of ethnic stratification between blacks and whites, between Indians and whites, and between Chicanos and whites in the United States.

In an ethnically stratified society, how do different ethnic groups adapt to one another, or what are the processes and outcomes of ethnic interaction or adaptation? Chapter 5 seeks to answer this question in the context of the United States. The chapter sets the stage for discussion by briefly reviewing the history of immigration to the United States. The pivot then shifts to a discussion of various approaches to ethnic adaptation, including assimilation theory, melting-pot theory, cultural pluralism theory, the ethnogenesis perspective, the internal colonialism perspective, and the class approaches. Finally, the chapter addresses the issue of interethnic unity versus separation.

Chapter 6 discusses ethnic differences in socioeconomic achievement. The chapter first presents empirical evidence on ethnic differences in socioeconomic achievements and then explores the determinants of these differences. Two categories of explanations are assessed: (1) Internal explanations, such as the biological argument, the cultural explanation, the social class approach, and the immigrant argument; and (2) external or structural explanations, such as the discrimination argument, the economic restructuring perspective, and the contextual perspective. The final section seeks a synthesis of the existing approaches.

The next three chapters consider interrelated topics of ethnic prejudice, ethnic discrimination, and racism, which shape ethnic stratification, ethnic adaptation, and socioeconomic achievement. Ethnic prejudice is the topic of chapter 7. This chapter begins with defining the concept of ethnic prejudice and its three dimensions. It proceeds with a review of empirical evidence on changes in ethnic prejudice in America. The focus of the chapter then turns to the examination of theories of ethnic prejudice, such as biological explanations, psychological theories, social learning theory, and conflict theory. The chapter closes with a synthesis of competing theories.

As a continuation of the previous chapter, chapter 8 is devoted to ethnic discrimination. Discussions include the concept of ethnic discrimination; various types of ethnic discrimination; and explanations of ethnic discrimination, including the prejudice hypothesis, functional/gain theory, class conflict theory, and social pressure theory. The chapter concludes with a discussion of the relationship between ethnic prejudice and ethnic discrimination.

Chapter 9 centers on racism, which is overlapped with ethnic prejudice and discrimination. While ethnic prejudice and discrimination apply to circumstances involving broadly defined ethnic groups in general, racism appertains to contexts strictly involving racial groups. This chapter examines the evolution of the concept "racism," presents a formal definition of this concept and its dimensions, analyzes racism in the English language and in American social institutions, and finally considers its effects on minorities and white Americans.

Chapter 10 analyzes ethnic segregation, an important dimension of ethnic interaction. The chapter provides an introduction to the concept and dimensions of ethnic segregation. The core of the chapter is residential segregation—the most common type of segregation that remains pervasive today. Discussions include measures, levels and trends, causes, and consequences of residential segregation. School segregation, which is still significant in American society, is also examined.

Ethnic interaction may not always result in assimilation or integration, and oftentimes it leads to ethnic conflict. Chapter 11 considers this facet of ethnic relations. The chapter first proposes a definition of ethnic conflict and delineates its various forms. The emphasis then switches to major theories of ethnic conflict, including cultural-clash explanation, human ecology theory, competition theory, the ethnic inequality argument, and class theory. It also analyzes Korean-black conflict in order to shed light on the causes of interminority antagonism. Efforts are also made to outline a more inclusive theory of ethnic conflict. The chapter discusses the scope, trend, and causes of "hate crime" against minorities as well.

Chapter 12 addresses ethnicity and politics, a topic that is important but inadequately addressed in the existing literature. This chapter analyzes ethnic differentiation in political party affiliation, political ideology, voting behavior, and political representation in government, and factors that influence differential power across ethnic groups.

Chapter 13 attempts to synopsize the burgeoning literature on the intersections and workings of race, class, and gender. The chapter highlights analytical approaches to the relationships among race, class, and gender, how the tripolar dimensions interlock to affect gender roles, work, power status, and sexuality, and how the triplicity interacts with social institutions.

Part III, Social Action Agendas and Future of Ethnic Studies, contains two chapters. Chapter 14 discusses current issues in ethnic studies that demand social actions, such as affirmative action and Proposition 209, illegal immigration and Proposition 187, the immigration debate, bilingual education and Proposition 227, and the English-Only movement. The pros and cons of each of these issues are presented and assessed.

The final chapter explores issues that are vital for the future development of ethnic studies. These include institutionalization of ethnic studies, academization versus politicization of ethnic studies, multiculturalism and ethnic studies, the study of whiteness and ethnic studies, and ethnic diversity and national unity.

CHAPTER 2

METHODOLOGIES OF ETHNIC STUDIES

It has largely been taken for granted that interdisciplinarity is the basic methodology of ethnic studies. However, what does interdisciplinarity mean? How does it relate to and differ from multidisciplinarity? What is the role of comparativeness in ethnic studies? What is comparative methodology? What are the comparative analytical strategies that can be used in ethnic studies? These questions have seldom been systematically addressed. This chapter provides a brief, yet comprehensive discussion of these important questions in ethnic studies methodologies.*

Interdisciplinarity, multidisciplinarity, and comparativeness are the overarching methodologies of ethnic studies. Nevertheless, this chapter begins with a brief introduction of several influential, traditional disciplinary methods, not only because they are still used extensively by ethnic studies scholars, but also because these methods provide indispensable background for understanding the ensuing interdisciplinary and multidisciplinary approaches that represent the most salient methodologies in ethnic studies. The reader who is familiar with these disciplinary methods may skip them and jump directly to the next section. The chapter then discusses interdisciplinary, multidiciplinary, and comparative method-

---

*While it is essential to include the entire chapter for courses such as Theories and Methodologies of Ethnic Studies, courses such as Introduction to Ethnic Studies may just highlight the key points of this chapter without going into technical details.

ologies, which constitute the kernel of the present chapter. The thrust of the discussion is on their basic characteristics, advantages, and disadvantages. The chapter also provides a terse introduction to discourse analysis, a method with a multidisciplinary nature which is gaining popularity among ethnic studies scholars, especially among humanities specialists.

TRADITIONAL DISCIPLINARY METHODS

Ethnic studies scholars have continued to use traditional disciplinary methods. In this section, a number of widely known methods such as field research, experiment, survey research, and content analysis is discussed. For a more in-depth examination of traditional methods, interested readers should consult texts in social science methodologies (e.g., Babbie 1995; Bailey 1994).

Field Research/Ethnography

Field research is a method that involves observations of social events or processes in a natural setting. Anthropologists are especially associated with this method and credited with its development as a scientific technique. The term *field research* is often used interchangeably with the term *ethnographic study* or *ethnography*.[1] Sometimes it is also referred to as observational studies, although observational studies could include observations in labs as well as in natural settings (Bailey 1994).

Several salient characteristics of field study are noteworthy. Field research occurs in a natural environment or the so-called "field," and the researcher imposes very little structure upon the setting. Observation is the most important way of data collection in field research. Observation includes two basic types: participant and nonparticipant. In participant observation, the researcher is a regular participant in the activities being observed. In nonparticipant observation, the researcher does not participate in group activities but simply acts as an outside observer. In praxis, participant observation is the most typical technique used in field research. Data produced by field research are qualitative.

---

1. Ethnography is a primary method used by cultural anthropologists to study relatively primitive cultures, but increasingly it is being used to analyze subcultural groups in America. The chief goal of ethnography is to describe a culture or subculture, including languages, customs, norms and values, religious ceremonies, and laws.

In a typical field study, the researcher normally follows these steps: gain entry into the field, develop rapport with members of the group being observed, observe events, write field notes, and analyze data. One classic example of field research is Herbert Gans's study (1962) of an inner-city Boston neighborhood called the West End and especially the native-born Italians who lived there. Gans, a sociologist and urban planner of upper-level background, moved into the working-class neighborhood in October 1957 and lived there for eight months. He used its stores, services, institutions, and other facilities as much as possible; attended as many meetings and gatherings as he could; visited neighbors and other West Enders; interviewed leaders, officers, and staff in community agencies and institutions, as well as other informants; and observed all the changes in the neighborhood. Gans recorded his data in field notes and placed them in a diary. He later analyzed them and produced a report.

Compared to other methods, field research can gather data on nonverbal behavior, can be conducted in a natural setting, and can follow changes over time. Limitations of field study include lack of control over study setting, difficulties of quantifying and coding data, small sample size, lack of ability to generalize findings to other settings, and lack of anonymity when studying sensitive issues.

Experiment

A popular method used by psychologists is experimentation. *Experiment* is a highly controlled method that seeks to establish a causal relationship between independent and dependent variables. A *variable* is any characteristic whose values vary from one case to another. A *dependent variable* is a characteristic whose values change as the values of independent variables vary. An *independent variable* is a characteristic whose values are independent of (or not affected by) values of other variables.

Unlike field research, experiment usually occurs in the laboratory. The goal of an experiment is to test whether empirical evidence supports a hypothesis about the relationship between one or more independent variables and one or more dependent variables. An experiment normally involves three steps: (1) the dependent variable is measured; (2) the dependent variable is exposed to the effects of the independent variable; and (3) the dependent variable is measured again to see if any changes have occurred.

In an ideal or true experiment, the experimenter can exercise several types of control. First, he/she has control over the environment for conducting the experiment and can control other extraneous factors that may influence the experimental outcomes. Second, the experimenter is able to control the assignments of subjects to the experimental group and the control group(s) through matching or randomization. Third, the experimenter can control the independent variable, also called an *experimental stimulus* (e.g., a video deemed to reduce racial prejudice). He or she can physically control the stimulus and administers the stimulus to the experimental group but not to the control group. Finally, the experimenter can measure the values of the dependent variable before administering the independent variable (the pretest) and after administering it (the posttest). The differences between pretest score and posttest score indicate the effect of the independent variable on the dependent variable.

An example should help illustrate how an experiment is conducted and used in ethnic studies. In a hypothetical study of antiblack prejudice, the researcher hypothesized that antiblack prejudice is in part caused by a lack of knowledge of black history. The aim of the experiment is to test whether this hypothesis is true. In this study, antiblack prejudice is the dependent variable (effect), and exposure to black history is the independent variable (cause). The researcher randomly selected subjects and assigned them to the experimental group and the control group. The use of the control group allows researchers to control effects of experiment itself and other extraneous factors. At the beginning of the experiment, each group of subjects was asked to fill out a questionnaire about their attitudes toward blacks (pretest). Then, a black history film (experimental stimulus) was shown to the experimental group but not to the control group. After the experimental group watched the film, *both* the experimental group and the control group were given the same questionnaire again (posttest). Responses to the posttest would allow the researcher to measure the later extent of antiblack prejudice for each subject and the average prejudice level of each group as a whole. If the experimental group showed a lower level of prejudice after the second administration of the questionnaire, we could conclude that the film indeed reduces antiblack prejudice, or more generally, exposure to black history does affect prejudice toward blacks. However, if the level of prejudice did not change significantly, we would conclude that the film does not have a significant effect on antiblack prejudice. This example is a typical experiment. In practice, there are a variety of experimental designs and techniques for doing experiments. For further details, please read the texts by Bailey (1994) and Babbie (1995).

Major advantages of experiments include: first, experiment is the best method in social sciences for establishing causation; second, it exercises rigorous control and reduces chances of error caused by extraneous factors; third, it provides the opportunity to observe changes over time; and fourth, the experiment is relatively easy to replicate.

Experiment has some disadvantages as well: first, total control in a natural setting is impossible; second, lab settings may be artificial; third, sample size of an experiment is usually small; and last, many questions on a massive scale or related to millions of people (e.g., social movements, urbanization, migration, economic cycle) are simply beyond the reach of experiments.

Survey Research

Survey research is most prevalent in such disciplines as sociology, political science, etc. *Survey* is a research method in which respondents provide answers to a series of questions or items. Surveys are particularly useful when answers to specific questions cannot be obtained through direct observations, such as racial attitudes, beliefs, and private lives of individuals. Data from surveys can be used in descriptive studies or explanatory studies.

Survey research entails the use of sample characteristics to infer population characteristics. A *population* is the total collection of all cases or units, which may be people, groups, organizations, geographic units, and societies. Each unit in the population is called a *sampling element*. A *sample* is a subset of the population. Probability sampling (also called random sampling) techniques such as simple random sampling, systematic sampling, stratified sampling, and cluster sampling are often used to ensure the equal chance of each case in the population to be selected and therefore the representation of the sample.

The main instrument of survey research is *questionnaire*, which is a series of questions or items to which respondents are asked to respond. Information on responses to the questionnaire could be obtained through mail (self-administered survey), personal interview, telephone interview, or computer assisted telephone interview. Examples of survey research include Gallup polls, the General Social Survey, and the National Longitudinal Study of Youth.

Unlike experimentation, survey research cannot directly establish a causal relationship between variables; as a correlational analysis it can only infer causation. Survey research cannot manipulate independent variable and environment; all it can do is statistical control. Survey research is usually cross-sectional, and results reflect conditions or opinions at a specific point in time.

However, compared to experimentation and field research, survey research has several advantages: (1) It permits the surveys of large populations using questionnaire. Sample size of a survey is normally much larger than that for an experiment and a field study. (2) If properly operationalized, survey results allow generalization from sample to population. (3) It could deal with the relationships between many variables and answer many questions at the same time.

Content Analysis

While field research is a qualitative method, experiment and survey research are quantitative methods. *Content analysis* is somewhere in between. Content analysis is a technique that transforms the manifest, verbal, qualitative content of text into objective, systematic, and quantitative data for analysis. Content analysis involves the frequency counting of words, phrases, paragraphs, articles, books, and so forth.

Content analysis can be used to study virtually any form of communication such as books, journals, magazines, newspapers, poems, letters, speeches, songs, and paintings (Babbie 1995). It can be used to describe patterns of communication and trends in text content, to analyze tone, style, stance, and perspective of texts, and to test hypotheses using statistical techniques and transformed quantitative data. For instance, content analysis is a good tool to answer such questions as "How have stereotypes of American Indians in novels changed over time?" "Is racism still significant in the mass media today?" "Do politicians' speeches reflect resentments against minority groups?" and so on.

Normally, the researcher proceeds with the following procedures: (1) draw a sample of documents for analysis, (2) decide the unit of analysis (e.g., word, symbol, sentence, paragraph, theme, item), (3) construct a set of mutually exclusive and exhaustive categories, (4) count and record the frequencies of those categories, and (5) analyze the results of frequency and percentage distributions. If statistical analysis is involved, the researcher may use a coding scheme to convert data into numbers and then perform statistical testing.

Content analysis saves time and money for data collection since it relies on existing documents; it allows longitudinal analysis if documents for more than one point in time exist; and it does not affect the subject being studied since documents have already been produced. However, content analysis has some disadvantages. It is limited to the study of recorded communication. In addition, validity and representation of selected categories are often a problem in content analysis (Babbie 1995).

As texts become increasingly computerized in the form of e-mail or electronic documents, computerized content analysis is emerging as an alternative to traditional content analysis. Various computer programs are being developed to carry out content analysis (Stone and Weber 1992). Examples include text-processing programs, which count word frequencies; categorization programs, which seek to classify words into categories; and statistical programs, which analyze the patterns of words or other units of analysis.

INTERDISCIPLINARITY AND MULTIDISCIPLINARITY

Despite their utility, traditional disciplinary methods do not define ethnic studies methodologies. What distinguishes the methodologies of ethnic studies from those of other disciplines is interdisciplinarity and multidisciplinarity because ethnic studies involves multiple disciplines of the social sciences and humanities.

As we know, monodisciplinarity is the methodology of *monodisciplinary research*, which involves the use of particular approaches of a single discipline. For example, field study dominates anthropological research; survey research overshadows other methods in sociology; psychology uses experiment. Monodisciplinary research aims at understanding specific subject matters using the conceptual frameworks and methods of a particular discipline.

In contrast, *interdisciplinary and multidisciplinary research* is characterized by the multiplicity of approaches. It involves the study of a subject from the assembled approaches of multiple disciplines or the integration of multidisciplinary approaches. This type of research seeks a more complete and thorough understanding of the subject from various dimensions and perspectives.

Compared to the monodisciplinary approach, the interdisciplinary and multidisciplinary approaches have several advantages. A chief advantage of these approaches is the use of the combined expertise of specialists across different disciplines and organizational boundaries. These approaches can bring disparate groups of researchers with distinct disciplinary training, backgrounds, and skills together to work on topics and concerns that lie beyond the boundaries of any one of those backgrounds.

Another major advantage is the furtherance of the interaction of disciplines. Interdisciplinarity and multidisciplinarity will facilitate cross-disciplinary exchange of concepts, ideas, and techniques, and development of a comprehensive framework for explanation of a social phenomenon.

Finally, through the combination and integration of multidisciplinary expertise and interdisciplinary interaction, the interdisciplinary and multidisciplinary approaches will ensure an optimum or comprehensive answer to the question being studied and grasp the whole of the subject.

Ethnic studies requires interdisciplinarity and multidisciplinarity because of the multifacets, complexity, and interdependency of ethnic phenomena. Ethnic groups and their interrelations can be best understood from multiple and integrated perspectives. Interdisciplinarity and multidisciplinarity are the most proper ways to discover truths about race and ethnicity and to make the structure of reality transparent. Race and ethnicity have become a focal point of interdisciplinary and multidisciplinary research in the United States because they are so salient in American life, and because for so long, they were sidetracked by the structures of intellectual skills and commitments.

The terms *interdisciplinary research* and *multidisciplinary research* are often used interchangeably. Nevertheless, there are nuances between the two. In multidisciplinary or pluridisciplinary research, disciplinary components stand independently and simply join together to study the same subject. Each separate discipline remains in isolation from the others, and different disciplines are assembled and juxtaposed. "Patchwork quilt" may be a proper analogy of this type of research. The multidisciplinary approach pursues knowledge through the simple combination of purely disciplinary approaches. That is, the research subject is decomposed into sub-problems and then solved by disciplinary approaches; the total solution is obtained as the coordinated sum of disciplinary solutions.

In interdisciplinary research, on the other hand, disciplinary components are integrated substantially. It is likened to a "seamless woven garment." The extensions and modifications of disciplinary contributions to interrelate them within a single research investigation characterize interdisciplinary research. Often specialists with different disciplinary backgrounds work together and produce joint, coordinated, and integrated research reports. The interdisciplinary approach quests for knowledge through the integration of disciplinary approaches, and it requires intensive cooperation of scholars in various disciplines to seek new concepts, relations, and methods.

Interdisciplinarity demands more work and sophistication than multidisciplinarity because the former entails the integration of disciplinary approaches rather than a simple mélange of different disciplinary approaches. In return, the interdisciplinary approach will yield results more fruitful than the multidisciplinary approach.

COMPARATIVENESS

Comparativeness is another overarching methodology of ethnic studies. While the premier position of the interdisciplinary and multidisciplinary methodologies in ethnic studies has long been recognized, the prominence of comparative methodology in ethnic studies is acknowledged only recently, partly because fruits of the past thirty years of research have allowed researchers to make comprehensive, meaningful comparisons. More and more scholars agree that comparative analysis is essential in ethnic studies (Ragin and Hein 1993; See and Wilson 1988). The prominence of the comparative approach has risen to such an extent that the nation's second Ph.D. program in ethnic studies, housed at UC San Diego, designed its program with a comparative emphasis (Hu-DeHart 1993). UC Berkeley, where the first Ph.D. program in ethnic studies is located, is also moving in the same direction. One noticeable signal is the renaming of the campus' Ethnic Studies Department to the Comparative Ethnic Studies Department.

Defining Comparative Methodology

What is comparative methodology? There does not seem to be a consensus among researchers. A narrow definition holds that only techniques whose goal is comparison can be deemed comparative methods. In a broad sense, however, comparativeness is a method for almost all social research since virtually all empirical social studies involve comparison of some sort, either comparison with other cases or comparison with itself over time. Hence, social research "in one form or other, is comparative research" (Lieberson 1985, 44).

In this book, I define *comparative methodology* as a set of techniques that attempt to describe and explain similarities and differences across social units (e.g., individuals, groups, categories, or societies). Note that this definition is broad enough to include both descriptive and explanatory comparative analyses and both similarity-oriented and variation-oriented studies. Nevertheless, according to this definition, only empirical social research with explicit attempts at comparison can be categorized as comparative studies.

Comparative methodology serves at least the following three purposes: First, it describes and explains similarities and differences across social units. This encompasses three specific dimensions: (1) find identicals across social units; (2) identify cross-unit differences; and (3) account for commonality and variation across social units in a characteristic. Second, it interprets specific experiences and trajectories of specific social units (e.g., groups, countries) in reference to other units. That is, comparatists are interested in cases themselves, and they attempt to understand the cases using other units as references. Third, it tests, refines, and advances social theories.

Comparative Analytical Strategies

To achieve the goals of comparative analysis, researchers have developed two general comparative analytical strategies: Case-specific comparison and cross-case comparison. Let me briefly describe these two strategies and then highlight some attempts of combining or integrating the two.

Case-Specific Comparison

The most common type of comparative analysis is case-specific comparison, sometimes also called case-oriented strategy. Case-specific comparison is a systematic analysis of similarities and differences across a few cases involved. Smelser (1976) dubbed this strategy "systematic comparative illustration."

Case-specific comparison possesses several characteristics. First, the number of cases in the analysis is usually small, so that in-depth, focused analysis is possible. Among available comparative studies of this type, cases are normally two to three, but seldom exceed ten. Second, case-specific comparison tends to be qualitative analysis of the cases included. Third, to assess causation this method treats each case as a combination of all relevant characteristics and compares cases with each other to uncover patterns of similarities and differences (Ragin 1987). Fourth, this method also tends to be historically interpretive (Ragin 1987, 3). Most comparatists are interested in historical sequences or outcomes and their causes across a set of similar cases.

Within the case-specific comparative method, there are several specific analytical strategies:

1. Two-case comparisons. In this strategy, researchers specify different outcomes of two cases and then trace these outcomes to different historical causes for each case. One example is the analysis of why the black slavery system was established and why there was no Indian slavery system in this country.

2. Within-unit comparisons over time. In this type of comparisons, outcomes of the same unit at two or more time periods are compared, and differential outcomes are attributed to different causes in different periods. For instance, the low social position of black Americans before the Civil Rights movement was largely an outcome of discrimination against them; nonetheless, the rise of a black middle class in recent decades can be partly attributed to the changing social conditions favorable to black social mobility after the movement.

3. Two-case comparisons supplemented by a third, varying case to bolster the two-group comparisons. This strategy is the same as the first one, except that a third case is introduced as a contrast or parallel to the two cases in order to reinforce the argument.

4. Identification of common characteristics of different cases to strengthen a preferred explanation. In this case, the primary purpose is to demonstrate that similarities in outcomes are associated with similarities of characteristics of two or more cases.

Cross-Case Comparison
This method is sometimes referred to as variable-oriented strategy. Unlike case-specific comparison, cross-case comparative method em-

phasizes variables and their interrelations. Cross-case strategy is a comparative method because it focuses on explaining *variation* across many different cases.

Cross-case comparison has several characteristics. First, the analysis requires a relatively large number of cases in order to generate reliable outcomes. Second, cross-case comparison is quantitative in orientation and conforms to the methodological norms of mainstream social sciences. Third, this method focuses on the anatomy of intervariable relationships across cases, rather than cases as wholes. Fourth, the usual goal of this approach is to engender generalizations about relationships among variables rather than to understand or interpret specific historical outcomes in a small number of cases or in an empirically defined set of cases.

There are a number of important differences between the two strategies (Ragin 1987, 54–55). First, the goal of the case-specific comparison is to explain different patterns of outcomes by different combinations of conditions, while the goal of the cross-case comparison is to explain variation across cases. The main interest of investigators who use the case-oriented approach is not to identify a single causal model that best fits the data but to uncover different causal models or historical conditions that account for different historical outcomes. On the other hand, researchers who use the variable-oriented approach are more interested in finding a universal causal model for explaining a phenomenon. Hence, the case-specific comparative strategy gives precedence to the goal of achieving causal complexity or heterogeneity, particularly multiple conjuncture causation, while, by contrast, the cross-case comparative approach underscores generality of causal conditions over causal complexity (Ragin 1987).

Second, the case-oriented approach uses theory to aid historical interpretation and to guide the identification of important causal factors, and empirical evidence is typically used to refine a theory; the variable-oriented strategy, by contrast, usually tests hypotheses or propositions derived from general theories, and contrary evidence provides a basis for rejecting a theory.

Third, the case-oriented strategy is limited in producing broad generalization and in its tendency toward particularizing, whereas the variable-oriented strategy may neglect particular historical conditions that account for variation in outcome or be limited in its tendency toward abstract and sometimes vacuous generalizations.

Finally, the case-specific comparative strategy is best suited for identifying patterns of similarities and differences, gaining knowledge of specific cases in analysis, and generating new theories with a small number of cases, while the cross-case comparison strategy is best suited for explaining differences across a range of cases and testing/refining theories about probablistic relationships between variables over the widest possible population of observations.

Currently, cross-case quantitative method seems predominant in mainstream social science research. However, this does not mean that case-specific comparative method is inferior and unusable. In fact, case-specific comparison has several advantages in comparison to the variable-oriented strategy. First, compared to the variable-oriented strategy, the case-oriented approach can more effectively examine the combined effects of social conditions on the phenomenon being explained, more directly analyze causal processes, and investigate them in context. Second, the case comparative approach can produce explanations for all instances of a phenomenon. It highlights the variation of each case and searches conditions that are associated with the variation. It can better describe and interpret the historical specificity of each case. Because of this feature, it is better suited for building new theories and synthesizing existing theories. Third, the case comparative approach forces the investigator to familiarize himself with the cases in the analysis. The variable comparative approach does not require a direct examination of the similarities and differences of cases involved; it entails the disaggregation of cases into variables and then examines them. In the case comparative approach, the investigator must examine each case directly and compare each case with other cases. Finally, case studies tend to be very sensitive to human agency and to social processes in general. These studies tend to see outcomes in terms of specific actions at specific historical junctures.

Combined and Synthetic Strategies

In addition to the two major strategies discussed above, there are other efforts to integrate the two. One type of integration is the development of a combined strategy that simply applies both major strategies to a specific problem. One example is quantitative cross-national analysis with case studies.

Another type of integration is a synthetic strategy that integrates several features of case-oriented and variable-oriented approaches. The synthetic strategy should at least include the following essential characteristics: (1) it should be capable of handling a large number of cases to protect researchers from the charge of particularism; (2) it should show concern for combinations of conditions and allow complex, conjunctural causation; (3) it should allow investigators to formulate parsimonious explanations; (4) it should provide a way for investigators to analyze the major features of social units and social processes, that is, the parts that combine in different ways to produce different wholes; and (5) it should also allow the testing of alternative explanations and meanwhile encourage the use of theory as a basis for interpretation. The ideal synthetic strategy should incorporate the best features of the case-oriented approach with the best features of the variable-oriented approach.

Issues in Comparison

Several issues demand particular attention in comparison. One is the comparability of cases. In order to achieve comparability, quantitative data and measurements must be standardized, and qualitative comparisons must have justifiable criteria.

Another issue is interpretability. A comparison is interpretable if it is possible to infer from it about the relationship between two or more variables.

To ensure comparability and interpretability, the unit of analysis should be given special attention. Researchers must make sure that comparison is made at the same level of analysis and must not jump levels to draw conclusions.

DISCOURSE ANALYSIS

Discourse analysis is a widely used research method among humanists (e.g., linguists, literary scholars, communications scholars) and has increasingly become recognized in the social sciences such as anthropology, psychology, sociology, and political science. Despite the predominant place of inter- and multidisciplinary and comparative methodologies in ethnic studies, the multidisciplinary characteristics of discourse analysis have made it especially appealing to ethnic studies scholars in recent years. Hence, this method deserves discussion.

What is discourse analysis? Scholars working in different disciplines have different interpretations and focus on different aspects of discourse. For example, descriptive linguists accent the structure of language used in communication. Philosophical linguists and formal linguists pay particular attention to semantic relationships between constructed pairs of sentences and their syntactic realization. Sociologists are primarily concerned about the structure of conversation in social interaction and its social contexts. Psychologists are more interested in the comprehension of short constructed texts or sequences of written sentences.

From an ethnic studies perspective, discourse analysis should be defined as broadly as possible to include different disciplinary emphases of the same approach but with a focus on social dimension because of the social nature of ethnic phenomena. Hence, *discourse analysis* may be defined as the study of written and spoken texts and their relationships with social contexts. Under this broad definition, scholars in different disciplines could retain their goals and emphases.

In discourse analysis, researchers analyze the structures of discourse, namely, text and talk. Discourse structures consist of surface structures and underlying (or latent) structures. *Surface structures* refer to the forms of language that can be seen or heard, such as sounds, intonations, gestures, graphics, syntax, letters, words, phrases, paragraphs, and the whole text as well as the order of lexical expressions.

Underlying structures refer to discursive meaning and action or interaction. Discursive meaning includes: (1) perspective, namely, the point of view from which events are seen, or more generally the position of the speaker or writer; (2) implicature, that is, implicit knowledge or meanings stored in actually expressed meanings; (3) coherence, including both local coherence—sequences of propositions or sentences—and overall coherence—sequences of topics in different parts of a long discourse; (4) level of description (generality or specificity) and degree of completeness; and (5) schemata (also called superstructure), or overall schematic forms or organizational forms of the overall meaning or topics of a discourse.

Another component of underlying discourse structures is discursive action and interaction, most apparent in spoken dialogue, but also found in such written communication as letters, e-mail, news reports, and textbooks. A basic premise of discourse analysis is that verbal utterances are actions (Austin 1962). Action and interaction in discourse may take several forms: First, speech acts, or verbal utterances such as assertions, questions, premises, complaints, requests, commands, orders, accusations, and threats. Speech acts may show the expression, enactment, and legitimation of power and dominance, or the delegitimation, exclusion, marginalization, derogation, defamation, and inferiorization of the powerless.

Second, turn taking, namely, exertion of power in changing turns of speech such as refusal to yield to another speaker, improper interruption, and curtailment of speech length. Third, impression formation or management, through moves of "saving face" and of positive self-presentation. Fourth, courtesy and deference, that is, the expression of politeness and respect by the speaker toward socially more powerful, higher-status, or older addressees on the one extreme, and the exhibition of discourtesy and disrespect toward less powerful, lower-status, or younger hearers on the other. Discourse analysis studies complex rules and strategies in discursive action and interaction in order to achieve effective, socially constrained communication.

Underlying structures are expressed or realized in surface structures. In other words, meaning, action, and interaction are carried out through palpable vocabulary, syntax, sounds, and intonations. Nevertheless, sometimes contradictions between surface structures and underlying structures can occur. For example, a boss, judge, or professor may seemingly make a "friendly request," but the "tone" of the request, featuring intonation, pitch, loudness, gestures, and facial expression, may convey the implication of an unfriendly command.

Not only does discourse analysis examine the detailed structures and strategies of written and spoken discourse, but it should consider the relationships between discourse and its historical, sociocultural, and political contexts (van Dijk, 1993). "Language and situation are inseparable" (Stubbs 1983). Thus, discourse analysis is the study of "text in context" (van Dijk 1993). Basic research tasks of discourse analysis include collecting, transcribing, or selecting texts, coding and comparing data, presenting and analyzing texts.

Discourse analysis has several advantages: (1) It can study both verbal and nonverbal texts; (2) it allows longitudinal study of changing texts; and (3) it can integrate multidisciplinary approaches.

There are at least two limitations with discourse analysis. First, discourse analysis is primarily limited to the study at the microlevel, so that it is difficult for use in the study of large-scale attitudes or behavior. And second, discourse analysis does not focus on product but on processes or activities.

SUMMARY

Since the majority of ethnic studies researchers are trained in a specific discipline, at the present stage, traditional disciplinary research methods are widely used in ethnic studies. This chapter has briefly introduced several influential disciplinary approaches such as field research, experiment, survey research, and content analysis. Field research is a qualitative method developed and popularized by anthropologists. Both experiment and survey research are quantitative methods. Experiment is most rigorous in the social sciences because of its ability to prove or disprove causation. Survey research is widely used by social scientists due to its ability to investigate a wide range of issues and to understand the population. Content analysis is a method that can transform qualitative data into quantitative data.

Moreover, the inter- and multidisciplinary nature of ethnic studies dictates the use of interdisciplinary and multidisciplinary methodologies. The interdisciplinary and multidisciplinary approaches are the most defining and overarching components of ethnic studies methodologies. Interdisciplinarity and multidisciplinarity assemble or integrate multiple disciplinary approaches and expertise to study ethnic phenomena.

In recent years, comparative methodology has been ascending and receiving growing recognition as the discipline matures. Case-specific comparison and cross-case comparison are the two most common analytical strategies of comparative methodology, which serve different purposes of research. It is also possible to combine and/or synthesize these two strategies.

Discourse analysis, a method with multidisciplinary nature, has been gaining popularity in ethnic studies. It is simply a study of texts in social contexts, involving the analysis of tangible text structures and hidden underlying discourse structures.

PART II
MAJOR ISSUES IN ETHNIC STUDIES

CHAPTER 3

THEORIES OF ETHNICITY

What is the nature of ethnicity? What forces create and sustain ethnicity? These are the basic questions that theories of ethnicity must answer. This chapter organizes the existing theoretical perspectives on the nature and basis of ethnicity into three schools of thought: the primordialist school, the constructionist school, and the instrumentalist school. It introduces and analyzes the basic ideas and specific variants of each school. Furthermore, the chapter presents a synthetic approach that attempts to integrate the competing theories of ethnicity.

CONCEPT OF ETHNICITY

Before we discuss the theories of ethnicity, it is essential to clarify the meaning of "ethnicity." At first glance, ethnicity is seemingly a straightforward concept, but in fact it is subject to different interpretations. Some understand it as ancestry, and others perceive it as physical attributes. The following familiar situation should help clarify the meaning of this concept.

You have been filling out forms all your life. They are required every time you apply for schools, jobs, scholarships, grants, and a myriad of other occasions. These forms often ask the question: "What is your ethnicity?" You are given categories to check, either broad categories such as white, black, Hispanic, Asian, and Native American, or specific categories such as Chinese, Japanese, Mexican, Puerto Rican, and so on.

What does the question *literally* mean in this context? The question can be rephrased as follows: What is your ethnic group membership? Which ethnic group are you affiliated with? Which ethnic group do you identify yourself with? If you agree with the interpretation of this question, then *ethnicity* may be defined as an affiliation or identification with an ethnic group. Other synonyms of ethnicity include *ethnic group membership*, *ethnic affiliation*, and *ethnic identity*. On the one hand, ethnicity is subjective since it is the product of the human mind and human sentiments. It is a matter of identification or a sense of belonging to a particular ethnic group (Yetman 1991, 2). On the other hand, ethnicity is objective because it must be based on some objective characteristics and is constructed by social forces and power relations. It is to a large extent independent of individuals' desires. On balance, ethnicity is the outcome of subjective perceptions based on some objective characteristics such as physical attributes, presumed ancestry, culture, or national origin. As mentioned in chapter 1, this book uses the broad definition of ethnic group, which includes both culturally defined ethnic groups and racial groups. Hence, affiliation or identification with a racial group is part of ethnicity.

The terms *ethnicity* and *ethnic group* are often used interchangeably. In actuality, although the two terms are closely related, there is a nuance dividing them. While ethnic group is a social group based on ancestry, culture, or national origin, ethnicity refers to affiliation or identification with an ethnic group.[1] This book treats them as two interrelated but separate concepts rather than as synonyms.

NATURE AND BASIS OF ETHNICITY: BASIC QUESTIONS

Theorists of both Marxism and modernism have predicted that as a society becomes industrialized and modernized, ethnicity will fade and eventually die out. Likewise, assimilationists and advocates of the "melting

---

1. In some contexts, interchanging the two terms will not make much difference in meaning, as in the questions, "What is your ethnicity?" and "What is your ethnic group?" In other contexts, however, the meanings of the two terms vary. For example, in the questions, "What determines ethnicity?" and "What determines ethnic group?" "ethnicity" and "ethnic group" are obviously not synonyms.

pot" paradigm have envisaged a withering of ethnic identification as a result of ethnic assimilation and amalgamation. However, none of these presages has materialized. On the contrary, not only has ethnicity remained a vital and important part of contemporary life, but its significance has been on the ascendence at certain times and in certain places.

In America, for instance, the vitality of ethnicity is undeniable. Ethnicity affects the opportunities of members of different ethnic groups in schools, jobs, income, housing, poverty, crime, and politics. Throughout the world, there is no sign that ethnicity is vanishing. In reality, the importance of ethnicity is even on the rise. As we have seen in the past ten years or so, the broad "Soviet" identity failed to override ethnic divisions in the former Soviet Union; ethnic division has torn Yugoslavia apart and led to the ongoing war in Bosnia; ethnic strife and separation have continued in Northern Ireland, Quebec, and other European countries; Israeli-Palestinian conflict has lingered on despite the peace-making process; ethnic collision between majority Hindus and minority Muslims and Sikhs in India has intensified; ethnic fighting between ruling Sinhalese and minority Tamils has killed eight thousand and forced more than 200,000 Tamils into refugee camps; in South Africa, racial tension remains despite the abolition of apartheid; and in Rwanda, ethnic warfare between the majority Hutu and the minority Tutsi erupted in 1994. Not only has conflict along the ethnic lines remained a constant global theme, but it has intensified in many parts of the world. Almost five million people lost their lives and more than fifty million were displaced in the maelstrom of intergroup conflict between 1990 and 1996. Ethnic memberships often demarcate the lines of intergroup conflicts. Throughout history people have often used ethnic distinctions to rank members of a society. The tenacity of ethnic identities verifies the centrality of ethnicity in modern human societies.

To understand the emergence and persistence of ethnicity, we need to answer the following two interrelated questions:

1. What is the nature of ethnicity? Is ethnicity something that is inherited or something that is constructed?

2. What determines ethnic affiliation or identification? In other words, what is the basis of ethnicity?

Theories of ethnicity attempt to answer these fundamental questions in ethnic studies. Over the years, scholars have developed many theories of ethnicity, which may be grouped into three schools of thought: (1) primordialism, (2) constructionism, and (3) instrumentalism. The remainder of this chapter first presents the central ideas of these three paradigms and some specific versions of arguments within each school and then focuses on the formulation of an integrated approach. It should be noted before proceeding that the three schools of thought are ideal types. Often a specific theory may not be pigeonholed under a single category. Nevertheless, most theories have a tendency to lean toward a particular school. It is the presence of an intrinsic underlying view that is used to classify a theory under a particular heading.

THE PRIMORDIALIST SCHOOL

How does the primordialist school answer the two questions posed above? Three arguments are at the heart of this school of thought. First, ethnicity is an *ascribed* identity or assigned status, something inherited from one's ancestors. For example, if your ancestors are Chinese, then you are also Chinese because you inherit physical and cultural characteristics from your forebears. Ethnicity is a very deeply rooted, primal bond to one's ancestral bloodline.

Second, as an important corollary of ascribed identity, ethnic boundaries, which demarcate who is a member of an ethnic group and who is not, are fixed or immutable. Ethnicity is static. If you were born Chinese, you will be forever Chinese, and you can't change your membership to another group.

Finally, common ancestry determines ethnicity. In other words, people belong to an ethnic group because members of that group all share common biological and cultural origins. "Primordialist" is used to characterize this school of thought because it stresses the role of primordial factors, such as lineage and cultural ties, in determining ethnicity. To primordialists, it is the primordial bonds that give rise to and sustain ethnicity (Geertz 1973; Isaacs 1975; van den Berghe 1981).

Within the primordialist framework, there are at least two variant views. The *sociobiological* perspective represented by Pierre van den Berghe emphasizes the importance of a sociobiological factor—kinship—in determining ethnicity. Van den Berghe (1981) argued that ethnicity is an extension of kinship. Ethnic affiliation originates from membership in a nuclear family, then an extended family, and finally the ethnic group.

Ethnic identity develops and persists due to the common ancestral bonds of group members. An implication of this view is that ethnicity will never perish because kinship always exists.

A second current of primordialism is the *culturalist* perspective, which underscores the importance of a common culture in the determination of ethnic group membership. According to this view, a common culture (e.g., a common language, a common religion) determines the genesis and tenacity of ethnic identity even in the absence of common ancestors. For instance, Hispanic identity is determined by a shared language, Spanish, rather than by people's shared ancestry. Different racial groups of people originating from the same country can form an ethnic group and develop a common ethnic identity even though they have no common biological bonds.

Grasping the sentimental or psychological origins of ethnicity, the primordialist school provides a plausible explanation for the rise and tenacity of ethnic attachment. However, primordialism contains several drawbacks. First, this perspective cannot explain why ethnic memberships or identities of individuals and groups change. Second, it cannot fully account for why new ethnic identities, such as Asian American, emerge among biologically and culturally diverse groups, and why ethnic identities wane and disappear. Third, it tends to overlook the larger historical and structural conditions that construct/deconstruct and reinforce/undermine ethnic loyalties. Finally, it neglects the economic and political interests closely associated with ethnic sentiment and practice (Glazer and Moynihan 1963; Greenberg 1980).

It is undeniable that ethnicity requires some common origins, such as common ancestry or common culture; but how important are common origins in determining ethnic affiliation, and is ethnicity completely ascribed? Primordialists tend to offer affirmative answers to these questions. Constructionists and instrumentalists, however, dissent.

THE CONSTRUCTIONIST SCHOOL

The primordialist school was the dominant way of thinking until the 1970s, and many people are still accustomed to this way of thinking today. Starting in the 1970s, the constructionist school began to ascend. The answers of the constructionist school to the two questions stand in sharp contrast to those of the primordialist school. Constructionists have advanced three major arguments: First, ethnicity is a socially *constructed* identity, something that is created. The emphasis of this school on the social construction of ethnicity breeds the label of "constructionist" school. Second, as an extension of constructed identity, ethnic boundaries are flexible or changeable. Ethnicity is dynamic. Lastly, ethnic affiliation or identification is determined or constructed by society. Ethnicity is a reaction to changing social environment.

The constructionist school also encompasses several different perspectives which emphasize different components. William Yancey et al. (1976) proposed an "emergent ethnicity" perspective. They downplayed the effect of cultural heritage and viewed ethnicity as an "emergent phenomenon" created by structural conditions. Focusing on the experience of Italian, Jewish, and Polish immigrants in America around the turn of this century, Yancey and his associates maintained that the formation, crystallization, and development of ethnic communities, cultures, and identities were shaped by structural conditions closely associated with the industrialization process in the host society and the positions of ethnic groups within it. Specifically, the industrialization process led to the creation or expansions of certain industries (e.g., the garment industry, steel industry, construction industry) and occupations associated with these industries; immigrant groups with different occupational skills moved into different industries and occupations at different times, leading to occupational concentrations of ethnic groups with similar life styles, class interests, work relationships; because of the transportation conditions at that time, immigrants working in the same industry and occupation tended to live in the same area, resulting in residential concentration; common occupations and residence led to the use of the same institutions and services, such as churches, schools, and financial institutions. All of these structural conditions resulted in the formation and development of Italian, Jewish, and Polish ethnic communities, ethnic cultures, and ethnic identities by reinforcing the maintenance of kinship and friendship networks (Yancey et al. 1976, 392). According to this view, ethnicity emerges as a response to structural changes in society. Yancey et al.'s work was among the pioneering attempts to explore the sources of ethnicity derived from the structural forces of society.

Jonathan Sarna, a historian, developed a so-called "theory of ethnicization," which somewhat differs from the emergent ethnicity perspective formulated by sociologists such as Yancey et al. Sarna (1978) maintained that ethnicity is created by two conditions: ascription and adversity. Ascription refers to the assignment of individuals to particular ethnic groups by outsiders such as governments, churches, schools, media, natives, and other immigrants. Adversity includes prejudice, discrimination, hostility, and hardship. Sarna contended that adversity forces members of the same group to unite and helps create group identity and solidarity. Sarna's theory probably understates the active role of ethnic groups in shaping their identities while inflating the effects of outside forces. However, the merit of Sarna's theory lies in its call to locate the creation of ethnic identity in relation to the larger society.

Other scholars focus on the resurgence of old ethnic identities and boundaries that previously existed. In other words, ethnic identity is constructed around formerly recognized historical boundaries. They found that "resurgent ethnicity" is particularly evident among white ethnic groups. For instance, quite a few studies (e.g., Alba 1990; Bakalian 1993; Kivisto 1989; Waters 1990) show that although ethnic boundaries among the white population are weakening due to intermarriage, language loss, religious conversion, or declining participation, white Americans increasingly identify with their group of origin. Some argue that social changes since the 1960s and shifting societal emphasis from assimilation into the Anglo culture to ethnic distinctiveness have resulted in resurgent ethnicity among whites. On the other hand, Gans (1979) contended that ethnic revival among whites is nothing more than "symbolic ethnicity," or symbolic allegiance to, love for and pride in the culture and tradition of the immigrant generation and the country of origin, without having to be incorporated in everyday behavior. Simply put, symbolic ethnicity is "feeling ethnic" rather than being ethnic.

The more recent *social constructionist* perspective explicitly emphasizes the social construction of ethnicity and race and the dynamic process of ethnic/racial formation. For example, Werner Sollars (1989) suggested the notion of "the invention of ethnicity." Challenging the primordialist assumption that ethnicity is an irrational form of cultural attachment, Sollars argued that ethnic identity is embedded in tradition, which is created, sustained, and refashioned by people. Joane Nagel (1994, 1996) contended that ethnicity is socially constructed and reconstructed by internal forces (i.e., actions taken by ethnic groups themselves such as negotiation, redefinition, and reconstruction of ethnic boundaries) and external forces (i.e., social, economic, and political processes and outsiders), and that ethnicity is a dynamic, constantly changing property of individual identity and group organization. Focusing on the centrality of race,

Michael Omi and Howard Winant (1994) demonstrated how the meanings and categories of race both shape and are shaped by the political process.

The constructionist school pinpoints the centrality of social construction in ethnic formation and retention; it highlights historical and structural forces that create and sustain ethnicity; and it better explains the volatility of ethnicity. Nevertheless, the constructionist school tends to ignore the ancestral basis of ethnicity and deemphasize the limitations of social construction. Like the primordialist school, it also pays insufficient attention to the role of political and economic interest in the construction of ethnicity.

THE INSTRUMENTALIST SCHOOL

Unlike the primordialist school and the constructionist school, the instrumentalist school views ethnicity as an instrument or strategic tool for gaining resources. Hence, the "instrumentalist" tag is affixed to this school. According to this theoretical framework, people become ethnic and remain ethnic when their ethnicity yields significant returns to them. In other words, ethnicity exists and persists because it is useful. The functional advantages of ethnicity range from "the moral and material support provided by ethnic networks to political gains made through ethnic bloc voting" (Portes and Bach 1985, 24). To Nathan Glazer and Daniel Moynihan (1975), who are among the pioneers of this school, ethnicity is not simply a mix of affective sentiments, but like class and nationality it is also a means of political mobilization for advancing group interests. Ethnic groups are also interest groups.

The most extreme version of instrumentalism attributes the acquisition and retention of ethnic membership or identity solely to the motivation of wanting to obtain comparative advantage. For example, Orlando Patterson (1975, 348) asserted that "The strength, scope, viability, and bases of ethnic identity are determined by, and are used to serve, the economic and general class interests of individuals." Hence, interests are the sole determinant of ethnic identity, and ethnic affiliation tends to be transient and situational as the benefits of ethnicity shift. A more moderate variant of instrumentalism combines advantages of ethnicity with affective ties. For instance, Daniel Bell (1975, 169) stated that "Ethnicity has become more salient because it can combine an interest with an affective tie." Cohen (1969) suggested that cultural homogeneity of people facilitates their effective organization as an interest group and boosts ethnic solidarity and identity.

Another recent formulation of instrumentalism is *rational choice theory* (Banton 1983; Hechter 1986, 1987; Hechter et al. 1982). As a social theory, rational choice theory assumes that people act to promote their socioeconomic positions by minimizing the costs of, and maximizing the potential benefits of, their actions. As an application to ethnic identity, rational choice theory maintains that ethnic affiliation is based on the rational calculation of the costs and benefits of ethnic association. For the advocates of rational choice theory, ethnicity is an option. People choose one ethnicity over another or avoid association with an ethnic group because of the utility or cost of such affiliation. Some people favor an ethnic affiliation because it is beneficial, while other people hide or deny an ethnic identity because it will bring disadvantages.

Rational choice theory can help us understand the change of ethnic identity, but it has limitations as well. First, ethnic choice is limited. Since ethnic choice is subject to ancestral constraints defined by a society, not everyone can freely choose ethnic identity. As Joane Nagel (1996, 26) stated, "We do not always choose to be who we are; we simply are who we are as a result of a set of social definitions, categorization schemes, and external ascriptions that reside in the taken-for-granted realm of social life." Alternative ethnic options become possible only when an ethnic status quo is challenged and superseded. Second, not all ethnic choices are rational and materialistic. Some people choose an ethnic affiliation not for material gains, rewards, or access to resources and services but for psychological satisfaction, which includes emotional fulfillment, social attachment, or recreational pleasure. The notion of symbolic ethnicity suggested by Herbert Gans (1979) comes closest to this function of ethnicity. This type of ethnic option is symbolic, nonrational, nonmaterial-driven.

AN INTEGRATED APPROACH

The foregoing review of the three schools of thought on the nature and basis of ethnicity reveals the varying degrees of validity of their arguments as well as their limitations. We do not have to rely on the either/or logic of thinking; rather, an integration of valuable ideas is possible and worthwhile. The balance of this section formulates an integrated approach of my own that builds upon some useful insights of these theories and incorporates strands from all three paradigms.

I argue that ethnicity (including race) is socially constructed partly on the basis of ancestry or presumed ancestry and more importantly by society, that the interests of ethnic groups also partly determine ethnic affiliation, and that ethnic boundaries are relatively stable but undergo changes from time to time. This argument contains four specific propositions.

Proposition 1. Ethnicity is partly ascribed because it is partly based on ancestry or presumed ancestry that normally carries certain physical or cultural characteristics and national or territorial origins.

Few people would deny the relevance of ancestry to ethnicity. "Perception of common ancestry, both real and mythical, has been important to outsiders' definitions and to ethnic groups' self-definitions" (Feagin and Feagin 1993, 9). For Max Weber (1961, 1:306), one of the founding fathers of sociology, ethnic groups are "human groups that entertain a subjective belief in their common descent—because of similarities of physical type or of customs or both, or because of memories of colonization or migration—in such a way that this belief is important for the continuation of the nonkinship communal relationships." Hence, ancestry must be an imperative condition for ethnic affiliation or identification.

The social construction of ethnicity or race cannot be undertaken without some reference to common ancestry or presumed common ancestry. Each individual is assigned by society to a particular ethnic group or identifies himself/herself with a particular ethnic group in part because of that person's ancestry or presumed ancestry. For instance, a person is categorized as Japanese American or identifies himself/herself as Japanese American, partly because his/her ancestors originated in Japan. Similarly, roots in Africa partly define people originating from that continent as "African Americans." The same rule applies to a person from Britain, Italy, Mexico, or any other country. "Hispanic American" is defined partly because of the shared language of various groups.

Ethnic choice also partly depends on ancestral ties. It is true that ethnic options have become increasingly open in America over time. Take the U.S. population census—a premier means of categorizing people's ethnicity and race—as an example. Before the 1960s, census takers checked the race/ethnicity category of the census form for individuals based on their observations of the physical characteristics of respondents.

Since the 1960s, individuals have been given the responsibility to check their racial/ethnic categories for themselves. People have had a certain degree of freedom to choose their ethnic affiliations or identities, but the freedom to choose is not absolute. If you are to select a category for a form, you cannot choose whatever you want. You make your choice at least partly based on your knowledge of your ancestry. Your choice has to be recognized by other people who make their judgment following a set of rules for ethnic categorization established by society. If a person of pure Chinese descent declared himself white, black, Latino, or Indian, most people would think he had made a mistake, or he was a liar or, even worse, insane.

The majority of people do not get to choose their ethnicity; they are born into it according to a set of rules defined by society. There are limitations to the learning of ethnicity. Listening to black music, learning Ebonics, and hanging around with black students won't make a nonblack person black. Similarly, enjoying Mexican food and learning to speak Spanish won't make one Mexican. The basic rule accepted by American society is ancestry in terms of the family tree.

Proposition 2. Ethnicity is largely constructed by society.

There are at least four mechanisms through which society constructs ethnicity. The first mechanism is that society largely determines people's ethnic group memberships through written or unwritten rules for assigning its members to different ethnic categories. Ethnic definitions and categories are social constructs and arbitrary decisions that reflect intergroup power relations. Individuals are often born into an ethnic or racial category defined by society, and they normally have little control over their ethnic group memberships. The story of Susie Guillory Phipps helps illustrate this point (*San Francisco Chronicle* 1982, 1983).

Susie Phipps, the wife of a wealthy seafood importer in Louisiana, looked white and always considered herself white, but on her birth certificate she was designated "colored" because her great-great-great-great grandmother was the black mistress of an Alabama plantation owner back in 1760.[2] According to a 1970 Louisiana law, any person with one thirty-second of "Negro blood" should be designated as colored regardless of

---

2. Phipps was exactly three thirty-seconds black. "Colored" and "black" are sometimes used interchangeably, such as in the National Association for the Advancement of Colored People—a prominent African American organization.

that person's skin color. In order to change her race from "colored" to "white," she sued the Louisiana Bureau of Vital Records in 1982–1983. Her attorney argued that designating a race-category on a person's birth certificate was unconstitutional and that in any case the one thirty-second criterion was inaccurate. However, she lost the case and the court upheld Louisiana's law quantifying "racial identity" and affirmed the legal principle of assigning persons to specific "racial" groups. Susie Phipps was made black because of the law decided by society.[3] Ironically, one drop of black blood made her black, but the bulk of white blood could not make her white.

Ethnic/racial categorization rules vary from one society to another, and therefore the same person could be categorized into different ethnic or racial groups in different societies. For instance, in the United States, ancestry, rather than physical appearance, plays a crucial role in determining one's ethnicity or race. In Brazil, however, a person's total physical appearance (e.g., skin color, hair texture, facial features) is the primary determinant of his/her racial classification. Hence, many lighter-skinned blacks in America would be defined as whites in Brazil. In addition to physical appearance, Brazil also uses other factors as ethnic or racial determinants. One of the important factors is social class. People with a higher social class status are more likely to be classified as white than those with a lower social status. The Brazilian saying, "a rich Negro is white, and a poor white is a Negro," vividly reflects this "money whitens" rule.

Sometimes, race/ethnicity-assigning rules, normally based on physical appearance or ancestry, may not be written in books but are widely acknowledged and practiced in society. In the United States, for instance, although the "one drop" rule was rejected, its influence has still lingered today. When members of white ethnic groups intermarried, the race of their descendants remained white. However, up to now the descendants of a white person and a black person are viewed as blacks in the eyes of the American public. Many immigrants with mixed ancestries of black and white from the West Indies often have a turning-black experience. For example, in Jamaica, an island nation in the West Indies, the mixed ancestry of black and white is a norm, and the mixed-blood Jamaicans are not defined as blacks in their society. However, when Jamaicans come to the United States, they and their descendants "become" black, even though many Jamaicans do not like to be so categorized. Although there

3. Susie Phipps's failed suit later prompted a legislative reform, which led to the abolition of the law in 1983 (*San Francisco Chronicle* 1983).

is no written rule governing the blood quantum of mixed-blood West Indians, apparently government officials who decided the race categories acted on the assumption that West Indians with any amount of African ancestry are black because of the influence of the "one-drop" rule.

The second mechanism of social construction of ethnicity is that social conditions can create new ethnic groups and identities. Among the many good examples is the formation of an ethnic group called Vietnamese Americans and their identity. Before 1975, there was no such group or identity as "Vietnamese American," because only a small number of Vietnamese resided in the United States at that time. The collapse of South Vietnam in 1975 generated a huge influx of Vietnamese refugees into this country. As a result, Vietnamese Americans and their identity were forged by the conclusion of the Vietnam War and its ensuing refugee arrivals. In general, immigration creates new ethnic groups because today's immigrant groups become tomorrow's ethnic groups.

Another example is the creation of "Asian American" identity. Prior to the 1960s, there was no such concept as "Asian American." There were, however, Chinese, Japanese, Filipinos, and Koreans. Each group identified itself with its national origin or even with its subnational/subethnic group (Cheng and Yang 1996). "Asian American" was a new ethnic identity created during the 1960s as Asian Americans deemphasized their separate group identities. Scholars label this new ethnic identity "Asian American panethnicity" (Espiritu 1992), which is the panethnic identity of all Asian American subgroups, including Chinese, Japanese, Filipinos, Koreans, Asian Indians, Vietnamese, and other Asian groups.

At least three important factors contributed to the construction of Asian American panethnicity. One was the racial lumping of diverse Asian groups into an umbrella category by government bureaucracies and the larger society (Espiritu 1992; Lopez and Espiritu, 1990). In some sense, Asian American panethnicity is an imposed identity (Espiritu 1992). Another important factor was the common economic and political interests of Asian groups. The political and social struggles of Asian Americans during the 1960s led them to realize that forming a coalition could better advance their economic and political interests and that the pan-Asian identity could be used as a strategic instrument to mobilize culturally diverse Asian groups for that purpose. Finally, it was the Asian American movement that gave rise to this pan-Asian identity as the young, native-born Asian Americans searched and coined the term "Asian American" for their political organizations (Espiritu 1992).

Similar examples include the construction of Hispanic American panethnicity by grouping "Mexican," "Cuban," "Puerto Rican," and other Hispanic groups together, and the creation of Native American panethnicity by lumping Eskimo, Aleut, Cherokee, Sioux, Pueblo, and several hundred other Indian nations into the broad American Indian category. In general, *panethnicity* refers to a panethnic identity and solidarity among subethnic groups that are considered homogeneous by outsiders. "Asian American," "Hispanic American," and "Native American" are all new ethnic identities constructed in the past several decades.

The third mechanism through which social environment determines ethnicity is that social conditions can change the ethnic membership or identity of individuals and groups. As mentioned in chapter 1, Asian Indians were defined by the government as white prior to the 1970s. The group organized to demand a reclassification to "Asian" during the 1970s. After a series of negotiation with the government and public hearings, they were finally pigeonholed as Asian Americans.

Ethnic switching to American Indians provides another illuminative case. The population census statistics show that between 1960 and 1990, the number of American Indians increased from 523,591 in 1960, to 792,730 in 1970, 1,364,033 in 1980, and 1,878,285 in 1990. The phenomenal growth cannot be explained by Indians' high fertility, decreased mortality, immigration, or change in the Indian definition. Nagel (1996) found that the major reason lay in the "ethnic switching" of people with some Indian lineage (primarily whites) to Indians. Before the 1960s, people with mixed ancestries of Indians and whites were unwilling to claim their Indian heritage due to stigma and disadvantages associated with Indians, and in the past several decades people with some Indian descent have reclaimed their Indian identity. Thus, ethnic group membership or identity is fluid.

Several social conditions were accountable for this ethnic switching phenomenon. First, the Civil Rights movement and the "Red Power" Indian political movements increased Indians' ethnic consciousness and ethnic pride, so that people were willing to switch back to being Indians.[4] Second, federal Indian urban and social policies (e.g., assimilation pro-

---

4. Some well-known events involving the Red Power movements included the nineteen-month occupation of Alcatraz Island beginning in 1969; the 1972 Trail of Broken Teaties; which culminated in a week-long occupation of the Bureau of Indian Affairs in Washington, D.C.; the seventy-one day siege at Wounded Knee, South Dakota, in 1973; and the 1975 shootout on the Pine Ridge Reservation in South Dakota.

grams beginning in the nineteenth century and urbanization programs after World War II) created an urbane, educated, English-speaking Indian community and led to the growing acceptance of Indians by the larger society. Finally, benefits given to Indians through some social programs such as affirmative action and settlement of land claims also stimulated ethnic switching to Indian, a point which will be emphasized in Proposition 3.

The fourth mechanism is that social structural conditions can heighten ethnic awareness and identities. Many structural conditions function as catalysts or stimuli of ethnic consciousness and identity. Government recognition or designation can lead to a group's self-consciousness and organization and can also increase identification and mobilization among groups not officially recognized. For example, the categorization of Vietnamese, Laotians, and Cambodians by the U.S. government in the census makes official their ethnic status and heightens their identities. On the other hand, the government recognition of Indochinese prompts other Asian groups such as Thai and Pakistanis to demand similar recognition, which helps increase the attachment of members to their own groups.

Government policies and practices can promote ethnic awareness and identities. For instance, the incarceration of Japanese Americans on the U.S. mainland during World War II heightened the ethnic boundaries and identities of Japanese Americans. This modern example substantiates the effect of adversity on ethnic identity suggested by Sarna (1978). During the Iran hostage crisis in 1980, the Carter administration required Iranians in America to report to the government for photos and fingerprints, and this practice promoted Iranians' self-awareness and identity. It should be noted that international context (U.S. Embassy staff in Iran were taken hostage during the Iranian revolution in 1980) was largely responsible for this government practice and the ensuing effect on Iranians' ethnic consciousness. Affirmative action policy in the United States increases the self-awareness of whites. Interestingly, affirmative action in India, which constitutionally guarantees parliamentary representation and government posts for Untouchables (outcast), has encouraged the collective identity and political mobilization of Untouchables and led to the formation of an Untouchable political party—the Republican Party (Nayar 1966; Rudolph and Rudolph 1967).

Ethnic identity can be enhanced by competition for economic and political resources. For instance, Min (1996) showed that economic competition and conflict between Korean Americans and African Americans in New York and Los Angeles heightened ethnic solidarity, awareness, and identity among Korean Americans, and the heightening effect was most evident among the young generations of U.S.-born Koreans. Competition for political access or control can promote ethnic identification. For example, the successful pursuit of political offices by ethnic candidates can increase group members' pride and willingness for identification. Ethnic mobilization or countermobilization during a political race can also heighten ethnic consciousness.

Proposition 3. Costs and benefits associated with ethnic group memberships partly determine ethnic affiliation or identification.

When ethnic choice becomes available, the costs and benefits of ethnicity play a pivotal role in determining the ethnic options of individuals and groups. These costs and benefits do not always exert their impact on ethnic options alone; often they function together with other social factors. People choose or avoid an association with an ethnic group in order to maximize their gains and minimize their losses. Self-interest in part determines ethnic options. For example, as mentioned earlier Asian Americans created the pan-Asian identity partly because this panethnic identity had the utility of uniting Asian groups and promoting their common interests. Asian Indians' campaign of reclassifying their racial category from white to Asian was in part motivated by benefits entitled to minorities, especially programs that provided contracts for minority-owned businesses. In the same vein, the ethnic switching of people with partial Indian ancestry to Indians in the latter half of this century can be partly accounted for by the changing social costs and rewards associated with American Indian identity (Nagel 1996). In addition, affirmative action benefits for college admissions, employment, and government contracting encourage ethnic identification with groups eligible for the rewards.

There are many other international examples that bolster the role of costs and benefits of ethnicity in determining ethnic choice. For instance, during apartheid in South Africa, many people applied to change their official ethnic affiliation in order to gain benefits available to whites and Coloureds and to avoid restrictions associated with black or African identity (Lelyveld 1985). In Sudan, members of the Fur group who mainly depended on agriculture for a living, switched to Baggara ethnicity, a group that engaged in the more lucrative animal husbandry (Haaland 1969).

Religious conversion—a form of ethnic switching—is also influenced by self-interest. In India, outcast Hindus switched to Islam, which allowed them to avoid untouchability. Some did the same conversion for employment purposes in colonial India (Nayar 1966). The British preference for Sikh military recruits led many Hindus to switch to Sikhism (Nayar 1966).

In general, beneficial ethnic membership encourages affiliation while socially costly ethnic membership stimulates avoidance and dissociation. Ethnic choice can be rational or nonrational (Nagel 1996). There are two kinds of utility or cost associated with ethnicity. One is material benefits or costs associated with ethnic group membership. Ethnic options based on these material considerations may be termed rational choice. The second type of utility or cost of ethnicity is psychological satisfaction or dissatisfaction associated with ethnic group membership. Ethnic choice based on this function of ethnicity may be called nonrational or symbolic choice.

Proposition 4. Ethnic boundaries are relatively stable, but they can change from time to time, especially when existing ethnic categories are challenged.

Even though ethnic boundaries are not immutable, we must recognize their relative stability. Since ethnic boundaries are crystallized and partly defined by ancestry that is socially recognized, they do not change quickly. Furthermore, although ethnic categories do shift, they seldom reshuffle completely in a short period of time. It is only when existing ethnic categories become problematic, often as a result of political challenges to the existent ethnic order, that ethnic boundaries begin to transform.

Their stability notwithstanding, ethnic boundaries are not fixed, but shift from time to time. There are several specific forms of boundary metamorphosis. First, ethnic boundaries can expand to include groups previously excluded. An example is the widening boundaries of whites in the United States. In 1795, Benjamin Franklin grumbled at German "aliens" whose presence intruded in the dominance of "purely white people" (Jordan 1968, 102, 143, 254). Early Irish immigrants were considered a separate race. Similarly, Italians, Jews, Greeks, Slavs, etc. were historically excluded from the white racial stock. However, these groups gradually became part of the white category.

Second, ethnic boundaries can upgrade from a lower level to a higher level. The creation of Asian American panethnicity and the ensuing

Table 3.1   Summary of Four Approaches to the Nature and Basis of Ethnicity

Approach	Primordialism	Constructionism	Instrumentalism	Integration
Nature	Ascribed identity; inherent ancestral traits	Socially constructed identity	Social instrument	Identity constructed by ancestry and society
Ethnic boundaries	Fixed	Flexible	Flexible	Relatively stable but changeable
Basis	Ancestry	Society	Costs/benefits	Ancestry, society, costs/benefits

panethnic boundaries engulfing Chinese, Japanese, Filipinos, Koreans, Asian Indians, Vietnamese, and other Asians are one case in point. While the specific Asian group boundaries still remain, new boundaries are constructed at a higher level.

Third, ethnic boundaries can shrink or split. For instance, the Clinton administration decided that for the 2000 census, the existing Asian and Pacific Islander American category of the race variable will be split into two categories: Asian American, and native Hawaiian and other Pacific Islander.

Finally, ethnic boundaries can disappear along with ethnic categories. For example, in the 1870 to 1890 U.S. censuses, there existed a total of eight racial categories: white, black, mulatto, quadroon, octoroon, Chinese, Japanese, and Indian. In the 1900 census, the three racial categories—mulatto, quadroon, and octoroon—were removed and have never been used since then.

In sum, ethnic identity and boundaries are constructed and reconstructed by individuals, ethnic groups themselves, other groups, and society as a whole. Ancestry, self-interests, and the larger economic, political and social structures all underlie the social construction of ethnicity. Ethnic choice is available to some individuals and groups at certain times and places; and the choice could be materialistically motivated (rational) and/or emotionally induced (nonrational). The main ideas of the integrated approach and the similarities and differences between this approach and the other three paradigms are summarized in Table 3.1.

IDENTITY OF MIXED-RACE PEOPLE

The issue of multiracial people has recently attracted increasing attention because mixed races have become more and more common among Americans as a result of interracial breeding. We do not have accurate data on how many people in America belong to the category of "mixed race." However, indirect evidence from the 1990 census puts that number in 1990 at about five million.[5]

What is the racial identity of people with mixed racial backgrounds? How do we determine the race of mixed-race people? These issues often confront societies with mixed-blood people. Undoubtedly, the identity of mixed-race people is also largely determined by society. Society makes written or unwritten rules to assign mixed-race people to a particular category. There are several commonly used categorization rules. One rule often used in the history of America is to use the race of one parent (usually mother) or the parent who is nonwhite to determine the race of a mixed-race child. For example, in the colony of Virginia in 1662 the race of a child whose father was white and whose mother was black was designated black. The guidelines of the 1920 census stated that "any mixture of White and some other race was to be reported according to the race of the person who was not white" (U.S. Bureau of the Census 1979). Another rule is the use of blood quantum, for which different societies use different quantitative criteria. For instance, the Bureau of Indian Affairs has long used one-fourth of blood quantum as a minimum requirement to define who is an American Indian for entitlement to certain government services (e.g., medical services). A large number of Indian tribal governments use blood criteria ranging from one-sixteenth to one-half to determine tribal membership. A third rule is the use of physical appearance. This is most common in daily life. People normally assume the race of mixed-race people based on how they look. A fourth rule is to designate a special category for mixed-race people. In Brazil, for example, "mulatto" is the category for people with mixed races of black and white. South Africa uses "colored" to designate people with black and white ancestries.

In the United States, there is no such category. In the past several

---

5. In the 1990 census, there was a category called "other race" for the variable "race." Normally, mixed-race people or those who did not wish to check white, black, Asian, or Indian chose that category. In 1990, the number of people who checked that category ws 9,804,847, among whom a significant proportion were Mexicans.

years, certain groups representing mixed-race Americans demanded the addition of a new category, "mixed race" or "multiracial," to the race variable for the 2000 census. They argued that without the separate category, it will be difficult to chart their numbers and provide them with adequate protection from some forms of discrimination. However, this demand is not simply an issue of adding a category. It will have impact on the distribution of resources and power. A separate category could cause underrepresentation of minority groups, affect the number and location of minority voting districts that are based on the numbers of people in different racial categories, and reduce government and private financing of minority programs that are tied to census figures.

After four years of study, in July 1997 a thirty-agency Clinton administration task force rejected the proposal to add the "multiracial" category to the 2000 census but recommended allowing mixed-race people to check off more than one racial category. The task force's recommendations were effectively adopted by the federal government. In October 1997, the Clinton administration announced that the "multiracial" category will not be used for the 2000 census, but it will allow mixed-race Americans for the first time to select more than one racial category for themselves. All federal agencies will be expected to conform to the new standards as soon as possible, but no later than January 1, 2003.

Currently, the multiracial category does not exist on most forms, and multiracial people can choose whatever category best serves their interest, but their choice has to be able to stand verification. Some people with multiple ancestries use ethnicity as a strategy to achieve their goals. For example, an ethnic studies instructor with mixed ancestries of Japanese and white at UC Berkeley checked the "Asian" category to increase her chance of admission when she applied for colleges in the early 1980s. Yet, five years later when her brother applied for graduate schools, he chose the "white" category because there were attempts to restrict the admissions of Asian students.

The environment one grows up with can have decisive effects on the identity of mixed-race people. For instance, a student of black and white descent at UC Berkeley was perceived as black because she looked black and sometimes she felt black. But she now considers herself white because her parents split when she was two and a half years old and she grew up with the white side of the family. Tiger Woods, the Masters golf champion of 1997, did not consider himself black or Asian, despite the initial black label given to him by the media. He stated that growing up, he learned his racial identity is "Cablinasian" because he is one-eighth Caucasian, one-fourth black, one-eighth Indian, one-fourth Thai, and one-fourth Chinese. His mother is partly Thai and partly Chinese, and his father is partly black, partly white, and partly Cherokee. His environment imparts a multiracial identity to him.

The identities of mixed-race people are especially fluid over time. The experience of Lisa Graham, who has a Filipino mother and a Caucasian father, provides a good example. The following excerpt of her narrative shows how her identity changed from American-white to Filipino and to half-Filipino and half-white.

> When I was younger, I used to say, "I am American, I am American. I am white." It was just because everybody seemed to be either black or white, a full race. . . . Starting in junior high, it became important for me to say that I was Filipino because of my mom. . . . I realize that the first thing I usually say now is, "I am Filipino," . . . But whenever I have said that, people usually responded with, "You are not full Filipino." So then I had to say that "I am half-white." But then I don't look white either. When I think of "white," I see light, light brown hair or blonde hair, and I don't look like that. . . . But now my whole attitude is changing. Now I say that I am half-Filipino and half-white. (Espiritu 1995, 202–203)

Multiple ancestries sometimes could cause discrepancies between self-identity and identity assigned by others. Professor Mary Waters of Harvard University told an interesting story about the difficulties a student of hers had in choosing her identity. The student had learned from her mother that she was an American Indian, with some heritage of black, Irish, and Scottish. When applying to colleges, she checked all the boxes on the applications that applied to her. After arriving at Harvard, she began to receive mail from the Black Student Association, and she was pressured by other black students to hang around with them. Apparently, Harvard had designated her to be black. She was not alone at Harvard. Her identical twin sister had also been admitted to Harvard University, and had checked the same boxes that she had when applying to colleges. However, the twin sister was receiving mail from the Native American Student Association and was being lobbied to attend their meetings on campus. Two genetically identical twins attending the same university were perceived as members of different ethnic groups. The story also confirms that ethnicity is socially constructed in complex ways by ancestry, social environment, and self-interest.

SUMMARY

Theories of ethnicity address what the nature of ethnicity is and why ethnicity emerges and endures. Primordialism, constructionism, and instrumentalism are the three existing paradigms formulated to answer these questions. Primordialism emphasizes the ascription of ethnicity, fixed ethnic boundaries, and the importance of biological and/or cultural inheritance. In contrast, constructionism accentuates the social construction of ethnicity, flexible ethnic boundaries, and the salience of social environment. Instrumentalism treats ethnicity as a tool for advancing self-interest and as a rational choice to minimize social costs and maximize socioeconomic rewards. An alternative theorization and synthesis of the three paradigms builds upon the cornerstone of the social construction of ethnicity and views social structure, ancestry, and the utility and cost of ethnic affiliation as ingredients contributing to the construction of ethnicity. It also attempts to balance the stability and dynamics of ethnic boundaries.

Social construction and determination also apply to the identity of mixed-race people as society assigns mixed-blood people to a particular category using such rules as the race of mother or a nonwhite parent, blood quantum, physical appearance, or a special mixed-race category. For mixed-race people, as opposed to those with single ancestry, an "ethnic option" seems more open to them, and their ethnicity is more dynamic, more complicated, and at times more afflicting.

CHAPTER 4
ETHNIC STRATIFICATION

Due to its universality and salience, ethnic stratification is at the heart of ethnic studies. To obliterate ethnic stratification and achieve ethnic equality, we must understand its origins. This chapter is divided into three major sections. The first section defines basic concepts relating to ethnic stratification. The second section focuses on theories of the origins of ethnic stratification. The third section examines the historical evidence of ethnic stratification in America in order to test the validity of the theories and to suggest where the theories of ethnic stratification may be perfected.

BASIC CONCEPTS

Several basic concepts must be defined before preceding, the first and most basic one being ethnic stratification itself. *Ethnic stratification* refers to institutionalized inequality among ethnic groups in a society. The word *institutionalized* is important. *Institutionalized* ethnic inequality means a system of ethnic relations and social rules that determines the unequal distribution of resources across different ethnic groups. Within this system, people come to expect differential rewards to different ethnic groups and to understand why they are rewarded in such a way. The inequality is not random, but follows a pattern and shows relative constancy and stability, and it is legitimized and justified. Frequently, scholars equate ethnic stratification with ethnic inequality (e.g., Farley 1995, 66). However, inequality in wealth and prestige could be due to noninstitutional factors such as individual qualities. The term ethnic stratification better captures the institutionalization of the social hierarchy across ethnic groups. "Structured ethnic inequality" is another expression of "institutional ethnic inequality."

In the same vein, *racial stratification* can be defined as institutionalized inequality among racial groups in a society. Racial stratification is a special case of ethnic stratification in which the institutionalized inequality is based on race. Racial stratification is an appropriate term in the context of institutionalized inequality among whites, blacks, Asians, and Indians in America. Due to the salience of racial stratification in the United States, it is easy to understand why racial stratification has been a focus of scholarly inquiry.

In an ethnically stratified society, different ethnic groups occupy different social positions. The ethnic group that occupies a dominant position in a society is a *majority group*, while the ethnic group that occupies a subordinate position in a society is a *minority group*.[1] The majority group enjoys a disproportionately larger share of wealth, power, and prestige, whereas the minority group shares a disproportionately smaller portion of these resources.

Unlike the conventional usage in everyday life, in the social sciences, majority group or minority group is defined in terms of relative power and status, not strictly in terms of the number or population size of a group. Number and power normally go hand in hand, but it is a mistake to assume that they are always correlated. For instance, under the apartheid system of South Africa, blacks, who constituted 75 percent of the country's population, were the numerical majority, but they were, by definition, a social minority group because they possessed a subordinate position in their society. The political and economic systems were controlled by whites until 1994 when Nelson Mandela was elected as the country's first black president. Even today, whites still control a disproportionately large part of the economy and wealth. Hence, blacks may still be a minority group today in South Africa. In the history of America, similar examples can be found in most colonies and in some areas of the American South. In 1910, for instance, African Americans accounted for more than

---

1. Sometimes, scholars define "majority group" and "minority group" in their broadest meanings to include nonethnic dimensions such as gender, sexual orientation, and disability.

55 percent of the population in Mississippi and South Carolina but they were completely excluded from all political offices in these two states (Yetman 1991, 11). Numerical majority does not necessarily guarantee social majority status.

Many commentators prefer the terms *dominant group* and *subordinate group* to the terms *majority group* and *minority group* because the former are more accurate than the latter (Yetman 1991). However, both sets of concepts may be used. Although dominant group and subordinate group are more precise in terms of meaning, these terms may have been tinted with too much political pigment for some people today, implying a repressive or hostile relationship between the two groups. In addition, the use of majority group and minority group has had a long history, and they are still widely accepted by scholars. Thus, this book continues to use majority group and minority group most of the time.

Furthermore, the status of majority group or minority group is not immutable. For instance, when the Catholic Irish first came to the United States they were considered by the dominant English to be a minority. Gradually, the Irish have become part of the majority group—white. Similarly, both Catholic Italians and Jews were treated as minority groups when they first arrived, and both have become part of the white category. Majority group or minority group status can change as the power and status of ethnic groups shift.

THE ORIGINS OF ETHNIC STRATIFICATION

The Prevalence of Ethnic Stratification

In multiethnic societies throughout the world, we seldom see egalitarian relations among ethnic groups. Ethnic stratification is the norm rather than the exception. In the United States, for example, before the Civil Rights movement, laws and government policies gave more social rewards to whites than to minorities. Although white privileges are seemingly not protected by laws and policies any more, the existing social structures still maintain whites at the top of the social hierarchy. Minority groups occupy lower positions than whites at varying levels in terms of power, wealth, and status.

In Canada, historically the English Canadians (Anglophones) were at the top of the ethnic hierarchy; the French Canadians (Francophones) ranked below the Anglophones and no higher than the noncharter groups (i.e., groups other than the Anglophones and Francophones); and the natives—Indians—stood at the bottom of the social hierarchy. Today the dominance of English Canadians still remains to some extent, but the inequality among white groups has declined and may be virtually nonexistent, as Raymond Breton (1989) argued. However, native groups continue to hold the lowest rung in all categories of social class.

Brazil is a racially mixed society. Three major color categories are *branco* (white), *prêto* (black), and *pardo* (mulatto). There are further divisions within each category. For instance, the mulatto includes *mulatto escuro* (dark mulatto) and *mulatto claro* (light mulatto). Whites and blacks are subclassified in terms of skin, hair, and facial features as well. Since hard lines between ethnic groups are not recognized, ethnicity is seemingly unimportant in the allocation of social rewards. Nevertheless, close scrutiny reveals a correlation between ethnicity and class. As Charles Wagley (1971) put it, "The darker the skin, the lower the class."

In South Africa, ethnic rank was delineated in the following order at least until 1994 and may continue today: whites at the top; colored (people of mixed white and black background); Asians (mainly Asian Indians); and Africans at the bottom. The last three categories constitute the black designation and follow a hierarchical order as well.

The above selected examples demonstrate the omnipresence of ethnic stratification in multiethnic societies. It should be noted, however, that human society was not always thus divided. Ethnic stratification did not exist at the beginning of a society. There was little or no ethnic stratification at the outset of ethnic interactions. Ethnic stratification has arisen over time. An important question then is: What conditions cause the emergence of ethnic stratification? This is a classic question in ethnic studies.

Preconditions of Ethnic Stratification

In order for ethnic stratification to arise, certain preconditions are necessary, though not always directly causal. Scholars have identified at least two of these (Noel 1968). First, there must be two or more ethnic groups in a society. If only one ethnic group exists, there will be no ethnic stratification since the same group will be at the top and at the bottom of the social hierarchy.

Second, different groups must come into contact in the same society.

If there is no group interaction, there will be no stratification. Different groups come into contact via several avenues. One channel is colonization, which occurs when the migrant group conquers and subordinates the indigenous group. A case in point was the colonization of Puerto Rico by the United States in 1898, which brought Puerto Ricans into contact with Americans. Another channel is annexation, a situation wherein one group annexes the territory of another group. Annexation can occur peacefully or violently. An example of peaceful annexation was the Louisiana Purchase from France in 1803, and an example of violent annexation was the annexation of most of the southwest including California, New Mexico, and Arizona from Mexico in the mid-nineteenth century as a result of the Mexican-American War (1846–1848). The third channel is migration, which could be voluntary or involuntary. Historically, most European immigrants came to America voluntarily while most Africans were sold here. Albeit required, two or more ethnic groups and intergroup contact are not sufficient to generate ethnic stratification. In order for ethnic stratification to take shape, there must be other direct conditions.

Causes of Ethnic Stratification

What underlying conditions cause the emergence of ethnic stratification? Several theories have been proposed to answer this question. Among the most influential ones are the social-Darwinian approach, the social-psychological approach, the functionalist approach, the conflict approach, and the Donald Noel hypothesis. Following is a brief overview of the five theories.

The social-Darwinian approach claims that ethnic stratification emerges because strong ethnic groups have a natural tendency to dominate or control weak groups. Domination motivated by a desire to increase material possessions and comfort is an instinct of human beings. Hence, strong groups will impose their wills on weak groups, and subdue them if they do not give in. Following the rule of the survival of the fittest, natural selection divides the dominant group and the subordinate groups in a social system. This approach is an application of Darwinian theory to the ethnic stratification of human societies. Hence, it is labelled the social-Darwinian approach.

This theory is problematic for at least two reasons. First, it reduces humans—the highest level of social animals—to lower-level animals. Second, the inborn desire of strong groups to subordinate weak groups is an unproven and untenable assumption. Whether human nature is essentially evil or good is both moot and irrelevant. Actions of domination may better be explained by the reward of potential gains than by any innate tendency.

The social-psychological approach contends that widespread individual prejudice against members of other groups causes ethnic stratification. In light of this approach, negative attitudes and beliefs about outgroups and their perceived undesirable characteristics and qualities beget discriminatory actions against them and, further, serve to legitimize both such actions and the outgroups' eventual subordination. When individual ethnic prejudice in a society reaches a critical level among a large number of prejudiced individuals, prevalent discrimination and the resulting ethnic stratification are inevitable. Hence, the fundamental source of ethnic stratification lies in individual psychological processes.

Undeniably, ethnic prejudice contributes to the genesis of ethnic stratification. Nonetheless, prejudice is certainly not the only determinant of ethnic stratification; nor may it be the most important one. The notion that attitudes alone explain the emergence of ethnic stratification is both simplistic and inadequate. Moreover, the origins of negative attitudes and beliefs about outgroups per se need to be explained and may be sought from group competition and conflict over limited resources.

According to *the functionalist approach*, ethnic stratification arises because it is functional or useful to the whole society. The ethnic hierarchy reflects varying positions of different ethnic groups, and multilayered ethnic strata are necessary to maintain social stability. Ethnic stratification is inevitable in a society with diverse ethnic composition. With ethnic diversity, the uneven distribution of wealth, power, and prestige among different ethnic groups is bound to emerge. Differential rewards for different groups are therefore justified, with the result that powerful groups gain a greater share of resources while weak groups obtain less.

A chief problem with the functionalist approach is that it does not acknowledge that ethnic stratification could be dysfunctional because it can cause ethnic conflict due to the uneven distribution of resources. It is doubtful that ethnic stratification does any good to the whole society, much less to minority groups. Furthermore, current disparity in the possession of resources does not justify ethnic domination.

The conflict approach argues that ethnic stratification is a result of group competition and conflict over scarce resources. It is created because the powerful group benefits from such stratification. The powerful group subordinates weak groups since domination gives it an upper hand in acquiring access to finite resources and in restraining the access of other groups to such valuable possessions. Ethnic stratification hence serves the interest of the dominant group. Societies with ethnic stratification will very likely experience conflict along ethnic lines.

This approach captures a key determinant of ethnic stratification—competition and conflict to serve self-interests. However, the causes of ethnic stratification are much more complex than the acquisition of resources alone. Competition and conflict explain the motivation of domination but cannot fully explain why a particular group becomes the target of domination and especially how one group can subordinate another. Other important factors must be taken into account as well.

Sociologist Donald Noel (1968) developed a *theory of the origin of ethnic stratification* by synthesizing some insights of the above theoretical perspectives. Noel identifies three conditions that cause the emergence of ethnic stratification. First, there must be ethnocentrism. *Ethnocentrism* refers to the tendency to judge other groups by the standards of one's own group. That is, one's own group is the center and the standard. Norms, values, and behaviors of other groups that are consistent with those of one's own group would be viewed as normal; those that deviate would be deemed abnormal or inferior. Ethnocentrism helps create ethnic boundaries, identities, and a sense of "we-ness"; it helps justify a double standard of morality for in-group members and for "outsiders," in which "insiders" are not subject to the normal rules concerning dishonesty, cheating, exploitation, and killing; and it helps legitimize actions against other "inferior" groups because of their perceived inferiority. Hence, ethnocentrism explains *whom* to dominate.

Second, there must be competition for the same scarce resources (e.g., land, water, jobs, money, prestige, and power) among ethnic groups. One ethnic group is motivated to subordinate another group because this subordination gives the first group advantages over the second group in gaining scarce resources that both groups compete for, a point suggested by the conflict approach. Even though two groups are not in direct competition, ethnic subordination can occur if one group has certain resources (e.g., labor, land) desired by the other group. Hence, competition for scarce resources explains *why* one group seeks to dominate another.

Finally, there must be unequal or differential power between ethnic groups. Power includes physical or military strength; technological advantages; possession of wealth, land, natural resources, special job skills or labor power, and valuable information; political power; size of the group; degree of organization; etc. One group must be powerful enough to dominate the others. If no group has enough power to control others, ethnic stratification will not occur. Unequal power is probably the most crucial factor, and it is unequal power that explains *how* to dominate.

Noel argues that only when all three conditions are present together will ethnic stratification emerge. Without ethnocentrism the groups would quickly merge and competition would not be structured along ethnic lines. Without competition, there would be no motivation and no rationale for instituting stratification along ethnic lines. Without differential power, it would simply be impossible for one group to achieve dominance and impose its wills and ideals upon the others.

To a great extent, Noel's theory is a synthesis of some valuable ideas from a number of approaches, and it provides a more plausible explanation for the emergence of ethnic stratification. However, Noel's theory is not flawless. As will be shown in the next section, class complicates the causal relationship.

THE GENESIS OF ETHNIC STRATIFICATION IN AMERICA

Having reviewed the theoretical perspectives on the origins of ethnic stratification, we now turn to the examination of historical evidence to see how well the theories, especially the most comprehensive theory—Donald Noel's theory—match reality. Three historical cases will be analyzed: (1) the emergence of the black slavery system, which best represents the stratification system involving blacks and whites in America; (2) the origins of Indian-white stratification as reflected in the conquest of Indians by European settlers; and (3) the genesis of Anglo-Chicano stratification as shown in the subordination of Mexicans.

The Emergence of the Black Slavery System

As the most recognizable ethnic stratification system in America, the black slavery system did not exist from the earliest black arrival in America. In 1619, twenty Africans were sold to the colony of Virginia, the first blacks who ever set foot in America (Takaki 1993, 53). However, the black slavery system did not begin to take shape until the 1660s.

Historians have demonstrated that in the first few decades of black arrivals, there was inequality between blacks and whites, but this inequality was relatively mild and uninstitutionalized. There is an abundance of evidence. At that time, many blacks were *temporary* indentured servants who were contracted to serve their masters for a limited period of time, normally four to seven years. After that period, they could become free citizens and receive land of their own (Franklin 1967, 71). Indeed, some African indentured servants later became successful farmers and landowners, and they themselves purchased African and/or white indentured servants. Although the servants under this arrangement were sometimes called slaves (Handlin 1957, 7–9), they "were not slaves in a legal sense" (Frazier 1957, 3). In other words, they were not permanent slaves at the beginning.

Furthermore, black indentured servants were not very different from many white indentured servants in terms of status. For example, in Virginia in 1665, the majority of the indentured servants were whites, mainly from England as well as Germany and Ireland, who were convicts, rogues, vagabonds, whores, cheats, and rabble in their home countries (Smith 1965). Africans made up only a small proportion of the population.[2] Both African indentured servants and many white indentured servants were brought to the New World involuntarily. They were all under some sort of indenture or involuntary servitude, and had comparable status (Hardlin and Hardlin 1950).

However, three or four decades later, the situation changed drastically. In 1661, the Virginia Assembly began to institutionalize black slavery. By the end of the 1660s, several colonies, such as Maryland and Virginia, had passed laws that legalized the slavery of blacks. In the next one hundred years, black slavery gradually became an institutionalized system. Blacks became permanent slaves with few legal rights, and their status was automatically passed on to their children.

Why did this happen? Several conditions contributed to the establishment of the black slavery system. Ethnocentrism was one of them. There is no doubt that ethnocentrism existed in seventeenth-century America. European settlers viewed blacks as inferior and had prejudice against them. For example, even before their settlement in America, the English had an array of negative images of Africans. Africans were viewed as "uncivilized," "dirty," "foul," "dark or deadly" in purpose, "malignant," "sin-

2. For instance, in 1650 there were only 300 blacks, who constituted 2 percent of the total 15,000 population in Virginia.

ister," "wicked," and "a people of beastly living, without a God, law, religion" (Takaki 1993, 51–52). They were believed to be cannibals who ate human flesh. Black inferiority was used to justify the enslavement of blacks.

Nevertheless, the white ethnocentric view of Africans was not sufficient to motivate European settlers to enslave blacks. There were benefits that white plantation owners could gain from the enslavement of blacks, namely, profit through plantation. The plantation system played a very important role in the development of slavery in this country. In order to run the plantation system, white planters needed cheap and dependable labor. Blacks were the ideal and desirable source of this labor for three reasons. They knew hot-weather farming techniques better than Indians and the Europeans; they were more easily available than Indians; and they were both exploitable and controllable.

Moreover, unequal power played a critical role in the emergence of the black slavery system. Obviously, the strong economic, political, and military power of white planters over Africans gave them advantage in subjugating blacks. But the question still remains. Since there were other weak groups such as Indians and white indentured servants, why did white planters enslave blacks but not those groups? The answer lies in the unequal distribution of power among the weak groups themselves.

White planters had a comparable amount of ethnocentrism against Indians, but Indians were not systematically enslaved and there was no Indian slavery system in America. The main reason was that Indians were in a stronger position to resist enslavement than blacks. Several specific conditions gave Indians some advantages over blacks. First, Indians proved to be much more difficult to enslave than blacks, since they could run away and rejoin their tribal groups, and tribal groups could attack plantations to free their people. Blacks, on the other hand, had none of these strengths. In a strange land, blacks had no place to escape; they lacked group solidarity, since they were imported from different parts of Africa and their families and tribal groups were deliberately broken up. Second, European settlers often depended on Indians for trade, which also put Indians in a better position than blacks. White planters depended on blacks for nothing except cheap labor. Hence, blacks became the group most vulnerable to enslavement.

There were also white indentured servants, and some (e.g., Catholic Irish) were subjected to certain degrees of ethnocentrism. However, white indentured servants escaped the fate of enslavement. The main reason, as with their Indian counterparts, rested in their stronger position relative to blacks. More specifically, white indentured servants suffered less racial prejudice than blacks and Indians; they were not racially identifiable if they ran away; and if they were permanently enslaved, the supply of prospective white indentured servants could be cut off since white debtors would not be willing to come to the New World to pay their debts.

Accordingly, Donald Noel's theory seems quite tenable because ethnocentrism, self-interest, and differential power all played some roles in the emergence of the black slavery system that clearly separated whites and blacks in terms of rights and privileges.

However, Noel's theory is not problem free in explaining the origins of the black slavery system. In particular, it fails to consider the role of class. In reality, class intersected with race to create the black slavery system. First, not all whites benefitted from the enslavement of blacks. It was mainly the white plantation owners who reaped profits from it, rather than the entire white group. At that time, only one-fourth of all southern white families owned slaves, and a mere 3 percent of the white planter-class families owned more than half of the slaves. White indentured servants and other white laborers did not have much to gain from black slavery but had much to lose because of it.

Second, black slavery was designed to be a solution for the problem of white class conflict. The white plantation class enslaved blacks in order to reduce their reliance on white indentured servants, who were armed and numerous and who could "erode their own economic advantage and potentially undermine their political hegemony" (Takaki 1993, 65). As Takaki (1993, 76) put it, "African slaves seemed to offer a solution to the problem of class conflict within white society. Slavery enabled planters to develop a disfranchised and disarmed black work force." That was why the white plantation class turned from preference for white indentured workers to preference for black slaves after Bacon's Rebellion in Virginia (Takaki 1993). Class conflicts among whites seemed to be what Takaki called the "hidden origins of slavery."

Hence, we need to modify Noel's theory by adding the class dimension in order to have a complete understanding of the origins of black-white stratification. The black slavery system was created not by ethnic factors alone, but by the interlocking of race and class. In particular, the conflicting interests and imbalanced power among the white planter class, the black indentured servants, and the white indentured servants were the crucial determinants in the invention of black slavery.

The Origins of Indian-White Stratification

The complexity of the interaction between Indians and Europeans cautions against any sweeping generalizations because exceptions almost always existed. Nevertheless, certain patterns can be identified. When the Europeans first arrived in America, the relationship between Indians and European settlers was generally equal. There was a period of peaceful coexistence and considerable cooperation between the two groups. The Thanksgiving Holiday originated in the legend that the Indians had helped the earliest Pilgrims at Plymouth survive the winter of 1621–1622. Many European settlers, mainly the Spanish, the French, and the British, depended on the Indians for survival. Both the Europeans and the Indians benefitted from the fur trade (Lurie 1991).

However, coexistence and cooperation were soon replaced by conflict and conquest. The Europeans subordinated and conquered Indians. Indian-white stratification was created. Several factors were accountable for the rise of this inequality: First, the white settlers had ethnocentric views of Indians. One early ethnocentric image of Indians constructed by European settlers was "lazy red savages," which served to justify the attempted enslavement and dislodgement of them by "hardworking whites." The "child of nature" was another early myth, which had great impact on the expectations of missionaries, especially Spanish ones, seeking to convert Indians to Christianity (Spencer, Jennings et al. 1977). On the other hand, the Protestant British viewed Indians as ungodly heathens unworthy of conversion and human association, and thus the inhumane treatment of Indians was legitimized. As Indian resistance to land seizure and the "civilizing" pressures of missionaries grew, new stereotypes such as "bloodthirsty savage" began to arise. These stereotypes provided land-seeking Puritans with justifications to hunt down Indians as they would animals.

Nonetheless, ethnocentrism alone did not lead to widespread subjugation of Indians. Stiff competition between the Europeans and Indians over land strongly motivated white settlers to subordinate Indians because of the gain—land. Unlike the Spanish, who were mainly interested in wealth and conversion of souls to Christianity, and the French, who were mainly interested in trade, the largely agriculture-oriented British settlers were attracted to North America primarily because of their desire for land (Garbarino 1976). This competition for land inevitably resulted in conflict.

Imbalanced power also explains the conquest of Indians. Firearms enabled white settlers to subdue Indians who only had knives and sticks. The growing number of white settlers further increased the power imbalance between whites and Indians. Because of unequal power, the Europeans conquered and subordinated Indians. They massacred Indians, seized their lands, and forced them to relocate to reservations where land was worthless and uninhabitable.

Thus, ethnocentrism, resource competition, and unequal power seemed to be important causes that led to the conquest and displacement of Indians. It is unclear from the existing literature that class played any significant role in the emergence of systematic Indian subjugation by whites. Perhaps race overshadowed class in the case of Indian-white stratification. Anyhow, the role of class and other factors warrants further investigation.

The Rise of Anglo-Chicano Stratification

The earliest contact between Anglos (or white Americans) and Mexicans on a sizable scale started in the early 1800s in today's southwestern United States. At that time, Texas, California, New Mexico, Arizona, Nevada, as well as most of Colorado and small parts of three other states, were part of Mexico. At the initial interaction, the relationship between Anglos and Mexicans, who were mostly mestizos—descendants of Spanish and Indians, may be characterized as mostly cooperation with limited competition. Some amount of competition notwithstanding, there was little ethnic stratification between the two groups. Both groups were ranchers, farmers, and landowners; and both groups lived side by side in a relatively equal status with substantial cooperation.

Early competition for land, and the Anglos' superior power and numbers, first manifested itself in Texas. The Mexican government's decision to abolish slavery in 1829 and Texas's independence from Mexico in 1836 accelerated the large influx of Anglo immigrants into Texas. This influx broke the balance of power. The increasing number of Anglo immigrants carried with them prejudice toward Mexicans and created new demands for land. As whites outnumbered Mexicans, they soon sought admission to the United States. As Texas was annexed to the United States in 1845, the power scale tipped totally in favor of Anglos. The past cooperation and equality between Anglos and Mexicans yielded to Mexican submission. Most of these new Mexican Americans, or Chicanos, were quickly deprived of their land either by American law or by force (Mirande 1987).[3] By 1900, even the largest and richest Mexican landowners had generally lost their land (Alvarez 1973). Accompanying this shift of economic power was a great upsurge in anti-Mexican prejudice, which justified the subordination of Mexicans in Texas.

Most of the rest of the southwest—California and Nuevo Mexico (which largely consisted of present-day Arizona and New Mexico)—became part of the United States in 1848 as a result of the Treaty of Guadalupe Hidalgo. This treaty awarded legal and political power to Anglos throughout the southwest, but it did not immediately result in ethnic stratification except in northern California where the Gold Rush commenced right after the treaty. In other areas, the subjugation of Mexicans came after a large inflow of whites in the 1870s and 1880s in much of southern California and later in New Mexico. This influx intensified competition for land as whites seized the lands of Mexican Americans and displaced them on lands and in jobs. The Anglo influx also heightened white ethnocentrism, which was used by Anglos to legitimize the mistreatment and displacement of Chicanos. The growing numbers of Anglos also gave them the status of a numerical majority, which further strengthened their political power. In various times and places throughout the southwest, the number of whites appeared to be correlated with the amount of inequality between Anglos and Chicanos.

The foregoing historical evidence again bolsters up Noel's hypothesis that ethnocentrism, competition, and unequal power together give rise to ethnic stratification, although the workings of the three factors vary from case to case in intricate manner. In every case, differential power was central in the genesis of ethnic stratification.

SUMMARY

Ethnic stratification means ethnic inequality that is codified, structured, or institutionalized. Similarly, racial stratification refers to structured inequality among racial groups. The latter can be viewed as a special case of the former. In the United States, racial stratification is prominent com-

3. Mexicans living in ceded territories were entitled to U.S. citizenship, and most became U.S. citizens (Meier and Rivera 1972). Ironically, Indians in the ceded territories with Mexican citizenship rights were denied the right to U.S. citizenship (Meier and Rivera 1972).

pared to the stratification of culturally defined ethnic groups. Majority group, also called dominant group, and minority group, also termed subordinate group, are defined in terms of the relative power and status of ethnic groups rather than group sizes, although power and group size are often correlated.

Ethnic stratification is typical in multiethnic human societies. The key question that needs to be answered is: How do we explain the emergence of ethnic stratification? In order for ethnic stratification to arise, there must be at least two preconditions: (1) there must be two or more ethnic groups; and (2) different groups must have interaction through colonization, annexation, and/or migration. What are the direct causes of ethnic stratification? This chapter has presented five theories that address this question. The social-Darwinian perspective maintains that ethnic stratification is a result of an inborn instinct on the part of stronger groups to control weaker groups. The social-psychological perspective views ethnic stratification as an outcome of widespread individual prejudice in a society. The functionalist perspective emphasizes the functional effect of ethnic stratification in maintaining social stability. The conflict perspective explains ethnic stratification in terms of group self-interest. Finally, as a synthesis of some of the foregoing theories, Donald Noel's theory argues that ethnic stratification can be explained by the combination of three conditions: ethnocentrism of ethnic groups, especially the most powerful group; group competition for scarce resources to advance self-interest; and unequal power among different ethnic groups, which is probably the most important determinant. Each of these theories has limitations. However, comparatively speaking, the Noel hypothesis offers the most comprehensive account of the origins of ethnic stratification.

The emergence of the black slavery system—an epitome of black-white stratification, the conquest of Indians by white settlers, and the subjugation of Mexicans or Chicanos all to a great extent support Noel's theory of the origins of ethnic stratification. What seems to be lacking, especially in the case of black-white stratification, is the interaction between class and race in the creation of ethnic stratification.

CHAPTER 5
ETHNIC ADAPTATION

Built on past and continuous immigration, the United States is probably the most diverse nation on earth, with people who have originated from almost every country in the world. The interaction or adaptation of different ethnic groups has always been at the hub of ethnic relations. This chapter begins with a brief description of the history of immigration to America. The main thrust of the present chapter is a review of major theoretical models concerning the processes and outcomes of ethnic interaction in America. The chapter introduces the main ideas of these theories, shows their logical development, and assesses their validity. It also briefly discusses which direction America should head toward in ethnic interactions and relations of the future, especially concerning the issue of intergroup unity versus separation.

A NATION OF IMMIGRANTS

In 1958, then-Senator John F. Kennedy (1958) called America "a nation of immigrants" in his book of the same title. Ever since, this phrase has become a well-known label describing our diverse nation. This tag was, and increasingly is, a precise descriptor of American population because everybody in America is an immigrant or a descendant of immigrants whose origins can be traced to somewhere else.

In the past, Native Americans were not viewed as immigrants since they were the aborigines or natives of this land. However, significant changes have taken place in recent years. For instance, a recent book by Abram Jaffe (1992) proclaimed Native Americans "the first immigrants." Social studies teachers at elementary schools have started to instill students with this notion. Despite the lack of definite archeological evidence, a widely accepted theory maintains that the ancestors of Native Americans crossed the Bering Strait from northeastern Asia to North America through a land bridge (Beringia) that connected the two continents between perhaps about 28,000 B.C. and about 10,000 B.C. Several different human groups from northeastern Asia—the northern Chinese, Japanese, Mongolians, and Siberians—walked across the land bridge at different times.[1] The land bridge began to disappear beneath the sea in about 10,000 B.C. as rising temperature caused the glaciers to melt. At the time of Beringia, there also existed the Mammoth Steppe, a vast northern grassland that extended from interior Alaska to the west and south of the Urals and perhaps as far as present-day Ireland (Guthrie and Guthrie 1980). People could wander back and forth across the Mammoth Steppe. The natives lived in Alaska by 25,000 B.C. and moved further to South America by 15,000 B.C. (Spencer, Jennings et al. 1977).

In 1492, funded by King Ferdinand and Queen Isabella of Spain, Christopher Columbus, an Italian sea captain from Genoa, "discovered" the continent of America. He named the people he met on a tiny Caribbean island "los Indios" (Indians). His voyage set European exploration of North America in motion.

The white Anglo-Saxon Protestants (WASPs) from England were the first major European group to settle in America.[2] Between 1607 and 1733, they established the thirteen English colonies (Virginia, Massachusetts, Rhode Island, Connecticut, New Hampshire, New York, New Jersey, Delaware, Pennsylvania, Maryland, North Carolina, South Carolina, and Georgia), which later formed the United States of America. They brought the English language, English customs, Protestantism, and other English cultural traditions to America. Following the English model, they established their preferred social institutions including the economic system,

---

1. The northeastern Asian origins of Native Americans were supported by dental evidence provided by Turner (1983, 1987).

2. The term "Anglo-Saxon" is sometimes used loosely to refer to the British groups including the English, the Scottish, and the Welsh. Sometimes, Anglo is a synonym for white.

political system, legal system, and educational system. In short, the WASPs established the dominant culture and social institutions to which other groups had to adjust.

In 1619, the English settlers began to import Africans, first as indentured servants and later as permanent slaves. As discussed in chapter 4, the first twenty blacks were sold to Virginia as indentured servants. As slave trade expanded, more Africans were sold into bondage.

Somewhat later than the English, other groups from western and northern Europe, such as the Dutch, Germans, Scandinavians, the Irish, Scots, Welsh, and the French also came to settle in America. The immigration of these western and northern Europeans is normally referred to as "old immigration."

Starting in 1848, large numbers of Chinese arrived as a result of the Gold Rush in California. Racism, economic competition, and politicians' opportunism led Congress to pass the Chinese Exclusion Act of 1882, which suspended the immigration of Chinese laborers for ten years and deprived Chinese immigrants of the right of U.S. citizenship. The 1882 Chinese Exclusion Act was renewed by the Geary Act of 1892 for ten additional years and extended indefinitely in 1904; it was not repealed until 1943.

After the 1882 Chinese exclusion, Japanese laborers were brought in as a replacement of Chinese laborers. They were later excluded from immigration as a result of the 1907–1908 Gentlemen's Agreement between the U.S. and Japanese governments; simply, the Japanese government promised not to issue additional passports to Japanese laborers in exchange for the U.S. government's permission for the Japanese laborers already in the United States to stay and to bring their families over.

In the late nineteenth century and early twentieth century, many immigrant groups from southern and eastern Europe immigrated to America, such as Italians, Jews, Poles, Hungarians, Russians, Greeks, Portuguese, Slavic peoples, Gypsies, Armenians, and so forth. This wave of immigration from eastern and southern Europe is usually referred to as "new immigration."

In the 1840s, part of Mexico was annexed to the United States mainly as a result of the Mexican-American War, and consequently some Mexicans became U.S. residents. The bulk of Mexicans started to pour in as political refugees following the Mexican Revolution in 1918, and they were followed by economic immigrants.

Starting in the early nineteenth century, significant numbers of Filipinos, Koreans, and Asian Indians were brought in by plantation owners and other employers to fill the vacancy left by Japanese laborers and to "divide and conquer" Asian laborers. The immigration of most Asian laborers was effectively banned after the Immigration of Act of 1917, which established a so-called "Asiatic Barred Zone."

Although Puerto Rico became a U.S. possession in 1899, significant Puerto Rican immigration to the U.S. mainland did not begin until the late 1920s and continued during the next several decades. The migration of the bulk of Cubans to the United States occurred after the Cuban Revolution in 1959 that overthrew the Fulgencio Batista regime and gave power to Fidel Castro.

The Immigration and Nationality Act of 1965 opened a new page in U.S. immigration history and provided more equal opportunities for immigration to people of all countries. For quota immigrants, a 20,000 per country annual quota was allocated to all Eastern Hemisphere countries effective in 1968 regardless of population size, and was extended to all Western Hemisphere countries in 1976. In addition, immediate relatives of U.S. citizens were not subject to the per country annual quota. In the post-1965 period, immigrant groups have come from many parts of the world, but Latin America and Asia have sent the majority of new immigrants to the United States. Among the largest new immigrant groups are Mexicans, Filipinos, Chinese, Vietnamese, Dominicans, Asian Indians, Cubans, Jamaicans, Koreans, Salvadorans, and other Indochinese. In recent years, immigration rates from the former Soviet Union, Poland, and Ireland have also risen.

Table 5.1 shows the numbers and percentages of immigrants by continent and from the top twenty immigrant-sending countries from 1820 to 1995. In these 176 years, about 61 percent of immigrants originated from Europe, about 25 percent from North and South Americas, some 12 percent from Asia, less than 1 percent from Africa, and even less from Oceania. The top twenty sending countries include many European nations, Mexico, Canada, several Asian countries, and a number of other Latin American countries.

Immigrants to the United States have originated from almost every country on earth. Each group came to America with its own culture and preferred social institutions. Each new group has had to interact with the dominant group and other groups, and it has had to adapt to the culture and social institutions of the host society. An important question is: What are the process and outcomes of ethnic adaptation or interaction?

Table 5.1. Numbers of Immigrants by Continent and from the Top 20 Sending Countries, 1820-1995

Continent/Country	Number	Percent
Continent		
Europe	37,865,895	60.9
North and South America	15,779,241	25.3
Asia	7,593,997	12.2
Africa	482,608	0.8
Oceania	234,940	0.4
Not specified	267,646	0.4
Country		
Germany	7,134,028	11.4
Italy	5,424,543	8.7
Mexico	5,378,882	8.6
United Kingdom	5,210,137	8.3
Ireland	4,776,548	7.7
Canada	4,401,315	7.1
Austria-Hungary	4,358,398	7.0
Soviet Union	3,690,916	5.9
Norway-Sweden	2,155,710	3.5
Philippines	1,324,815	2.1
China	1,125,679	1.8
Cuba	813,927	1.3
France	806,786	1.3
Korea	734,202	1.2
Dominican Rep.	728,684	1.2
Greece	716,404	1.2
Poland	716,388	1.1
India	638,150	1.0
Vietnam	606,341	1.0
Jamaica	517,488	0.8
Grand total	62,224,327	100.0

Source: INS (1997).

APPROACHES TO ETHNIC ADAPTATION

Many theories have been formulated to portray the process and outcomes of ethnic interactions or relations. This section introduces the most influential ones, including the Anglo-conformity perspective/assimilation theory, the melting-pot perspective, the cultural pluralism perspective, the ethnogenesis perspective, the internal colonialism perspective, and the class approaches.

The Anglo-Conformity Perspective/Assimilation Theory

An ideology that had been prevalent for a long time in the thinking and practice of America is the Anglo-conformity perspective. Historically, Anglo-conformity was strongly promoted after the Revolutionary War and World War I. Early in this century, President Theodore Roosevelt forcefully argued that Anglo-conformity was the ideal toward which we should strive. Anglo conformity means conforming to the Anglo culture and institutions—the dominant and standard way of American life. Assimilation theory is another term for the Anglo-conformity perspective. Unlike the terms *integration* and *adaptation, assimilation* implies a one-directional change, or absorption of one group or culture by another.

The basic idea of the Anglo-conformity perspective or assimilation theory is that after many generations, all immigrant or ethnic groups will inevitably and completely assimilate into the dominant Anglo culture and institutions. That is, each new immigrant group will eventually lose its cultural traditions and social institutions; learn the dominant group's language (i.e., English), norms, values, behavior, customs, laws, and world view; and become incorporated into the dominant economic, political, legal, and education systems. Ethnic interaction results in a total absorption of the new immigrant group by the dominating group. The basic idea is graphed in Figure 5.1a.

How does assimilation take place? There are differing descriptions. The two most influential models are Robert Park's Race Relations Cycle and Milton Gordon's stages of assimilation. Park's theory, developed in the 1930s, represents one of the earliest formulations of the assimilation process. Park (1937) outlined four stages of the so-called "race relations cycle": (1) Different groups come into *contact* through migration or exploration. (2) Contact sets in motion a *competition* between different groups for scarce resources such as land, water, and capital, and competition often

Figure 5.1. Three Perspectives on Ethnic Adaption

ORIGINAL
CULTURE SYSTEM
               TIME   CULTURE SYSTEM
AFTER ADAPTION

Adaption over Generations

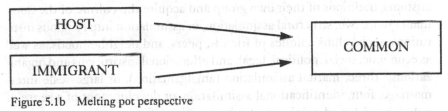

Figure 5.1a   Anglo-conformity perspective

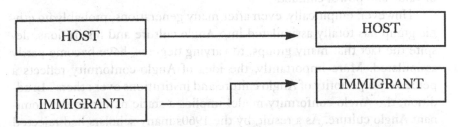

Figure 5.1b   Melting pot perspective

Figure 5.1c   Cultural pluralism perspective

Source: Andrew Greeley, *Ethnicity in the United States*, John Wiley and Sons, 1974.

causes conflict. (3) Competition and conflict are followed by a temporary *accommodation* stage in which conflict subsides and a dominant group and a subordinate group emerge. Laws, customs, and rules are established to regulate intergroup conflicts and relations. (4) The final outcome of group interaction is *assimilation* of smaller or weaker groups into a larger or dominant one. Park (1937) maintained that the four-stage cycle is universally applicable, and the sequence is "apparently progressive and irreversible."

In spite of its contribution, Park's model has been subject to much criticism over the years. Critics assert that the cycle is not universally applicable, may be incomplete, and may be reversible; and that the outcome of contact may not be assimilation, but exclusion, pluralism, or continuous ethnic stratification.

Another well-known model is Milton Gordon's seven stages of assimilation. In his now-classic book *Assimilation in American Life* published in 1964, Gordon (1964) suggested that assimilation normally goes through seven stages: one, cultural assimilation, also termed acculturation, a process in which members of an immigrant group relinquish the language, customs, traditions of their own group and acquire the culture of the dominant group; two, structural assimilation, or assimilation into religious institutions, social clubs, cliques of friends, peers, and neighborhoods, as well as economic, social, political, legal, and educational institutions and organizations;[3] three, marital assimilation (amalgamation), or large-scale intermarriage; four, identificational assimilation, or development of a sense of peoplehood based solely on the host society; five, attitude receptional assimilation, or absence of prejudice; six, behavioral receptional assimilation, or absence of discrimination; and last, civic assimilation, or absence of value and power conflict.

However, empirically, even after many generations, probably no ethnic group has totally assimilated into Anglo culture and institutions, despite the fact that many groups, to varying degrees, have become partly assimilated. More importantly, the idea of Anglo-conformity reflects a perceived superiority of Anglo culture and institutions over others'. In addition, the Anglo-conformity model implies a static nature in the dominant Anglo culture. As a result, by the 1960s many scholars had rejected the idea that assimilation is inevitable or desirable (see Yinger 1961).

---

3. Note that Gordon is too limited in restricting structural assimilation at the primary group level. Both primary structural assimilation, interaction in close, personal settings, and secondary structural assimilation, interaction in impersonal settings, should be part of structural assimilation.

Another model, melting-pot theory, began to catch widespread attention at the beginning of the twentieth century.

The Melting-Pot Perspective

The "melting pot" has been a very popular image of American society. It was popularized by a play, *The Melting Pot*, written by English-Jewish writer Israel Zangwill and presented on Broadway in 1908. The underlying idea of melting-pot theory is that as a result of ethnic interaction, both the host group and the immigrant group will blend together culturally and biologically, creating a new group called "American" and a new culture called "American culture." America is analogous to a big pot, and different ethnic groups and cultures are just like different ingredients. They are all melted in the same cauldron. Both the host group and culture and the immigrant group and culture disappear, and both contribute to the new group and new culture, as shown in Figure 5.1b.

The melting pot is certainly a very appealing idea. It is free from the ethnocentric pigment of Anglo conformity and represents equal relation between ethnic groups. Furthermore, it symbolizes dynamic and progressive changes in society. It is surely an ideal.

Is America a melting pot? Does the melting pot accurately describe what has occurred in America? Few scholars today have given an affirmative answer to these questions. As Lawrence Fuchs (1990, 276) stated, " 'Melting pot' was not and never had been the best metaphor to describe the dynamics of ethnic diversity and acculturation, certainly not for Indians or blacks, not even for immigrants and their children." Although the melting process occurs within certain boundaries, it has yet to happen in the big national pot (see, for example, Hirshman 1983). Look at intermarriage, the avenue through which biological blending befalls. A pioneer study by Ruby Jo Reeves Kennedy (1944) of intermarriage from 1870 to 1940 in New Haven found that white intermarriage occurred across nationality lines but seldom crossed religious lines. Intermarriage tended to occur within each of the three religious groups—Protestants, Catholics, and Jews. She labelled this phenomenon a "triple melting pot." Rigid religious lines of intermarriage have loosened in contemporary times; nevertheless, racial lines of intermarriage are still difficult to traverse today, despite the evidence that the numbers of interracial couples have gradually risen in the past two decades. What about cultural blending? No evidence has indicated that the dominance of Anglo-Saxon

Protestant culture in American culture has fundamentally changed, although some new elements from other cultures have been added. The entry of many diverse immigrant groups into American society has not led to new social structures or new social institutions.

In short, available evidence suggests that the single-melting-pot model does not capture American ethnic verity. Today, most researchers consider "the melting pot" a myth rather than a reality. It is unrealistic, and it has never been found in practice. A more accurate descriptor of American reality may be "multiple melting pots" or more precisely a "salad bowl."

The Cultural Pluralism Perspective

While Anglo-conformity theory and melting-pot theory prescribe the homogenization process of ethnic interaction, the cultural pluralism perspective emphasizes the differentiation process of ethnic interaction. The basic idea (Figure 5.1c) is that ethnic interaction over time will result in the coexistence of the dominant culture and the ethnic culture. That is, after interaction, the ethnic or immigrant group preserves its own culture, but it also to some extent acquires the dominant culture (e.g., learns to speak English as the common language of communication, follows the norms and values of society, and participates in the overall economic and political life of the nation). Cultural diversity is the outcome.

In recent decades, there have appeared other metaphors that express the same or similar idea of cultural pluralism. One is "multiculturalism," which connotes the existence, mixture, and penetration of many cultures. "Mosaic," a picture made of many small pieces of mixed, colorful stone, glass, etc., is another metaphor that conveys the similar idea. "Salad bowl," another comparable metaphor, vividly depicts the idea of intermingling and coexistence without melting within the common cauldron. For Fuchs (1990, 276), "salad bowl" is not an appropriate metaphor because "the ingredients of a salad bowl are mixed but do not change." To capture the dynamic nature of ethnic relations, he suggests the metaphor "kaleidoscope," which is complex and varied in form, pattern, and color, and continuously shifting from one set of relations to another. A common theme of these metaphors is that a positive whole is produced by parts that are very different.

Does cultural pluralism reflect American reality? The answer is yes. Cultural pluralism has always accompanied America, from the colonial period to the birth of the nation until now. Cultural pluralism springs from religious diversity, to language diversity, and to diversity of ethnic institutions and organizations. As Milton Gordon (1961) put it, "Cultural pluralism was a fact in American society before it became a theory—a theory with explicit relevance for the nation as a whole." Historically, cultural pluralism was not a reigning ideology of ethnic interaction. However, there is indication that it will be in the future.

The Ethnogenesis Perspective

The ethnogenesis perspective proposed by Andrew Greeley (1974) is an integration of assimilation theory, melting-pot theory, and cultural pluralism theory that incorporates the ideas of partial assimilation, partial retention of ethnic culture, and the modification and creation of ethnic cultural elements in the same framework. Literally, "ethnogenesis" means "the creation of ethnic groups" or "ethnicization." The main argument of this perspective is that over time, immigrant groups will share more common characteristics with the host group, but they still, to varying degrees, retain and modify some components of their ethnic culture, and they also create new cultural elements in response to the host social environment by incorporating their own culture and the host culture.

Figure 5.2 presents the complex model of the ethnogenesis perspective for intergroup adaptation. According to Greeley (1974), at the beginning the host group and the immigrant group may have some things in common. For instance, the Irish could speak English, and some groups were Protestants. As a result of adaptation over generations, the common culture enlarges. The immigrant group becomes similar to the host group, and the host group also becomes somewhat similar to the immigrant group. However, the immigrant group still keeps some elements of its culture and institutions, modifies some of its cultural and social structural characteristics, and creates some new cultural elements in response to the challenge of the host society. The result is a new ethnic group with a cultural system that is a combination of the common culture and its unique heritage mixed in the American crucible. Similar to the cultural pluralism perspective, the ethnogenesis perspective embraces the ideas of partial assimilation and ethnic cultural preservation, but it differs from the cultural pluralism perspective in that it emphasizes cultural change and the creation of new ethnic culture.

Empirical evidence abounds to support this theory. Partial assimila-

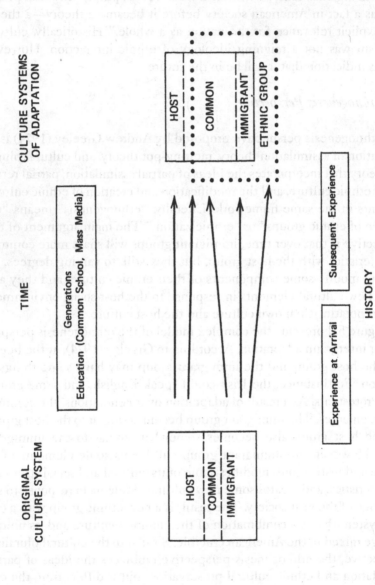

TIME

ORIGINAL
CULTURE SYSTEM

HOST
COMMON
IMMIGRANT

Education (Common School, Mass Media)
Generations

CULTURE SYSTEMS
OF ADAPTATION

HOST
COMMON
IMMIGRANT
ETHNIC GROUP

Experience at Arrival
Subsequent Experience

HISTORY

Figure 5.2. Ethnogenesis perspective

tion into the dominant culture is an undeniable fact for every immigrant group, especially European ones. Partial retention of ethnic cultures can be found at all times for almost all groups. The modification of ethnic cultural components is not uncommon. One example is Jewish Americans' celebration of *Hanukkah* (sometimes also spelled *Chanukah*). Historically, Hanukkah was not a very important Jewish holiday. However, American Jews have elevated Hanukkah to a status somewhat equivalent to "Jewish Christmas," partly because Hanukkah occurs very close to Christmas, and partly because it is an opportunity to keep Jewish culture alive. Activities during Hanukkah now resemble those of Christmas but with Jewish uniqueness, such as giving gifts to children, festive gathering, sending holiday cards, lighting and displaying candles in a menorah, and so on.

African Americans' invention of the *Kwanzaa* holiday is probably the best example of the creation of ethnic cultural elements in response to the host environment. "Kwanzaa" means "first fruits" in Swahili. The holiday runs from December 26 to January 1—parallel to the Christmas season. It is a family-centered holiday related to traditional African harvest festivals. During the holiday, African Americans light seven colorful candles (three red, three green, and one black), each representing one of the seven values or principles: unity, self-determination, collective work and responsibility, cooperative economics, purpose, creativity, and faith (Madhubuti 1977). Each day, participants light one candle and discuss its principle. Other items used for celebration include a unity cup for the pouring of libations; fruits, representing the rewards of a harvested crop; and dried corn, representing children and the future. African Americans exchange simple gifts, preferably handmade. In Los Angeles, an annual Kwanzaa parade is held.

The Kwanzaa holiday was created in 1966 by Ron Karenga (now known as Maulana Karenga), professor of black studies at Cal State Long Beach. Karenga invented this holiday because he believed that it was important for African Americans to have a holiday created by themselves in order to bring African Americans, who have been torn from their cultural roots since the slave trade, together to celebrate their heritage and their achievements. It is a time to recommit to the holiday's principles. Today, twenty million people of African descent celebrate Kwanzaa—including islanders of the Caribbean, South Americans, Europeans, and even Africans.

Some scholars maintain that assimilation theory, melting-pot theory, the cultural pluralism perspective, and the ethnogenesis perspective may well depict the adaptation experience of European groups, but may not be able to explain the adaptation experience of minority groups such as African Americans, Asian Americans, Hispanic Americans, and Native Americans. The reasons are twofold. First, the experience of the minority groups is different from that of European groups, because of their differences in racial characteristics, national origins, and cultural traditions. These minority groups suffer more prejudice and discrimination than European groups. Some minority groups may not be allowed to assimilate and may not be welcomed. Second, assimilation into the dominant culture and social structure may not be a desired outcome for minority groups.

In order to account for the adaptation experiences of minority groups, scholars have proposed theories of adaptation that depart largely from the foregoing theories. These theories emphasize conflict, inequality, oppression, exploitation, discrimination, and resistance of subordinate groups to the dominant group. Two influential approaches along this line are discussed below: the internal colonialism perspective and class approaches.

The Internal Colonialism Perspective

One well-known theory dealing with unequal, asymmetric, repressive intergroup relations is the internal colonialism perspective. Internal colonialism should not be confused with external colonialism. *External colonialism* refers to the control of a country's economy and political system by an external colonial power. External colonialism occurs outside one's national boundaries. An example is the colonization of America by Britain before the founding of the United States. *Internal colonialism,* on the other hand, refers to the subordination and oppression of minority ethnic groups by the dominant group within a country. Internal colonialism does not equate with ethnic enclaves such as Chinatown, Koreatown, or Little Saigon. It does not require a spatial concentration. It is an analogy about the relations between the dominant group and the minority group.

According to the internal colonialism perspective, the dominant group is like the colonizer, and the minority group is like a colony or a colonized people. Although other processes also go on, the most important characteristic of ethnic interaction or relations is that the majority group colonizes, controls, and exploits the minority groups within a nation (see Blauner 1972).

Advocates of this theory, notably Robert Blauner, provide historical examples of internal colonization, oppression, subordination, exploitation, and discrimination. For example, African Americans were enslaved for more than two hundred years, and they were like a colony within America. Native Americans were conquered, killed, and driven to reservations; and they were like an internal colony in America. With land taken from them, Chicanos were subordinated and treated as a colonized people. In the nineteenth century, the Chinese were excluded from immigration, denied U.S. citizenship, and forced to seek refuge in Chinatowns in isolation; they were nothing more than a colonized people. During World War II, more than 110,000 Japanese Americans on the U.S. mainland, over two-thirds of them U.S. citizens, were treated as enemy aliens and were incarcerated in concentration camps without trial for the "crime" of being a Japanese. They were like an internal colony. To Blauner, internal colonization best describes the adaptation experience of minority groups. Abundance of historical evidence notwithstanding, it is unclear whether and to what extent internal colonialism still applies to today's ethnic relations. While minorities tend to believe that there is at least some validity in this model for today's society, many white Americans show reservations or hesitancy about it.

The Class Approaches

To some theorists, ethnic relations cannot be understood solely by looking at race or ethnicity, and class division is an even more dominant dimension. Talking only about repressive ethnic relations disguises the more fundamental issues—class relations. A complete understanding of the subject requires an analysis of ethnic relations in the framework of class relations.

One of the first theorists who adopted a Marxist class approach was William E. B. DuBois, a black scholar and civil rights activist. DuBois underscored the inextricable connections between racial oppression and class oppression. The interaction of the two dimensions explains the unequal relations between whites and blacks. Oliver Cox, who drew on the ideas of DuBois, emphasized the role of class in racial oppression. In his 1948 book entitled *Caste, Class and Race*, which studied black-white relations in the South, Cox (1948) argued that the racial exploitation of black Americans was essentially part of capitalist exploitation of labor. He stated, "As a matter of fact, the struggle has never been between all blacks and all white people—it is a political class struggle" (Cox 1948, 573). Hence, the capitalist class's profit making and the need for cheap labor are the root of racial/ethnic subordination. This approach tends to reduce racial/ethnic oppression and exploitation to class oppression and exploitation.

A contemporary version of the class approach is Edna Bonacich's split labor market perspective (Bonacich 1972). This theory argues that in a capitalist society, the working class and the capitalist class of the dominant group do not share interests, nor do they benefit to the same extent from the subordination of minority groups. According to Bonacich, the desire to maximize profits motivates employers of the dominant group to recruit minority group workers because they are cheaper, docile, less unionized, and manipulatable by the capitalist class to break strikes organized by dominant group workers. However, the recruitment of minority workers hurts dominant group workers because they are more likely to be displaced and to receive lower wages and less benefits. To protect their own interests, workers of the dominant group will try to exclude minority group workers or, more frequently, to restrict their access to good, high-paying jobs. The result is a split labor market: high-paying jobs for dominant group workers on the one hand, and low-paying jobs for minority group workers on the other. Hence, minority group workers suffer from double discrimination—discrimination from both the capitalist class and the working class of the dominant group. They are subordinate to both classes of the dominant group. Nevertheless, the root cause of racial exploitation and subordination of minorities is the capitalist class's profit-making drive.

We have reviewed a number of influential theories regarding ethnic interaction and relations in America. It should be noted that there is no single American experience. Different groups follow different trajectories. Hence, no single theory can explain the adaptation experience of all groups at all times. Each theory may contain some partial truth, and each garners some empirical support. Some theories fit the experience of European groups while others fit the experience of other minorities. The applicability of these theories also varies across different times and places.

COMING TOGETHER OR FALLING APART?

Is there an ideal model of ethnic interaction or adaptation for America? What should be the direction of ethnic interactions or ethnic relations in the near future? How should different ethnic groups interact with one another? The answers to these questions naturally vary across individuals and groups. In my opinion, a more ideal model can still be found in the national motto—*e pluribus unum*, namely unity in diversity, or unity based on diversity.

Anglo conformity or assimilation is unity in a wrong way. Melting pot is unity in mirage, if not in Utopia. Internal colonialism is not unity oriented. Regardless of what approaches are taken, the following three principles should be kept in mind when dealing with ethnic relations in the future:

1. *Equality*. All groups should maintain equal relations. Any model or practice that rests on the superiority and domination of one group over another or on any other unequal relations between groups is neither acceptable nor workable. Any notion, either conscious or subconscious, that people of African, Asian, Latino, and Indian origins or of a particular white ethnic origin are un-American or less American is unacceptable and should be eradicated.

2. *Diversity*. Ethnic diversity is an essential ingredient of American national identity. Diversity is a basic fact in American life. We can't ignore the tremendous diversity among ethnic groups in this country. The negation of ethnic diversity is tantamount to ostrichism. There is nothing wrong with ethnic pride and the preservation of ethnic culture. America's strength is in the richness of its cultural diversity. We must learn to respect the cultures of other groups, and we must learn to live with our differences.

3. *Unity*. Unity includes interethnic or interracial unity. All groups, whites, blacks, Latinos, Asians, and Indians, can and should work together because of our common interests. We should not overemphasize our differences because it could beget separatism. Disunited, we fall. Unity also includes national unity. That is, all groups should work together to maintain national unity. The imperative of national unity ought to be given the same recognition as the reality of diversity.

A big challenge facing America in the twenty-first century is to build a stronger and more humane multiethnic society in which individuals are free to express their ethnic traditions and interests within the framework of national identity, to make ethnic diversity a source of national unity rather than division, and to strengthen the *unum* even as *pluribus* becomes more visible. Let us maintain ethnic equality, celebrate ethnic diversity, and promote and reinforce national unity.

SUMMARY

The brief history of immigration to the United States has shown the development of ethnic diversity in America. In an ethnically diversified society, the interaction or adaptation of different ethnic groups is inevitable. What mode and outcome best represent the American experience? What model should be the direction of ethnic adaptation for America in the near future? These are the questions addressed in this chapter.

Scholars have formulated the models of ethnic interaction in very different ways. The Anglo-conformity perspective envisions a disappearance of ethnic culture and institutions and a total assimilation of an ethnic group into the dominant Anglo culture and institutions. The melting-pot perspective foresees a disappearance of both the dominant culture and the ethnic culture and the creation of a brand new group and culture through fusing both. The cultural pluralism perspective emphasizes the retention of ethnic culture and the coexistence of the dominant culture and the ethnic culture. The ethnogenesis perspective integrates assimilation, melting pot, and cultural pluralism in a more complex fashion, with an attempt to explain the real adaptation process of ethnic groups, especially European groups.

Projecting interaction between the dominant group and minority groups in a more antagonistic fashion, the internal colonialism perspective stresses the internal colonization of minority groups by the dominant group within the same country. The class approaches suggest examining ethnic antagonism and oppression in a class framework by highlighting the crucial role of the capitalist class in making profit and causing ethnic conflict and subordination.

These theories are to varying degrees valid for the experience of specific groups in specific places and specific times. For the foreseeable future, multiculturalism as a framework for American ethnic relations seems to be gaining momentum. In any event, equality, diversity, and unity should govern future ethnic relations in the United States.

CHAPTER 6
ETHNIC DIFFERENCES IN SOCIOECONOMIC ACHIEVEMENT

Socioeconomic achievement is an important barometer of ethnic adaptation and mobility. This chapter first reviews some statistical evidence on ethnic differences in socioeconomic achievements. It then focuses on the question of why socioeconomic achievement rates differ among ethnic groups and presents major theories explaining group differences in socioeconomic achievement. The final section seeks a synthesis of the existing approaches.

DIFFERENTIAL SOCIOECONOMIC ACHIEVEMENTS

Historically, ethnic groups differed substantially in socioeconomic status due to apparent discrimination against new groups and especially minority groups. As a result of the Civil Rights movement and other social changes in American society, opportunities have gradually become more and more equal over time for all groups. However, the latest empirical evidence from the 1990 U.S. census indicates that the gaps across ethnic stripes in socioeconomic achievement, such as educational attainment, occupational status, income, employment status, and poverty status, have not vanished but have remained substantial.

Table 6.1 shows the socioeconomic indicators of broad ethnic groups in 1990. In terms of education, Asian Americans were generally better educated than other groups. For instance, about 37 percent of Asian Americans had a bachelor's degree or higher compared to 22 percent of whites, 11 percent of blacks, 9 percent of Hispanics, and 9 percent of Native Americans with such degrees. About 59 percent of Asian Americans had college experience, the highest of all groups. Overall, Hispanics, rather than blacks or Indians, were the least educated group. The large percentage (31 percent) of Hispanics in the lowest-level category was partly due to the fact that more than one million former illegal immigrants from Mexico and other Latin American countries with low levels of education had been legalized under the 1986 Immigration Reform and Control Act and were counted in the 1990 census.

Corresponding to educational attainment, Asian Americans were more likely than other groups (even somewhat more likely than whites) to be in the professional, managerial, and other white-collar occupations and less likely to be manual laborers. Again, Hispanics showed the lowest occupational status overall. African Americans and Indians fared slightly better than Hispanics, but significantly worse than whites and Asians. Asians, on the other hand, were more likely to be service workers than whites.

In terms of median family income, Asian Americans stood at the highest level while Native Americans registered the lowest level. However, since family income depends on the number of earners in the family, a better indicator of income is per capita income.[1] Statistics on per capita income reveal that whites, rather than Asians, had the highest level of income. Asians lagged $2,511 behind whites, despite their higher levels of education and occupational status. American Indians and Hispanics were at the bottom.

Poverty levels of families and individuals were the lowest among whites and the highest among Indians and blacks. Whites were least likely to be unemployed whereas American Indians were most likely. The unemployment rate of Asians was parallel to that of whites while black and Hispanic unemployment rates were close to that of Indians.

Not only do differences exist among broad ethnic groups, but there

---

1. Statistics from the 1990 census indicate that Asian families on average had more workers than white families. This fact partly explains why Asians had a higher level of median family income than whites.

Table 6.1 Socioeconomic Indicators of Broad Ethnic Groups, U.S. 1990

	White	Black	Hispanic	Asian	Native American
Education (25 years old and over)[a]					
% Less than 9th grade	8.0	13.8	30.7	12.9	14.0
% 9th to 12th grade	12.9	23.2	19.5	9.5	20.5
% High school graduates	31.4	27.9	21.6	18.5	29.1
% Some college	25.6	23.8	19.1	22.5	27.2
% Bachelor's degree or higher	22.0	11.4	9.2	36.6	9.3
Occupation (%—employed persons 16 years old or over)[a]					
Professional/managerial	28.5	18.1	14.1	30.6	18.3
Technical/sales/admin. support	32.6	29.4	25.9	33.2	26.8
Services	11.5	22.1	19.2	14.8	18.5
Precision/craft/repairs	11.6	8.2	13.1	8.0	13.7
Operators/fabricators/laborers	13.4	20.8	22.9	12.1	19.4
Farming/forestry/fishing	2.4	1.5	5.0	1.2	3.3
Median family income, 1989	$37,628	$22,429	$25,064	$41,251	$21,750
Per capita income (persons in households), 1989	$16,326	$ 9,019	$ 8,444	$13,815	$ 8,367
% Families below poverty level	7.0	26.3	22.3	11.6	27.0
% Persons below poverty level	9.2	29.5	25.3	14.1	30.9
Unemployment rate (%—persons 16 years or over)	5.0	12.9	10.4	5.3	14.4

Source: Bureau of the Census (1993), *1990 Census of Population: Social and Economic Characteristics*, Tables 42–49.
Note: Whites refer to non-Hispanic whites; Asians include Pacific Islanders.
[a] Total may not add up to 100% due to rounding errors.

Table 6.2 Educational Attainment and Household Income of Selected European Groups

Group	Years of schooling	Household income (1986 dollars)
British	13.4	$34,100
French	13.1	$32,500
Irish	12.6	$31,050
Swedish	13.5	$31,700
Dutch	12.0	$29,600
German	12.6	$31,000
Italian	12.3	$31,800
Jewish	14.5	$48,700
Greek	11.9	$34,100
Hungarian	12.8	$34,800
Polish	12.3	$30,400
Russian	12.8	$29,990

Source: Smith (1991)

are also variations across specific groups within each broad group. Table 6.2 presents data on educational attainment and household income of selected European groups. Although the differences among most European groups were relatively small, Jews outshone all other groups on both variables. Empirical evidence from other studies indicate that the Jews were highly educated and highly professional and managerial. For example, a recent poll by *Los Angeles Times* (Getlin 1998) found that nationwide 87 percent had at least some college experience, among whom 35 percent attended graduate school, and that 40 percent were professionals and 24 percent managers. Compared to their total population of about six million or 3 percent of the total U.S. population, they are highly overrepresented among academics, attorneys, corporate executives, and other professionals. For instance, Feagin and Feagin (1993, 154) believed that about 20 percent of the nation's lawyers were Jewish; Steinberg (1974, 101, 103) reported that in 1969 Jews accounted for almost 9 percent of the total university or college faculty and 17 percent at the top-ranking universities and 13 percent at the top-ranking colleges; between 6 to 8 percent of senior executives in U.S. corporations were Jewish in the mid-1980s. Jewish Americans are among the nation's Nobel Prize winners, distinguished scholars, finest writers, movie moguls, musicians, artists, entertainers, journalists, educators, and business leaders.

Table 6.3   Socioeconomic Indicators of Major Asian American Groups, U.S. 1990

	Chinese	*Japanese*	*Filipino*	*Indian*	*Korean*	*Vietnamese*
Education (25 years old and over)[a]						
% Less than 9th grade	16.8	5.6	10.4	7.3	10.2	20.4
% 9th to 12th grade	9.6	6.9	7.0	7.9	9.6	18.5
% High school graduates	14.5	26.0	16.3	11.6	24.9	17.5
% Some college	18.3	27.0	27.0	15.1	20.9	26.3
% Bachelor's degree or higher	40.7	34.5	39.3	58.1	34.5	17.4
Occupation (% — employed persons 16 years old or over)[a]						
Professional/managerial	35.8	37.0	26.6	43.6	25.5	17.6
Technical/sales/admin. support	31.2	34.4	36.7	33.2	37.1	29.5
Services	16.5	11.1	16.8	8.1	15.1	15.0
Precision/craft/repairs	5.6	7.8	7.4	5.2	8.9	15.7
Operators/fabricators/laborers	10.6	6.9	11.0	9.4	12.8	20.9
Farming/forestry/fishing	0.4	2.7	1.5	0.6	0.7	1.4
Median family income, 1989	$41,316	$51,550	$46,698	$49,309	$33,909	$30,550
Per capita income (persons in households), 1989	$15,133	$19,761	$13,709	$18,054	$11,374	$9,057
% Families below poverty level	11.1	3.4	5.2	7.2	14.7	23.8
% Persons below poverty level	14.0	7.0	6.4	9.7	13.7	25.7
Unemployment rate (%— persons 16 years or over)	4.7	2.5	5.1	5.6	5.2	8.4

Source: Bureau of the Census (1993), *1990 Census of Population: Social and Economic Characteristics*, Tables 106–112.

[a] Total may not add up to 100% due to rounding errors.

Despite the high levels of average educational attainment and occupational status, significant variations do exist among major Asian American groups as shown in Table 6.3. For example, Asian Indians were highly educated, highly professional and managerial, and had a very high economic status. The Vietnamese, in contrast, showed the lowest levels of socioeconomic achievement in educational attainment, occupational status, income levels, poverty levels, and unemployment rate. Their occupational status and per capita income resembled those of African Americans, and their poverty levels paralleled those of Hispanics and approached those of Indians and African Americans.

Table 6.4 Socioeconomic Indicators of the Three Largest Hispanic Groups, U.S. 1990

	Mexicans	Puerto Ricans	Cubans
Education (25 years old and over)[a]			
% Less than 9th grade	36.5	22.5	26.1
% 9th to 12th grade	19.3	24.1	17.3
% High school graduates	20.5	24.5	19.2
% Some college	17.5	19.4	20.9
% Bachelor's degree or higher	6.3	9.5	16.5
Occupation (%—employed persons 16 years old or over)[a]			
Professional/managerial	11.6	17.1	23.2
Technical/sales/admin. support	23.6	31.9	34.1
Services	18.5	18.5	13.2
Precision/craft/repairs	14.2	10.2	11.7
Operators/fabricators/laborers	25.9	21.0	16.5
Farming/forestry/fishing	7.2	1.3	1.3
Median family income, 1989	$24,119	$21,941	$32,417
Per capita income (persons in households), 1989	$ 7,442	$ 8,470	$13,965
% Families below poverty level	23.4	29.6	11.4
% Persons below poverty level	26.3	31.7	14.6
Unemployment rate (%—persons 16 years or over)	10.7	12.4	6.9

Source: Bureau of the Census (1993), *1990 Census of Population: Social and Economic Characteristics*, Tables 115–121.

[a] Total may not add up to 100% due to rounding errors:

Table 6.4 displays socioeconomic indicators of the three largest Hispanic groups in 1990. Apparently, Cubans had the highest levels of socioeconomic achievement in terms of all the indicators. Mexicans showed the lowest levels of educational attainment, occupational status, and per capita income. Puerto Ricans registered the highest levels of poverty and unemployment.

The foregoing statistics paint a complex picture of differential socioeconomic achievement across ethnic groups, both broad ethnic groups and specific ethnic groups. It is more than black and white and more than culture and discrimination. They prompt us to think about why.

EXPLAINING ETHNIC DIFFERENCES
IN ACHIEVEMENTS

How do we explain the large differences across ethnic groups in socioeconomic achievement? This question has increasingly become a focus of scholarly inquiry. Many explanations have been proposed. Roughly, these explanations may be divided into two broad categories: internal explanations and external explanations (Yetman 1991). Let us examine these two categories of explanations.

Internal Explanations

Internal explanations mainly use the characteristics of particular ethnic groups to explain their differences in socioeconomic achievement. They are labelled "internal explanations" since these theories emphasize factors internal to an ethnic group as opposed to external conditions of the larger society.

Internal explanations view ethnic differences in socioeconomic achievement primarily as a result of ethnic differences in group qualities and characteristics (Yetman 1991). A group's possession of desirable qualities and characteristics such as good cultural traditions, good work ethics, and higher levels of premigration education and occupational status explains its higher level of socioeconomic performance, whereas a group's poor showing can be largely attributed to a lack of such valuable traits. Proponents of internal explanations believe that these qualities and characteristics can be passed on and maintained from generation to generation and that the transmission and perpetuation of cultural and behavioral characteristics determine the variation in socioeconomic status across groups. An implied assumption of internal explanations is that opportunities provided by society are fairly equal for all ethnic groups. With relatively equal opportunities, variation in qualities and characteristics explains variation in socioeconomic achievement across groups.

A number of arguments may be pigeonholed under the rubric of internal explanations. The most widely acknowledged include the biological argument, the cultural explanation, the social class explanation, and the immigrant argument. This section reviews the main arguments of these theories and the relevant empirical evidence.

The biological argument

According to this argument, differences across ethnic groups in biological or genetic factors such as genes and intelligence determine ethnic differences in socioeconomic achievement. In other words, a group fares better socioeconomically because it is biologically superior to other groups, and poor performance of a group is due to its biological inferiority.

In the nineteenth century and the early twentieth century, this kind of argument was widely held among many academics and politicians. For instance, the lower socioeconomic status of the Irish compared to Anglo-Saxons during the great migration period was attributed to Irish biological inferiority (Feagin and Feagin 1993). The Irish were derided as the "missing link" between the gorilla and the human race. Biological inferiority was also deemed decisive to the poor socioeconomic status of immigrants from southern and eastern Europe at the turn of this century, such as Italians (Feagin and Feagin 1993).

Today, the biological argument has lost its legitimacy. Few scholars still hold any belief in biological determinism. However, that does not mean this argument has perished. There are still a handful of ardent believers who advocate the biological determination of ethnic differences in socioeconomic achievement. One example is *The Bell Curve*, a book published in 1994 by two researchers—Richard Herrnstein, late professor of psychology at Harvard University, and Charles Murray, research fellow at the American Enterprise Institute.

Herrnstein and Murray (1994) argued that there were genetic differences in intelligence across ethnic groups. Based on the data from the National Longitudinal Study of Youth, Herrnstein and Murray found that the mean scores of IQ (measured by the Armed Forces Qualification Tests) for white Americans, black Americans, and East Asians (including Chinese, Japanese, and Koreans) were 103, 86.7, and 106, respectively. They focused on black-white differences since the number of cases for East Asians was relatively small (N=42). Herrnstein and Murray went on to argue that the lower level of African Americans' socioeconomic performance as seen in graduation from college, occupational status, income, poverty, unemployment, and welfare dependency can be largely explained by their lower level of intelligence, a genetic factor. They claimed that if IQ score is controlled, differences between whites and blacks in graduation from college, occupational status, income, poverty, and unemployment become much smaller. Hence, genetic differences are the most important determinant of socioeconomic achievement.

Their argument has received little support in the academic community. A main problem with their argument is that an IQ test does not measure inborn intelligence. Most genetics specialists would not say that genes explain IQ. Groups may have differences in mean IQ score, but the differences are largely a result of environment, rather than genetic inheritance. For instance, black children received a lower mean IQ score largely because they were less likely to attend better schools and were less prepared for the IQ test than white children. Their poorer prenatal and childhood nutrition may impede their later ability to do well on the IQ test. Culturally biased questions on the IQ test using white, middle-class norms may favor whites over blacks, although great efforts have been made to reduce such biased items. Herrnstein and Murray did not prove that the differences in mean IQ score are due to genetic differences. The fact that black children did not score higher on the IQ test than white children does not mean that they were born dumber than whites. Furthermore, intelligence is not the only determinant of socioeconomic performance, and it may not be the most important factor. Factors such as equal opportunities and resources are probably more important.

The cultural explanation

A very popular theory is the cultural explanation. The cultural argument contends that ethnic differences in socioeconomic achievement are determined by group differences in cultural characteristics such as norms, values, beliefs, attitudes, customs, and habits learned in the family and the community. Hence, some ethnic groups can pull themselves up the socioeconomic ladder by their own bootstraps and can overcome even severe discrimination because they have some desirable cultural traditions such as respect for education, future orientation, motivation for achievement, hard work, thrift, perseverance, and sacrifice. On the contrary, groups that lack those cultural traits are prone to failure.

Economist Thomas Sowell has formulated one of the most articulated versions of the cultural argument. To Sowell, cultural inheritance is "more important than biological inheritance," and cultural differences in values, attitudes, skills, and morality explain variations in socioeconomic achievement among American ethnic groups. As Sowell (1981, 282, 284) put it, ethnic groups "that arrived in America financially destitute have rapidly risen to affluence, when their cultures stressed the values and behavior required in an industrial and commercial economy." On the other hand, "groups today plagued by absenteeism, tardiness, and a need for constant supervision at work or in school are typically descendants of people with the same habits a century or more ago."

The socioeconomic success of Jews is often used as an example to support the cultural argument. It has been observed that large numbers of Jews and Catholics (primarily Italians and Polish) immigrated from Europe to the U.S. at the turn of this century, but within a generation the Jews outperformed their Catholic counterparts in gaining white-collar jobs and higher income. Several studies (Glazer 1958; Strodtbeck 1958; Strodtbeck, McDonald, and Rosen 1957) have argued that Jewish socioeconomic achievement was a result of their cultural traditions, such as a reverence for education, a strong belief in self-reliance for success, and the instillation of achievement orientation by the Jewish family. Especially, their respect for schooling and scholarship was derived from the intellectual tradition of orthodox Jewish culture. In contrast, parents of Catholic immigrants perceived little value in education and did not push their children for educational attainment (Strodtbeck 1958).

Similarly, the achievements of the Chinese and Japanese are often attributed to their respect for education, high aspirations, hard work, perseverance, self-reliance, and frugality. In particular, during World War II, Japanese Americans were incarcerated in concentration camps and suffered the grossest deprivation of basic civil rights in modern U.S. history. Nevertheless, in less than a generation after the incarceration they had become one of the most affluent, socially accepted, and generally respected groups in America. Their ethnic culture, which emphasized values and behavior compatible to those of the American middle class, was a key reason (Caudill and DeVos 1956).

On the other hand, the poor achievement of African Americans is often deemed to be associated with the deficiency of their cultural tradition. For instance, Lemann (1986, 35) asserted that a "distinctive culture is now the greatest barrier to progress by the black underclass, rather than either unemployment or welfare." This "ghetto culture" includes norms, values, and behaviors that tolerate or support teenage pregnancy and single motherhood, gang activities, the rejection of doing well in school, and a weak sense of accomplishing one's goals through one's own efforts. This claim is similar to the culture-of-poverty theory first suggested by Oscar Lewis (1959, 1965). Seeking a link between cultural orientation and social structure, Fordham and Ogbu (1986) argued that the orientation toward reduced academic effort among some black students was an "oppositional" response to white institutions and white standards. They found that some black students viewed doing well in school as a "white thing," and they often felt obliged to neglect school work in order to be accepted by their peers and be popular. In conjunction with group culture, the controversial Moynihan Report (U.S. Department of Labor 1965) attributed the most important cause of continuing black poverty to the black family structure, characterized by a high proportion of single-mother-headed families and the passing on of such "family values" to future generations.

Culture may partly explain why some groups fare better than other groups, but culture alone cannot give us a complete answer. Other characteristics of an ethnic group as well as larger societal conditions also affect its performance. A cultural argument tends to minimize or dismiss the role of external factors (Yetman 1991). Furthermore, the importance of culture in determining socioeconomic achievement is moot. Empirical evidence (e.g., Hill and Ponza 1983) suggests only a weak correlation between such values as motivation for achievement, future orientation, and parental sense of efficacy, and whether people can move out of poverty and how long they stay on welfare.

The social class explanation

Unlike the cultural argument, which pinpoints the prominence of culture, the social class explanation places more weight on the role of a group's class position. The social class explanation argues that ethnic groups' social class positions at the time of immigration to America largely account for their current differences in socioeconomic achievement. In other words, a group that arrived with a higher social class position or socioeconomic standing is more likely to succeed later than a group with a lower starting point. Hence, class backgrounds of ethnic groups are most important.

For instance, Stephen Steinberg (1981), a strong advocate of the social class position argument, emphasized the crucial role of class backgrounds in determining the socioeconomic achievement of different groups. Like other scholars, he also compared the socioeconomic achievements between Jewish and Catholic (i.e., Italian and Polish) immigrants who arrived at the turn of this century, but he came to a very different conclusion about why the Jewish immigrants later fared significantly better than the Catholics. According to Steinberg (1981), the better performance of the Jews was not mainly due to their cultural traditions but due to their higher status at their arriving time. He showed that only about one-fourth of all Jews entering the U.S. between 1899 and 1910 were illiterate as opposed to more than half (54 percent) of Southern Italians and one-third (35 percent) of Poles; two-thirds of Jewish immigrants were skilled workers, professionals, and merchants while only one-sixth of Italian immigrants and one-sixteenth of Polish immigrants were in these categories; more than two-thirds of Italians and three-fourths of Polish were unskilled laborers or farmers as compared to about one-seventh of their Jewish counterparts; Jewish immigrants mainly came from towns and cities of eastern Europe and had extensive experience with manufacturing and commerce, whereas many Italians and Poles came from rural areas and had little experiences with industry and business. The skills and backgrounds of Jewish immigrants enabled them to land better jobs than unskilled Italians and Poles and facilitated their children's entry into the professions later on.

Steinberg showed how social class affected the occupational mobility of Jews and Catholics within the academic profession. If the parents were professionals, managers, and businessmen, their children were more likely to get into these occupations. It was not simply Jewish cultural values that extolled education and learning, but the class factor that interacted with cultural values. "Cultural values are activated and given significance by their social class circumstances" (Steinberg 1981, 132). Hence, the social class of different ethnic groups has played a crucial role in influencing the socioeconomic status of their descendants.

Although social class position is not the only determinant of a group's socioeconomic performance, it is surely a very important one. Asian Americans are another supporting example in point. The high levels of educational attainment and occupational status of many Asian Americans are largely due to the selective immigration of educated and professional Asian immigrants. Many obtained a college degree prior to immigration to the United States, and some acquire additional training after immigration. Educated and professional Asian immigrants further push their children to pursue higher education and a professional path.

Another example is Cubans. Cubans fare much better than Mexicans and Puerto Ricans largely because the bulk of earlier Cuban refugees were former high-ranking government officials, professionals, and businessmen, who came after the 1959 Cuban Revolution. Their resources, experiences, and knowledge enabled them to succeed socioeconomically in the United States after arrival.

The immigrant argument

The immigrant argument contends that the length of time a group has spent in the host country is a critical factor in explaining variations in socioeconomic achievement. Some new groups are not doing well simply because time has been too short for them. After several generations, today's new immigrants will inevitably replicate the experience of European ethnic groups and move into the American mainstream. Hence, ethnic socioeconomic success is only a matter of time.

Few would disagree that time makes a significant difference since mobility is a long process. All else being equal, the longer a group has been in the United States, the higher its level of achievement. Over generations, group disparity in socioeconomic status should diminish. However, counterevidence exists. African Americans, the majority of them being native born, have been in America for several centuries, but their average socioeconomic status lags far behind whites and even behind the largely immigrant-composed Asians. American Indians, an indigenous group with few immigrants, trail even behind African Americans. Thus, there must be other factors not captured by time and other factors internal to ethnic groups themselves.

External Explanations

In contrast to internal explanations, external explanations accentuate factors external to ethnic groups or structural factors as the most important determinants of ethnic differences in socioeconomic achievement. The basic assumption of external explanations is that opportunities and resources provided by society are not equal for different ethnic groups. Some groups, such as white ethnic groups, fare better because they have more opportunities or face fewer constraints or barriers, while other groups, such as African Americans and American Indians, fare worse because they have fewer opportunities or confront more constraints and impediments.

There are at least three versions of external explanations: the discrimination argument, the economic restructuring perspective, and the contextual perspective. The first stresses the role of discrimination against certain racial/ethnic groups, the second underscores the role of the changing opportunity structure, and the last highlights an array of reception contexts.

The discrimination argument

An often-heard explanation is the discrimination argument, which contends that different degrees of discrimination encountered by different groups cause unequal opportunities and the resulting differences in socioeconomic achievements among groups. Whites have suffered the least racial discrimination and therefore have accomplished the highest level of socioeconomic status; the so-called *caste minorities* such as African Americans, American Indians, Chicanos, and Puerto Ricans have endured the most severe discrimination and therefore have remained at the bottom of the socioeconomic hierarchy; Asian Americans' discriminatory sufferings lie somewhat in between, leading to their middle position in the socioeconomic hierarchy (Ogbu 1978). Racial discrimination was and still is a major obstacle to socioeconomic mobility for minority groups.

There is no doubt that historically minority groups have suffered substantially more discrimination than whites, leading to their lower socioeconomic achievement. For instance, in a comparative study of blacks and white immigrants from the 1880s to the 1950s Stanley Lieberson (1980) found no evidence that blacks were less interested in education than white immigrants; rather, various forms of discrimination against blacks and their children explained their lower educational attainment. Feagin (1991) demonstrated that blatant discrimination against blacks is still a significant problem. Feagin and Feagin (1993, 235) maintained that past and continuing discrimination are the likely reason for black poverty, unemployment, and underemployment. Massey and Denton (1993) argued that racial prejudice and discrimination are the main cause of residential segregation and poverty.

Undeniably, historical and contemporary discrimination partly accounts for the lower achievement rates of some groups than other groups. However, the discrimination argument is not without criticism. William Julius Wilson (1987), for instance, argued that racial discrimination cannot solely or even mainly explain the unemployment, poverty, female-headed households, and welfare dependency of inner-city minorities. Social structural changes are also responsible for many problems. Sowell (1981) also downplayed the role of discrimination against minority groups. He contended that one cannot be sure about how important discrimination is in causing differences in socioeconomic achievement. For instance, the quick recovery of Japanese Americans in less than a generation after the interment proves that discrimination is not a severe barrier to socioeconomic advancement. Sowell also claimed that the economic success of black immigrants from Jamaica shows that racial discrimination is not insurmountable.

It is also inaccurate to state that one minority group has undergone less discrimination than another minority group. In fact, different minority groups have experienced *different kinds* of discrimination. Slavery suffocated African Americans; conquest and land seizure asphyxiated American Indians; subordination stifled Chicanos; and exclusion and denial of citizenship throttled Asian Americans. In particular, most Asian groups were not eligible for U.S. citizenship until the 1940s and 1950s. They were granted citizenship rights much later than all other minority groups. Thus, the historical discrimination experience of Asian Americans was not qualitatively different from that of other minority groups. Today, Asian Americans are still facing the problems of perpetual foreigner stereotyping, the glass ceiling, and political powerlessness.

The economic restructuring perspective

While the discrimination argument stresses the role of human discriminatory actions, the economic restructuring perspective underlines the significance of impersonal structural changes. This latter theory argues that a transformation from a manufacturing-based economy to a service-based economy causes changes in employment opportunities that have disproportional effects on different ethnic groups; as a result, some groups get stuck at the bottom of the economic ladder. Hence, it is the larger impersonal structural forces that are mainly accountable for unequal levels of achievement.

William Julius Wilson (1987) maintained that great changes in the economic structure such as "the shift from goods-producing to service-producing industries, the increasing segmentation of the labor market, the growing use of industrial technology, and the relocation of industries out of the central city" have offered educated blacks unprecedented job opportunities in the growing government and corporate sectors and meanwhile have had negative effects on uneducated, inner-city blacks. On the one hand, production jobs that require no advanced skills are relocated from inner cities to suburbs, the Sun Belt, or abroad; on the other hand, the jobs available in inner cities require highly technical competence and extensive training, which many inner-city blacks lack. Hence, this economic "mismatch" between the types of available jobs and the qualifications of inner-city blacks leads to the temporary or permanent unemployment of many black residents, thereby creating a black underclass.

Several studies have demonstrated the effects of this economic restructuring on African Americans. For example, Kasarda's study (1989) found that during the 1970s the number of jobs available for people with less than a high school diploma decreased tremendously in New York City (604,980), Chicago (292,420), Philadelphia (175,700), Detroit (162,760), Boston (129,240), and Cleveland (84,880). Hill and Negrey (1985) reported that due to economic recession, about half of the black male workers in durable goods manufacturing in five Great Lakes cities lost their jobs between 1979 and 1984. Wilhelm (1980) noted that the changing economic structure together with other factors such as automation, high educational requirements for jobs, and racism have rendered many African Americans useless and permanently unemployed. Other studies also found that Native Americans (Bureau of Indian Affairs 1987) and Puerto Rican Americans (Tienda 1990) also suffered disproportionately from the economic restructuring.

Not all agree with the mismatch hypothesis. Saskia Sassen (1988) found that in major urban centers the economic restructuring created more highly professional and technical jobs that demanded high credentials and training, and meanwhile expanded lower-paying service jobs such as housekeepers, gardeners, janitors, hotel workers, restaurant workers, cashiers, and garment industry workers. These jobs seemed to match the qualifications of uneducated inner-city black residents. Why have these jobs eluded black workers? Waldinger (1986-87) argued that distinctive economic niches of immigrant groups, through in-group network recruitment, played an important role. Ethnic network recruitment has a particular effect on native-born blacks, who are excluded from employment opportunities controlled by immigrants as well as by native-born whites.

The economic restructuring perspective opens our eyes to broader social processes that constrain individual and group attainment and cause their differential achievements.

The contextual perspective

Alejandro Portes and Ruben Rumbaut (1996) suggested a contextual approach, which stresses the *"contexts of reception"* for immigrant incorporation that interact with individual human capital characteristics and time to produce differential results in socioeconomic achievement for different groups. Portes and Rumbaut highlighted the three most relevant contexts of reception. The first context is immigration policies of the host government. Immigration policies determine whether the immigration flow of a country is allowed, what kind of people and how many of them can come, and in what way they can enter (e.g., family reunification, occupational skills, refugees). This context largely determines the social class position of a group and its later incorporation and success. The second context is the labor market conditions in the host country. These conditions include stages in the business cycle; demand for specific kinds of labor; regional wage differential; and presence or absence of prejudice and discrimination of employers toward immigrant groups. The economic prospects of a group largely depend on this context. The third context is the ethnic community. Whether the ethnic community exists and what type of community is available can have immediate and significant impact on group members. The existence of an ethnic community can mitigate new members' cultural shock, shield them from outside prejudice and discrimination, assist them in overcoming initial economic hardships through the provision of information on employment and language training, and provide them with financial resources for entrepreneurial undertakings. Furthermore, ethnic communities with a significant proportion of professionals and entrepreneurs offer group members more opportunities in employment and business than predominantly working-class communities. All these contextual conditions interact with individual skills and resources, leading to a plurality of outcomes.

TOWARD A SYNTHESIS

The above two camps of theories differ substantially in their emphases. The internal explanations emphasize primarily the backgrounds, attitudes, and behaviors of particular ethnic groups, whereas the external explanations accentuate the attitudes, practices, and structures of the larger society. With the exception of the biological argument, each of the theories examined above seems to capture an essential dimension of the whole picture, but none of them can stand alone to claim a grasp on the totality. Despite some inconsistencies, the two categories of explanations complement more than contradict each other. A synthesis of both is possible.

I argue that the combination and interaction of external factors and internal factors surely offer a better explanation of ethnic socioeconomic differential. Culture, class position, and length of time are no doubt important variables. With equal opportunities, ethnic groups are ultimately responsible for their own accomplishments. A higher starting point gives a group advantages in adaptation and facilitates its entry into the mainstream. Premigration experience largely determines the orientation of a group after immigration. Culture makes some differences. However, the importance of culture is subject to debate. "Cultures are not 'superior' or 'inferior.' They are better or worse adapted to a particular set of circumstances" (Sowell 1981, 285). Some groups are more successful in one aspect but less successful in another. Groups that value long-term investment, such as education, are more likely to climb the socioeconomic ladder later on than groups that seek quick profit and instant benefits. The transmission of certain desirable values such as emphasis on education, orientation for achievement, future orientation, self-reliance, and perseverance is better realized in high status families irrespective of race or ethnicity. In this sense, class position is perhaps more important than culture. Class facilitates the transmission of certain values and beliefs, and values promote class mobility. Class and culture interact in a complex way. All else being equal, the length of time in the host country is positively associated with socioeconomic achievement.

The large societal context is certainly relevant. It provides a backdrop that either permits or prohibits and either promotes or impedes groups' socioeconomic achievement and a framework in which social forces interact with groups' characteristics and resources. Unequal opportunities explain unequal outcomes in performance. Impersonal structural factors and receptional contexts have their own influences.

It is the *interaction* of the large social contexts with the characteristics and adaptation strategies of ethnic groups that ultimately determines the outcome. Equal opportunities are pivotal. Without equal opportunities, no group can make it even though it tries very hard. However, equal opportunities do not automatically produce the same outcomes for all ethnic groups. A group has to locate itself in the structure. It has to work hard to win social recognition and respect rather than wait for government assistance. Social forces are impersonal but they can to some extent be changed or mitigated by social actions. For instance, discrimination has gradually decreased through persistent human efforts. Although we may not be able to change the postindustrialization process, we can adapt to the changing social environment.

Questions often arise about the relative importance of internal and external factors. A universal answer to this question appears inconceivable. The importance of these factors depends on specific groups at specific times. Take African Americans as an example. Before the Civil Rights movement, external factors played a decisive role in determining their achievement. More than two centuries of slavery deprived them of their basic human rights and stigmatized the entire group. Systematic racial discrimination and segregation denied their access to valued and scarce resources in school, employment, housing, politics, and social life. Discrimination made their socioeconomic achievement impossible or extremely difficult. The result was their bottom position in the social hierarchy.

However, since the 1960s opportunities have gradually opened to all groups as a result of the Civil Rights Act of 1964 and changes in social policies, including affirmative action programs. That is why we have seen the rise of a black middle class, which is doing very well socioeconomically. Because of changing structural conditions, internal factors have gained greater importance.

Why did African Americans on average not fare well? An important reason lies in the existence of a black underclass, which possesses little education and skills, often lacks jobs, and lives in poverty. The averaging of all black Americans generates a bleak picture of the group. However, a closer look at African Americans reveals two black Americas: a middle-class black America and an underclass black America (see, for example, Grant, Oliver, and James 1996).

SUMMARY

Empirical evidence points to substantial variation in socioeconomic achievement across different ethnic groups. Why achievement rates differ concerns scholars and policy makers. The explanations can be grouped into two categories: internal explanations and external explanations. The former use factors internal to ethnic groups to explain their differences in socioeconomic achievement while the latter highlight the importance of factors external to ethnic groups.

Internal explanations assume that opportunities for all ethnic groups are basically equal. Success or failure of a group depends on its qualities and characteristics such as cultural traditions, class position, and so on. Within internal explanations, there are four major arguments. The biological argument underscores biological or genetic factors in explaining ethnic differences in socioeconomic achievement. This argument had quite a few supporters in the past but it enjoys little legitimacy in the academic community today. The cultural explanation accentuates the importance of culture, as found in norms, values, beliefs, and habits that are learned in the family and the community. The social class explanation emphasizes the class position of an ethnic group at the time of arrival. The immigrant argument stresses the importance of length of time in the host society.

External explanations focus on external or structural factors beyond the control of ethnic groups in determining socioeconomic achievement. External explanations presume unequal opportunities across ethnic groups. This chapter has identified three main external explanations: The discrimination argument attributes differential outcomes to differences in discriminatory experiences encountered by different groups; the economic restructuring perspective links the differences in achievement with the differential opportunities caused by economic restructuring; and the contextual perspective emphasizes the underlying roles of immigration policy, labor market conditions, and the ethnic community.

A more complete explanation of ethnic differences in socioeconomic achievement lies in the collection and interaction of many determinants at different levels: individuals' human capital; groups' cultural traditions, class positions, and lengths of time in the host country; and unequal opportunities, structural changes, and different contexts of reception in the larger society. The importance of these factors are group-dependent, time-dependent, and place-dependent.

CHAPTER 7
ETHNIC PREJUDICE

Prejudice is a general term that refers to negative attitudes or opinions about a social group such as an ethnic group, racial group, gender group, sexual-orientation group, class, and so on. This chapter focuses on ethnic prejudice, which is probably the most important type of prejudice. The notion and theories of ethnic prejudice, as well as analytical methods for it, can be applied to the analysis of other types of prejudice with some modifications. This chapter addresses the following questions: What are the meaning and dimensions of ethnic prejudice? How has ethnic prejudice changed over time in America? What causes ethnic prejudice? Ethnic prejudice and ethnic discrimination are often used together and even interchangeably. However, despite their intimate relationship, they are two different concepts. Ethnic discrimination will be the focus of the next chapter. Ethnic prejudice and ethnic discrimination are also associated with the notion of racism, which is the topic of chapter 9.

THE NOTION AND DIMENSIONS OF
ETHNIC PREJUDICE

What is ethnic prejudice? *Ethnic prejudice* usually refers to negative attitudes or beliefs regarding an ethnic group and its members that are based on faulty or inadequate information. For simplicity, *ethnic prejudice* is often abbreviated as *prejudice* in what follows. According to this definition, prejudice comprises attitudes or opinions, not actions. For example, refusal to sell a house to blacks based on their race is discrimination while the dislike of blacks due to their presumed violence is prejudice. Literally, ethnic prejudice may include positive attitudes or opinions. For instance, one may prefer dating Japanese women because of the perception that Japanese women are meek and gentle, or may believe that Jews are particularly intelligent, or may perceive blacks as good athletes. However, scholars usually avoid positive prejudice and focus on negative attitudes and beliefs, because negative attitudes and beliefs overshadow positive ones in frequency and intensity and because scholars are most concerned about the consequences of negative attitudes and how to deal with them. As Aboud (1988) put it, "The most salient characteristic of prejudice is its negative, hateful quality. This negativity defines prejudice." Moreover, prejudice is a prejudgment based on wrong or inadequate information. It is a *categorical judgment* based on the group membership of individuals. Prejudice differs from objective observations about average differences among different groups. For instance, the statement that "American Indians are much more likely to live under poverty than white Americans" is not a prejudice but a fact; however, it is prejudiced to assume every American Indian is poor.

The concept of ethnic prejudice includes three dimensions: cognitive (what people believe is true), affective (what people like or dislike), and conative (what people incline or tend to behave or do) (Allport 1954). (1) *The cognitive dimension. Cognitive prejudice* refers to false beliefs about a group based on faulty or insufficient information. Most frequently, false beliefs are generated through stereotyping. *Stereotyping* is a process of overgeneralizing about the characteristics of a particular group based on erroneous or inadequate information. A stereotype is an overgeneralization or exaggeration that ignores individual differences within group. There are countless examples of ethnic stereotypes: African Americans are oversexed; Indians are drunkards; Asian Americans are treacherous; Italian Americans are associated with the Mafia; and the Jewish are money hungry. As you can see, these stereotypes are doubtlessly false characterizations of these groups. Stereotype is the most typical form of cognitive prejudice, and many ethnic prejudices take the form of ethnic stereotype. (2) *The affective dimension. Affective prejudice* refers to negative feelings about a group, such as fear, hatred, dislike, disgust, uneasiness, contempt, or suspicion. It has to do with sentiments, emotions, or feelings. The affective and cognitive dimensions of prejudice may be intertwined. For example, a feeling of dislike or uneasiness toward another group may be associated with a person's stereotype toward that group. (3) *The conative dimension. Conative prejudice* refers to the tendency of the mind toward acting against members of another group. Note that the conative dimension is the *propensity* or *predisposition* to act if a situation comes up, not what one actually does. For instance, one thinks he/she would turn down a request for a date from a black student (he/she may act differently when it actually occurs); one would be inclined to reject members of another ethnic group for membership in his/her fraternity or sorority; and one would be prone not to live in a black neighborhood.

TRENDS IN ETHNIC PREJUDICE IN AMERICA

How has ethnic prejudice in America evolved over time? With modernization and universalized education, one would expect a trend of decreasing ethnic prejudice. Is there any empirical evidence to buttress this conjecture? Let us examine the results of some surveys on changes in stereotypes—a main form of cognitive prejudice—and on changes in the affective and conative dimensions of prejudice.

A pioneer study of stereotypes by David Katz and Kenneth Braly (1933) asked students at Princeton University to check a list of the characteristics that best represented the ten groups: Blacks, Germans, Italians, Irish, English, Jews, Americans, Chinese, Japanese, and Turks. Later studies have replicated this checklist approach for certain groups at Princeton University and Arizona State University (Gilbert 1951; Gordon 1973, 1986). Table 7.1 shows the results of these studies for blacks—the group that is most prejudiced against—over a fifty-year span. The data confirm a clear trend of steady declines in the traditional stereotypes of African Americans such as "lazy," "superstitious," "ignorant," "happy-go-lucky," and "stupid." These studies also found that stereotypes of Jews (e.g., "shrewd," "mercenary," "grasping," and "sly"), of Chinese (e.g., "superstitious" and "sly"), had also decreased over time. These trends are encouraging and indicate progressive attitudinal shifts.

While the data suggest that stereotypes are less socially acceptable, they by no means indicate the disappearance of ethnic stereotypes in society. There are at least three reasons. First, the respondents were college students, and less educated people may respond very differently. Second, subtle forms of stereotypes remain prevalent. Third, old stereotypes of

Table 7.1   Stereotypes of Black Americans, 1932–1982

Stereotype	1932	1950	1969	1982
Lazy	75%	32%	18%	18%
Superstitious	84%	42%	10%	9%
Ignorant	38%	24%	8%	9%
Happy-go-lucky	39%	17%	5%	1%
Stupid	22%	10%	2%	1%

Source: Adapted by permission from Leonard Gordon, "College Student Stereotypes on Blacks and Jews on Two Campuses: Four Studies Spanning 50 Years." *Sociology and Social Research* 70 (1986):200–21.

African Americans are being replaced by new ones. For example, Gordon (1986) showed that the stereotypes of African Americans as "aggressive," "sly," "loud," and "arrogant" increased significantly.

Scholars have also developed scales to measure the affective and conative dimensions of prejudice. The most notable measure is the *social distance scale* developed by Emory Bogardus (1933). This scale measures people's willingness to be associated (or to assume a degree of intimacy) with other groups through marriage, through joining the same club, through living in the same neighborhood, through working in the same occupation.

The seven degrees of social distance or contact is indexed by the following items and their scores, which indicate one's willingness to admit members of another group:

1. to close kinship by marriage;

2. to my club as personal chums;

3. to my street as neighbors;

4. to employment in my occupation;

5. to citizenship in my country;

6. as visitors only to my country; and

7. would exclude from my country.

A score of 1 means no social distance or no affective and conative prejudice, and a score of 7 indicates the highest degree of social distance or affective and conative prejudice. The higher the score, the higher the degree of social distance or prejudice.

Myriad studies have used this scale, and the results of several major studies are summarized in Table 7.2 (see Owen, Eisner, and McFaul 1981). Several observations can be made from this table: First, affective and conative prejudices have generally decreased over the years as indicated by the falling scores. The mean scores decreased from 2.14 in 1926 to 1.93 in 1977. Second, generally groups that originated from northern and western Europe were ranked the highest, followed by groups from southern and eastern Europe, and minority groups were ranked at the bottom. Third, relative positions of some groups have changed due to relations with foreign nations, such as the plummeting rankings of Germans and Japanese after World War II. Finally, with a few exceptions, the rankings have remained fairly stable over time. The respondents to these studies were primarily white college students. Nevertheless, the scale was also administered to black Africans, black Americans, Chicanos, Puerto Ricans, and Asians. The resulting rankings were similar, though every group put itself at the top.

Other studies of racial attitudes indicate that white acceptance of black Americans has steadily increased and conative prejudice has continued to decline (e.g., Firebaugh and Davis 1988; Schuman, Steeh, and Bobo 1985). For instance, the percentage of whites who favored school integration increased from 32 percent in 1942 to 70 percent in 1965 and to 93 percent in 1985. White Americans who rejected any laws against black-white intermarriages rose from 38 percent in 1963 to 60 percent in 1972 and to 73 percent in 1984. White Americans who did not object to interracial friendship between blacks and whites increased from 52 percent in 1963 to 78 percent in 1982. Firebaugh and Davis (1988) found that the declines in prejudice were due to both the replacement of older, more prejudiced cohorts by younger, less prejudiced ones and attitude change itself. However, a recent study of trends in racial attitudes of young white adults between 1984 and 1990 (Steeh and Schuman 1992) reported no significant upward or downward changes in racial tolerance among this group. Hence, there was no resurgence in prejudice in the general population in the 1980s, but changes in prejudice varied across groups.

Table 7.2 Changes in Social Distance by Score and Rank, 1926–1977

Rank	I 1926 Group	Score	II 1946 Group	Score	III 1956 Group	Score	IV 1966 Group	Score	V 1977 Group	Score
1	English	1.06	Americans (U.S. White)	1.04	Americans (U.S. White)	1.08	Americans (U.S. White)	1.07	Americans (U.S. White)	1.25
2	Americans (U.S. White)	1.10	Canadians	1.11	Canadians	1.16	English	1.14	English	1.25
3	Canadians	1.13	English	1.13	English	1.23	Canadians	1.15	Canadians	1.42
4	Scots	1.13	Irish	1.24	French	1.47	French	1.36	French	1.65
5	Irish	1.30	Scots	1.26	Irish	1.56	Irish	1.40	Italians	1.65
6	French	1.32	French	1.31	Swedish	1.57	Swedish	1.42	Swedish	1.68
7	Germans	1.46	Norwegians	1.35	Scots	1.60	Norwegians	1.50	Irish	1.69
8	Swedish	1.54	Hollanders	1.37	Germans	1.61	Italians	1.51	Hollanders	1.82
9	Hollanders	1.56	Swedish	1.40	Hollanders	1.63	Scots	1.53	Scots	1.83
10	Norwegians	1.59	Germans	1.59	Norwegians	1.66	Germans	1.54	Native Americans	1.84
11	Spanish	1.72	Finns	1.63	Finns	1.63	Hollanders	1.54	Germans	1.87
12	Finns	1.83	Czechs	1.76	Italians	1.89	Finns	1.67	Norwegians	1.93
13	Russians	1.88	Russians	1.83	Poles	2.07	Greeks	1.82	Spanish	1.98
14	Italians	1.94	Poles	1.84	Spanish	2.08	Spanish	1.93	Finns	2.00
15	Poles	2.01	Spanish	1.94	Greeks	2.09	Jews	1.97	Jews	2.01
16	Armenians	2.06	Italians	2.28	Jews	2.15	Poles	1.98	Greeks	2.02
17	Czechs	2.08	Armenians	2.29	Czechs	2.22	Czechs	2.02	Negroes	2.03
18	Native Americans	2.38	Greeks	2.29	Armenians	2.33	Native Americans	2.12	Poles	2.11
19	Jews	2.39	Jews	2.32	Japanese Americans	2.34	Japanese Americans	2.14	Mexican Americans	2.17
20	Greeks	2.47	Native Americans	2.45	Native Americans	2.35	Armenians	2.18	Japanese Americans	2.18
21	Mexicans	2.69	Chinese	2.50	Filipinos	2.46	Filipinos	2.31	Armenians	2.20
22	Mexican Americans	—	Mexican Americans	2.52	Mexican Americans	2.51	Chinese	2.34	Czechs	2.23
23	Japanese	2.80	Filipinos	2.76	Turks	2.52	Mexican Americans	2.37	Chinese	2.29
24	Japanese Americans	—	Mexicans	2.89	Russians	2.56	Russians	2.38	Filipinos	2.31
25	Filipinos	3.00	Turks	2.89	Chinese	2.68	Japanese	2.41	Japanese	2.38
26	Negroes	3.28	Japanese Americans	2.90	Japanese	2.70	Turks	2.48	Mexicans	2.40
27	Turks	3.30	Koreans	3.05	Negroes	2.74	Koreans	2.51	Turks	2.55
28	Chinese	3.36	Asian Indians	3.43	Mexicans	2.79	Mexicans	2.56	Asian Indians	2.55
29	Koreans	3.60	Negroes	3.60	Asian Indians	2.80	Negroes	2.56	Russians	2.57
30	Asian Indians	3.91	Japanese	3.61	Koreans	2.83	Asian Indians	2.62	Koreans	2.63
	Mean	2.14	*Mean*	2.12	*Mean*	2.08	*Mean*	1.92	*Mean*	1.93
	Spread in distance	2.85	*Spread in distance*	2.57	*Spread in distance*	1.75	*Spread in distance*	1.56	*Spread in distance*	1.38

Note: The term Negroes was used in the original studies.

Source: Carolyn Owen, Howard Eisner, and Thomas Mc Faul, "A Half-Century of Social Distance Research: National Replication of the Bogardus' Studies," Sociology and Social Research 66 (1981), adapted from Tables 1, 2, 6, and 7.

THEORIES OF ETHNIC PREJUDICE

What are the causes of ethnic prejudice, or, why do people have prejudice against members of another ethnic group? Theories addressing this question abound. These theories may be divided into four categories: biological theories, psychological theories, social learning theory, and conflict theory.

The Biological Explanations

Until the first quarter of the twentieth century, most explanations of ethnic prejudice had mainly focused on biological determination (Rose 1990). These theories attributed the cause of ethnic prejudice to genetic factors such as the biological inferiority of a group or innate dislike for out-groups. There were two currents of biological determinism: (1) the biological inferiority explanation, and (2) the innate tendency explanation.

The biological inferiority explanation maintains that ethnic prejudice exists because the ethnic group being prejudiced against is biologically inferior. Ethnic prejudice is thus viewed as a natural reaction to the factual inferiority of the group being prejudiced against. According to this view, what is to be blamed for ethnic prejudice is not the actor of prejudice (i.e., the person who has prejudice) but the victim of prejudice. Obviously, this is a victim-blaming approach.

By the early twentieth century, the biological inferiority explanation had lost its legitimacy. Instead, another biological argument, which I label the "innate tendency" explanation, arose. *The innate tendency explanation* contends that people have an innate tendency to like the members of their own group and to dislike out-group members, and this inborn tendency breeds ethnic prejudice. The biological instinct explains ethnic prejudice, because people fear the different and the unknown. Do people have an innate tendency to like their own kind and dislike members of other groups? No convincing evidence exists.[1] Liking or disliking of people of another ethnic group is a result of social learning rather than inheritance. Not knowing another group may be a precondition for the emergence of prejudice, but ignorance or unfamiliarity itself is not sufficient to produce prejudice (see Simpson and Yinger 1985). In this contemporary age, the biological explanations of prejudice have been replaced by social and psychological theories.

---

1. It would be interesting to do an experiment to see how newly born infants react to strangers of different races and to trace their changes in reactions over time.

Psychological Theories

Psychological theories find the sources of ethnic prejudice in psychological processes. These theories emphasize how prejudice toward other ethnic groups can satisfy certain psychic needs of individuals or how it can complement the general personality structure of certain people. The primary source of prejudice is placed within individuals rather than social forces.

Several psychological theories of prejudice are influential. One early approach is *scapegoat theory*, better known as *frustration-aggression theory*. This theory views prejudice as an outcome of scapegoating a weaker group by a stronger group or a result of transferred aggressions caused by frustrations. The idea flows as follows: When members of an ethnic group fail to achieve their desired goals such as better jobs, good schools, political power, etc., they become frustrated. Frustration tends to express itself as aggression or hostility (Dollard et al. 1939). Since it is difficult to locate the real source of frustration and to safely attack the source, frustrated members direct or transfer their aggression toward a substitute target or scapegoat, which is often a vulnerable ethnic group incapable of resistance. Ethnic prejudice is produced in this frustration-aggression process. Hence, prejudice serves as a safe outlet of displaced aggression and helps the maintenance and enhancement of self-esteem.

The situation of frustration, aggression, and scapegoating may be a common experience. For instance, when a person experiences frustration at work (e.g., is scolded by his boss), he is likely to become hostile and to divert his hostility toward his wife and/or children. However, this theory has met many criticisms: First, frustration may not necessarily cause aggression since humans can tolerate high levels of frustration (Allport 1954). Second, frustration is neither the only nor the most important cause of aggression (Geen 1972). Third, aggression is not always directed at a scapegoat. Sometimes it is directed inward at oneself, or it may be directed at the real source of frustration. Fourth, this theory does not explain why one particular vulnerable group is chosen as a scapegoat over other weak groups. The weakest group is not always the target of displaced aggression. Hence, frustration-aggression theory may not be able to offer a full explanation of ethnic prejudice.

Another early psychological approach is *authoritarian-personality theory*. This theory was developed by Theodore Adorno and his associates at

UC Berkeley in the late 1940s with an initial attempt to explain why anti-semitism and fascism were widely accepted in Nazi Germany and was later generalized to account for prejudice at large. Adorno et al. (1950) argued that prejudice, including antisemitism and negative attitudes against blacks and other minorities, is related to a personality structure called "authoritarian personality."

Adorno et al. outlined nine symptoms or characteristics of the authoritarian personality:

1. conventionalism: rigid commitment to conventional values;

2. authoritarian submission: uncritical acceptance of in-group authority;

3. authoritarian aggression: aggressiveness toward people who do not conform to conventional norms;

4. anti-intraception: an opposition to the subjective or imaginative and a resistance to examine inner self;

5. superstition and stereotype: superstitious beliefs and stereotypical thinking;

6. power and toughness: a preoccupation with strength versus weakness, dominance versus submission, and alignment with powerful figures;

7. destructiveness and cynicism: a destructive view of humans and a cynical view of life;

8. projectivity: a tendency to project unconscious emotions and the belief that the world is a wild and dangerous place; and

9. sex: an exaggerated concern with the sexual behavior of other people.

To document the relationship between authoritarian personality and ethnic prejudice, Adorno and his colleagues used data from responses to a questionnaire based on a nonrandom sample and constructed attitude scales using questionnaire items. They found positive correlations between authoritarian personality measured by the F scale (potentiality for fascism) and prejudice measured by the A-S scale (antisemitism) and the

E scale (ethnocentrism against Negroes, Japanese, Mexicans, and other minorities). That is, people who scored high on the F scale also scored high on the A-S scale and the E scale.

Furthermore, Adorno et al. established that the authoritarian personality originated from a person's early socialization experience in the family. Persons with the authoritarian personality were raised in families in which parents assumed dominant relationships with children, used harsh and punitive forms of discipline, and maintained clear authority. Consequently, the children distanced themselves from their parents and even harbored hostility and resentment toward them. Hence, these people would treat others in the way they were treated by their parents.

To be fair, the contributions and limitations of this theory must be seen in the historical context. This is a landmark study of prejudice that inspired many other studies and renovations later on. However, there are several deficiencies in this theory. First, its methodological flaws tend to undermine its validity. These methodological problems include, among others, the use of a nonrandom sample; defectively constructed attitude scales; possible interviewer or coder bias; and the failure to control other important variables. Second, the study only dealt with fascist (right-wing) authoritarianism but not liberal and radical (left-wing) authoritarianism. Finally, the theory fails to take into account social environmental factors and it does not explain why prejudice is created in the first place. Hence, at best the authoritarian-personality theory is an incomplete explanation of prejudice.

A new current developed in the past two to three decades in psychology has revitalized psychological approaches to prejudice. These new approaches may be pigeonholed under the rubric of "*cognitive theory of prejudice.*" This theory includes a variety of versions or variants, such as belief congruence theory, which argues that dissimilar or incongruent beliefs cause ethnic prejudice; accentuation theory, which contends that differences between individuals falling into various categories are overestimated (accentuated), while differences within the same category are underestimated (assimilated); and the theory of illusory correlation, which explains the emergence of stereotypes as the result of the co-occurrence of infrequent negative behaviors (e.g., violent acts) and minority status (Hamilton and Gifford 1976).

According to cognitive theory, since the ability of human beings to process information is limited while the social world is complex, we tend to oversimplify the available information about ethnic groups, which leads to biased judgments (see, for example, Hamilton 1981). Hence, ethnic prejudice is the product of the discrepancy between humans' finite capability of processing enormous, complex information and our tendency to oversimplify accessible information on ethnic groups. The primary cognitive process leading to ethnic prejudice is categorization, the mental process of classifying people or subjects based on their common characteristics. Categorization allows the organization of enormous information and avoids information overload. On the other hand, categorization without sufficient information often causes simplification and biases. The outcome is prejudice. Unlike the preceding two theories, categorization may not require hostile attitudes toward the outgroup, intergroup competition, personal gains, or other motivational factors (Hamilton 1981).

This new approach moves away from the traditional approaches that view prejudice as intentional and motivational. It suggests that prejudice may be unintentional and unconscious. There is an important difference between the cognitive approach and the other two early psychological theories. According to scapegoat theory and authoritarian-personality theory, ethnic prejudice arises because the mental process or personality of the persons who have prejudice is abnormal. Prejudice is a result of intrapersonal conflict or maladjustment. Prejudiced persons are sick or irrational. However, according to cognitive theory, people with prejudice are normal people with normal mental capacity. They become prejudiced due to the lack of information and/or ability to categorize voluminous information. They are therefore victims of simplified mental processes—overgeneralization.

Cognitive theory has met increasing recognition because it can better explain why almost everybody has some degree of prejudice although most people do not have abnormal mental status. By treating the emergence of ethnic prejudice as part of "normal" mental processes, cognitive theory better explains the psychological process of prejudice generation. However, the psychological process is only one of many that engender ethnic prejudice; there are also social processes we must look into.

Social Learning Theory

Rather than conceiving of ethnic prejudice as an outcome of biological or psychological processes, most sociologists tend to see it as a product of the social environment. Social learning theory is one of the approaches in line with this perspective.

The fundamental idea of social learning theory is that ethnic prejudice is learned and transmitted in the process of socialization. People acquire prejudice from the social milieu around them. Especially, agents of socialization such as parents, peer groups, schools, communities, and the mass media play important roles in the transmission process. If your parents, peers, teachers, and community leaders are prejudiced, negative attitudes and beliefs are likely to be passed on to you. If you internalize (i.e., come to accept on your own) these attitudes and beliefs, you will become prejudiced. People are taught to be prejudiced.

Ethnic prejudice is acquired through the processes of selective exposure to certain kinds of values and behavior; through role models such as parents and other figures; through reward for conformity and punishment for nonconformity; and through internalization. Prejudice could also be acquired through limited interactions with members of certain groups and the ensuing generalizations about them.

Studies have found that socialization during childhood is critical in the development of prejudice. Parents play a very important role in imparting prejudice to their children. Socialization in adult lives remains important in shaping people's attitudes toward other groups. The mass media have become increasingly influential in the socialization process, as people acquire ethnic prejudice from TV, movies, advertisements, and popular literature.

In brief, social learning theory underscores the effect of external forces on the formation of individual prejudice, and emphasizes socialization and observation as bases for the development of ethnic prejudice.

Does this theory provide a good explanation of ethnic prejudice? The reactions are mixed. Social learning theory is powerful in explaining how ethnic prejudice is transmitted and sustained and why it varies from person to person or from time to time for the same individual. For these merits, it is highly regarded by most social scientists and those who struggle against racial prejudice. A practical implication of this theory is that education can help reduce prejudice. Although social learning may not be the only cause of ethnic prejudice, it is certainly an important one. Nevertheless, this theory is not without limitations. In particular, it does not explain the *origin* of ethnic prejudice. Why and how is prejudice created in the first place before it can be passed on from generation to generation? What is its origin? Why do prejudiced attitudes against a particular group flow and ebb in a cyclical fashion over time? Social learning theory has little power to answer these questions. However, the answers to these questions may be found in competition and conflict over resources. Here is where conflict theory comes in.

Conflict Theory

Conflict theory argues that intergroup competition, real or imaginary, for scarce resources breeds ethnic prejudice. According to conflict theory, if two ethnic groups compete for the same natural resources (e.g., land, water), socioeconomic resources (e.g., jobs, schools, wealth, prestige), or political resources (e.g., political offices, power), one group may perceive threats from the other group. Members of one group are likely to harbor hostile feelings or other negative attitudes toward members of another group. Ethnic prejudice arises in this process of group competition. Hence, prejudice has an economic and political basis. The central idea of the conflict theory of prejudice is that prejudice is created by some members of an ethnic group to justify discriminatory actions against another ethnic group.

Evidence about the relationship between competition and prejudice abounds. DuBois demonstrated that white prejudices toward blacks were aroused when blacks appeared to be job competitors. John Dollard (1938) showed how prejudice against German immigrants in America in an early small industrial town did not exist but intensified as their competition with native-born whites for jobs became keen. The stereotypes of Italians as "organ-grinders, paupers, slovenly ignoramuses" began to spread as a result of competition intensified by the economic depressions of 1893 and 1907 (La Gumina 1973). The Chinese immigrants in the mid-nineteenth century were welcomed when they first arrived. Soon after their competition with white workers mounted, their initial positive image of an "honest," "hard-working," "law-abiding" people was superseded by negative ones such as "yellow peril," "clannish," "conniving," "deceitful," "mouse-eating." More recently, Cummings (1980) demonstrated that working-class whites who were in direct competition with black workers in the labor market were more racially bigoted toward blacks than better-paid and more secure whites not in direct competition with them. Tsukashima (1986) found that blacks who experienced unfair treatment or exploitation by Jews in their economic transactions were much more likely to have antisemitic attitudes than blacks who had no such experiences.

The strengths of other theories are the weaknesses of conflict theory. While conflict theory accounts for the origin of a major portion of ethnic prejudice, it does not address its transmission. Furthermore, the sources of prejudice can be very diverse including personality development, socialization, and cultural influence, and they vary depending on the level of analysis.

OVERALL ASSESSMENT AND SYNTHESIS

From the above review of existing theories, we can see that no one theory alone can explain ethnic prejudice in its entirety, since ethnic prejudice is not a product of any single process. With the exception of biological explanations, all other theories have certain merits. However, not all these theories are equally useful, and some are more useful than the others. For example, conflict theory and cognitive theory may better explain the emergence of ethnic prejudice. Social learning theory may better account for how ethnic prejudice is transmitted and sustained. Other psychological theories may have explanatory power as to why some members of an ethnic group have a stronger tendency toward prejudice than other members at the individual level. Some of these theories are complementary to each other. Conflict theory and social learning theory are macrotheories that focus on societal causes of prejudice, while psychological theories are microtheories that highlight individual causes. It would be useful to integrate some aspects of conflict theory, social learning theory, cognitive theory, and maybe other psychological theories.

The complexity and multicausal nature of prejudice calls for a synthesis and a multiple-causation explanation. I would argue that ethnic prejudice is a result of the multiple processes and has multiple determinants. The main determinants may be summarized as follows:

1. At the societal level, economic, political, and social competition for the same sources gives rise to the emergence, growth, and fall of ethnic prejudice. Ethnic prejudice arises as a rationalization and justification of discriminatory actions against competing groups.

2. At both the individual and society level, ethnic prejudice is maintained and transmitted through socialization by families, groups, communities, and social institutions. Prejudice against a particular group is disseminated in the socialization process as individu-

als internalize the negative attitudes and beliefs about other groups embedded in their culture.

3. At the individual level, the limitations of human cognitive ability and the complexity of the social world cause ethnic prejudice through the simplification and distortion of the characteristics of ethnic groups.

The hodgepodge and interaction of these multifaceted factors together provide a more complete and satisfactory explanation.

SUMMARY

This chapter has defined ethnic prejudice as negative attitudes or beliefs about an ethnic group and outlined its three dimensions: (1) cognitive prejudice, or false beliefs or thoughts, which is often expressed as stereotypes; (2) affective prejudice, or negative feelings or emotions; and (3) conative prejudice, or the predisposition to take action against members of other groups. Empirical evidence shows that some ethnic stereotypes have declined over time, although new ones have been created, and that affective prejudice and conative prejudice have also decreased as measured by the social distance scale and other attitude variables.

A plethora of theories have attempted to account for *why* ethnic prejudice takes place. The biological explanations locate the sources of ethnic prejudice either in the biological inferiority of the victims of prejudice or in the inborn tendency to dislike members of other ethnic groups. These explanations have long been rejected by most scientists. Social and psychological approaches have taken their place in contemporary times.

Three psychological theories are influential. Scapegoat theory/frustration-aggression theory perceives ethnic prejudice as being a result of the frustration-aggression-scapegoating process. Authoritarian-personality theory treats ethnic prejudice as an expression of authoritarian personality. Both scapegoat theory and authoritarian-personality theory view ethnic prejudice as a consequence of abnormality—either abnormal mental processes or abnormal personality. By contrast, newly developed cognitive theory sees ethnic prejudice as a result of contradiction between limited human capacity in processing immense and complicated information and a human predisposition to oversimplify information. This theory also considers prejudice as an outcome of the normal mental process, which occurs when oversimplified or insufficient information produces biases and misjudgment.

Sociological theories emphasize social forces that give rise to ethnic prejudice. Social learning theory focuses on how ethnic prejudice is maintained and transmitted in the socialization process, while conflict theory stresses group competition for scarce resources as the initial factor generating ethnic prejudice.

By integrating the useful elements of some of the above theories, especially conflict theory, social learning theory, and cognitive theory, a multicausal approach provides a more complete explanation of ethnic prejudice.

CHAPTER 8
ETHNIC DISCRIMINATION

Discrimination has many dimensions including ethnic, gender, age, disability, and sexual orientation. This chapter deals with the ethnic dimension of discrimination. A significant problem in America today, ethnic discrimination deserves our serious attention. To understand this phenomenon, this chapter begins with the clarification of the concept of ethnic discrimination. It then outlines the major types of discrimination from various dimensions. The subsequent review of existing theories of ethnic discrimination seeks to fathom the causes of ethnic discrimination. Finally, the relationship between ethnic prejudice and ethnic discrimination is examined.

CONCEPT OF ETHNIC DISCRIMINATION

At first glance, ethnic discrimination appears to be an unmistakable concept. In fact, it is not. How to define ethnic discrimination is still a debatable issue. In chapter 7, we learned that prejudice is tied to attitudes and beliefs while discrimination has to do with actions or behavior. But what kinds of actions can be termed ethnic discrimination? Two common definitions exist in the literature on discrimination. One frequently used definition is that *ethnic discrimination* refers to actions taken by members of the dominant group that have negative effects on members of minority groups (e.g., Feagin and Feagin 1993, 15). One important implication of this definition is that only the majority group can discriminate against minority groups, not vice versa. The situation of discrimination against minority groups by the majority group is probably most common since the dominant group has the vantage point to do so. However, this definition may not cover all possible occurrences of discrimination. For instance, is it possible that one minority group can discriminate against another minority group? Can members of the majority group be discriminated against? If the answers to these questions are affirmative, then the above definition does not apply to these circumstances.

Other scholars prefer a broad definition of ethnic discrimination (e.g., Healey 1995; Levin and Levin 1982). According to this definition, *ethnic discrimination* is defined as unequal or unfair treatment of individuals on the basis of their ethnic group membership. This definition applies to all possible types of discriminatory actions: the majority group against a minority group, a minority group against the majority group, or one minority group against another minority group. I prefer this broad definition, and I would treat the narrow definition as a special yet important case of the broad definition.

TYPES OF ETHNIC DISCRIMINATION

There are many terms pertaining to discrimination. Depending on the level, intention, and expressed form, types of discrimination may be classified into several symmetrical pairs. Three of the most important are discussed below.

Individual versus Institutional Discrimination

In terms of levels of action, discrimination can be divided into individual discrimination and institutional discrimination. This is perhaps the most important distinction involving ethnic discrimination. *Individual discrimination* refers to discriminatory actions taken by individuals. This type of actions occurs when individuals unfairly treat other individuals or groups based on their race or ethnicity. For instance, a personnel manager rejects Mexican job applicants; a homeowner refuses to sell his house to black homebuyers; an employer pays a lower salary to equally qualified Filipino workers than he pays to white workers.

Institutional discrimination has greater impact than individual discrimination. *Institutional discrimination* refers to laws, policies, or practices of social institutions and their related organizations that favor one ethnic group over another. One example is the Jim Crow laws ratified by the Supreme Court in its 1896 *Plessy v. Ferguson* ruling, which permitted legal segregation between blacks and whites in public facilities (e.g., bars, barbershops, drinking fountains, toilets, ticket windows, waiting rooms, hotels, restaurants, parks, playgrounds, theaters, and auditoriums) throughout the South in the last century. The High Court ruled that separate facilities were legal so long as they were equal. In practice, southern states never provided equal facilities to blacks. This was certainly institutional discrimination. The Jim Crow laws were not nullified until 1954. The Japanese incarceration during World War II is another perfect example. The U.S. government ordered more than 110,000 Japanese Americans on the U.S. mainland, the majority of them American citizens, to relocate to concentration camps in the name of wartime evacuation, an action based on their ethnicity. No evidence of espionage committed by Japanese Americans has ever been found. Ironically, German and Italian Americans, whose countries of origin were also at war with the United States, were spared such discriminatory treatment.

Note that individual (micro) discrimination and institutional (macro) discrimination are interdependent. From a macro standpoint, biased social structures provide an environment in which individual discriminatory behavior is tolerated and shielded. From a micro standpoint, institutional discrimination is realized by discriminatory agents through their formulation and enforcement of discriminatory laws, policies, and practices. Individual discrimination is consonant with existing macrostructures of ethnic inequality in the system.

Intentional versus Unintentional Discrimination

In terms of motive, discrimination may be pigeonholed into intentional discrimination and unintentional discrimination. *Intentional discrimination* refers to discriminatory actions taken purposively. It is motivated by prejudice or intent to harm (Feagin and Feagin 1993). An example is the intentional steering of Latino homebuyers to low-income, Latino-concentrated neighborhoods by real estate agents. Another example is the deliberate restrictions on the admission of Jewish American students to many colleges and universities in the period from the 1920s to the 1950s. Some universities used discriminatory quotas on Jewish students, and many schools employed such covert methods as "character tests" and "geographic balance" for an entering class, to limit Jewish admissions. As a result, Jewish student enrollment decreased from 40 percent to 15 percent at Columbia University and from 21 percent to 10 percent at Harvard University. Jewish admissions to major medical schools and law schools also dropped.

Unintentional discrimination refers to discriminatory actions taken without intention to hurt. Some laws, policies, and practices are developed without a conscious intent to discriminate, and may appear ethnically neutral and impersonal. Nonetheless, their effects are discriminatory against certain ethnic groups. For instance, raising the cost of college tuition seems to be a race-neutral practice. It does not intend to discriminate against minority groups. However, it has more negative effects on blacks and Hispanics than on whites because of their lower average family incomes. The results of this policy are discriminatory since it partly leads to higher proportions of blacks and Hispanics who do not have sufficient resources to attend colleges than whites. Hence, it is more important to consider the *effect* of a particular law, policy or practice on ethnic groups than it is to consider the *intention* of the law, policy or practice.

Overt versus Covert Discrimination

In terms of expressed form, we could classify discrimination as either overt or covert. *Overt discrimination* is discriminatory action that is obvious or blatant. A recent housing discrimination case serves as a good example (Guillermo 1998). In 1996, five Stanford female students of Asian descent were bluntly rejected for renting an apartment by the landlord, Janette Hybl, because of their race. Hybl told the students that she already had "good, white American applicants." "You people are ruining this country," she said, and, "White people need to stick together." Finally, she reportedly chased the women from her property, shook her fists, and yelled, "Go back to your country." In August 1996, the five women sued Hybl in federal court for violations of federal and state fair housing laws and civil hate crime laws. The case was recently settled with Hybl's reimbursement of $300,000 to the girls.

In contrast, *covert discrimination* is discriminatory action that is hidden or difficult to detect or document. An example is employment tokenism; namely, a few nonwhite employees are hired as "tokens" or "window dressing" to show that an organization provides equal employment opportunities for all ethnic groups. Another example is the subtle restriction of Asian American students' enrollment at UC Berkeley in the 1980s. During the 1984 admission cycle, UC Berkeley made two policy changes: (1) It raised the high school GPA for regularly admissible applicants from 3.75 to 3.9; and (2) the Asian Students in Asian American Educational Opportunity Program would no longer be exempted from "redirection" (i.e., could be sent to other UC campuses) (Chan 1990, 180). Seemingly, these new admission policies were not discriminatory and appeared to be ethnically neutral. However, they had noticeable negative effects on Asian students for two reasons. First, Asian students tended to have higher GPAs than standardized test scores, and raising the minimum GPA would blunt Asian students' competitiveness and reduce their likelihood of admission. Second, the redirection of Asian students to other UC campuses away from the San Francisco Bay area discouraged Asian students from applying to UC Berkeley because the redirection meant an added expense for many Asian immigrant families who could not afford to have their children live in dormitories rather than at home. These two policies were discriminatory in nature, but it was difficult to prove so. In fact, the FBI investigation of the incident did not end up with an indictment. Discrimination today is more likely to take the covert form than in the past.

The foregoing classification of discrimination only serves analytical purposes. In reality, different types of discrimination overlap in a specific case of discrimination. For example, the case of housing discrimination against the five Stanford Asian students by Hybl is individual, intentional, and overt, while the case of restricting Asian student enrollment at UC Berkeley is institutional, unintentional/intentional, and covert.

THEORIES OF ETHNIC DISCRIMINATION

A critical question in the study of ethnic discrimination is: Why do people discriminate against other ethnic groups, or what causes ethnic discrimination? Theories of discrimination seek to address this question. In comparison to the abundance of theories of prejudice, theories of ethnic discrimination have been underdeveloped. Few existing publications give this question a systematic treatment despite its importance. Very often, explanations of discrimination and explanations of prejudice are blended despite the differences between prejudice and discrimination. This section briefly reviews four groups of theories of ethnic discrimination in hopes of stimulating further integration and expansion of our knowledge about this issue.

The Prejudice Hypothesis

The traditional treatment of discrimination frequently assigns ethnic prejudice as the main cause of ethnic discrimination. That is, ethnic discrimination is a direct outgrowth of ethnic prejudice when negative attitudes and opinions toward a particular group are translated into biased actions or behavior. For example, James Jones (1997, 10–11) sees discrimination as the "behavioral manifestation of prejudice" and as negative behavior "based on negative attitudes" toward a group.

While few would deny that ethnic prejudice can cause ethnic discrimination, there are several limitations on the prejudice argument. First, ethnic prejudice does not always induce ethnic discrimination. Prejudice probably exists among nearly all people, but most people do not take discriminatory actions, either because of the existence of other complex social circumstances or because of the fear of legal consequences. Second, ethnic prejudice may not be the most important cause, and is certainly not the only cause, of ethnic discrimination. Other important determinants must be taken into account. Third, the relationship between prejudice and discrimination is not one-directional but interactive, as will be discussed in the next section of this chapter.

A classic example should help illustrate some of the foregoing points. In 1934, Richard LaPiere (1934) and a Chinese couple travelled about ten thousand miles together in the United States. They stopped at sixty-six hotels or motels and at 184 restaurants and cafeterias. At that time, the level of prejudice and discrimination against the Chinese was very high, but they were refused service only once in 250 occasions. After the trip, LaPiere mailed a questionnaire to each of the owners visited, asking whether they would accept "members of the Chinese race" as customers. Among those who responded (51 percent), 92 percent of the hotel owners and 93 percent of the restaurant owners said that they *would not* accept the Chinese as guests. Hence, attitude and behavior are not always consonant. What caused the discrepancy? Possibly, the monetary gain overshadowed their prejudice. Moreover, the well-dressed, well-mannered Chinese couple did not fit the negative stereotypes of Chinese. In addition, the companionship of a distinguished-looking white man may have further eased the resistance to the Chinese. Another parallel study with African Americans conducted by psychologists B. Kutner and his associates (1952) obtained similar results.

These examples prompt us to think about the role of prejudice in the discrimination-generating process and the possible roles of other factors. The recent trend in the research of discrimination is directed toward conditions other than prejudice. Let us now turn to other explanations of ethnic discrimination.

Gain/Functional Theories

Jack Levin and William Levin (1982) developed a *functionalist theory* of ethnic discrimination. They acknowledged that competition between ethnic groups for scarce resources will translate into ethnic prejudice and discrimination. They argued that discrimination develops and persists because it has important system-maintaining functions, especially for members of the dominant group. They identified two important social functions of discrimination for the majority group: (1) to acquire and maintain economic advantages in profit, wage, job, and land; and (2) to maintain political power.[1] Discrimination protects the dominant group's superior hold on opportunities and helps maintain the status of the majority group and the continuing subordination of minority groups. They also asserted that in addition, discrimination against minorities may reduce competition between a minority group and the majority group and increase the solidarity and identity of the minority group.

Another similar theory may be labelled *material and psychic gain theory*. This theory stresses that the motivation of discrimination against members of other ethnic groups is attributable to the material and psychological gains of the discriminator. In other words, discrimination satisfies the discriminator's psychological and material needs. For instance, Becker (1957) argued that prejudiced whites discriminate against black workers either because doing so provides a psychological gratification in distancing themselves from blacks or because prejudiced whites can gain financial compensation (e.g., paying lower wages to black workers) for their "psychic loss." Banton (1983) applied a modified version of Becker's theory to housing discrimination. He found that some white people refused

---

1. Levin and Levin (1982) did not make a clear distinction between prejudice and discrimination. Another function they discussed is the performance of unpleasant or low-paying jobs, which pertains to prejudice.

to sell their houses or rent their apartments to blacks because they feared that the entry of blacks into the neighborhood might cause them financial loss by lowering their property values and might increase their sense of insecurity. Using the data on a large number of cities in the United States in 1950, 1960, and 1970, Glenn (1966) and Dowdall (1976) showed that white Americans gained occupational benefits from the subordination of African Americans.

Class Conflict Theories

Class conflict theories contend that ethnic discrimination can be better understood in the framework of class struggle, and that it is an extension of class conflict. One of the most influential class analyses of discrimination is Edna Bonacich's split labor market perspective. Bonacich (1972) contended that discrimination against minority group workers derives from the class struggle between employers and workers. Employers recruit minority workers in pursuit of lower labor costs and higher profit margins. In protecting their own interests, white workers act to exclude minority workers or force them to take low-paying, less desirable jobs. Hence, while minority workers are exploited by the capitalist class and discriminated against by the white working class, white workers are the primary beneficiary of ethnic discrimination.

Many Marxist analysts disagree with Bonacich's claim that the white working class benefits most from ethnic discrimination. Instead, they argue that the primary beneficiary of discrimination against minority group workers is the capitalist class rather than white workers. The idea is that by treating workers of different ethnic groups differently, the capitalist class can prevent workers from uniting together to demand higher wages and benefits. Through ethnic discrimination, employers weaken workers' solidarity, reduce the power of labor unions, manipulate strikes, and pocket more profit for themselves. Hence, this "divide and conquer" strategy serves the interests of capitalists the most and punishes the minority workers the most.

Social Pressure Theory

Social pressure theory maintains that social pressures can cause discrimination in the presence or absence of prejudice. Under certain circumstances, social pressures, normally from one's own group, force some members to discriminate against members of other groups although they themselves may not be prejudiced. That means, group members are expected to conform to group norms; otherwise, they may be isolated or ostracized by their own group.

In an influential social experiment under controlled conditions, DeFleur and Westie (1958) asked forty-six white students to take part in a national campaign for racial integration. Half of the students had favorable attitudes about blacks and the other half had unfavorable attitudes. Each subject was asked to have a picture taken with a black person of the opposite sex and to sign a release agreement allowing the photo to be used in various phases of the campaign. The researchers found that nine of the presumably unprejudiced students were less willing than the average to sign the photo releases and that five of the presumably prejudiced students were more willing than the average to have their photos used. DeFleur and Westie contended that the discriminatory behavior of the purportedly unprejudiced students (i.e., their unwillingness to sign the release agreement) was caused by peer group pressures. Other follow-up studies (Green 1972; Linn 1965) all agreed that peer pressures in different social situations were important in causing discrepancy between expressed attitudes and actual behavior. Hence, differential discriminatory actions of individuals are the results of their reactions to various social circumstances.

INTERPLAY OF ETHNIC PREJUDICE AND ETHNIC DISCRIMINATION

The relationship between ethnic prejudice and ethnic discrimination is interactive and reciprocal. Ethnic prejudice can cause ethnic discrimination when negative attitudes are manifested in discriminatory actions. For example, the stereotype that blacks are untrustworthy and violent can cause an apartment manager to turn down a black home seeker. On the other hand, prejudice is partly a result of discrimination. For instance, discrimination may contribute to the high unemployment and low wages of blacks, which may in turn generate or reinforce the belief that blacks are inferior. Hence, prejudice and discrimination form a vicious circle.

However, the prejudice-discrimination reciprocity does not necessarily mean that ethnic prejudice and ethnic discrimination always go hand in hand. Prejudice may not always lead to discrimination, and vice versa.

There are four possible outcomes of prejudice-discrimination interaction corresponding to Robert Merton's (1949) typology, which combines the two dimensions in different ways.

1. Neither prejudice nor discrimination. This is an "unprejudiced nondiscriminator" or a person who is neither prejudiced nor discriminatory. His/her attitude and behavior are consistent.

2. Prejudice followed by discrimination. This so-called "prejudiced discriminator" is both prejudiced and discriminatory. His/her attitude and behavior are also consonant.

3. Prejudice without discrimination. This "prejudiced nondiscriminator" is prejudiced but not discriminatory. He/she refrains from discriminating because he/she is either afraid of consequences such as lawsuits and jail or does not want to take discriminatory actions. His/her attitude and behavior are dissonant. For example, a person who does not like black people but takes no actions against them is a prejudiced nondiscriminator.

4. Discrimination without prejudice. This "unprejudiced discriminator" is not prejudiced but is discriminatory. The person discriminates because of pressures from prejudiced family members, peers, clients, or communities and/or possible financial losses caused by the departure of patrons. His/her attitude and behavior are contradictory. An example of this type is a white small business owner who himself is not prejudiced against black people but who refuses to hire black workers for fear that his prejudiced white customers will not patronize his business again.

In reality, the first three outcomes are more common. Type 4 does occur in some instances, but it is the exception rather than the rule. However, we cannot assume that ethnic prejudice and discrimination always go together.

SUMMARY

There are two common definitions of ethnic discrimination. One emphasizes the asymmetric relationship between the dominant group and minority groups and defines ethnic discrimination as actions taken by the dominant group that hurt minority groups. The other seeks to encompass all possible circumstances and defines ethnic discrimination as differential or unfair treatment of individuals because of their group membership. I prefer the broad definition since it covers all possible types of discrimination.

Ethnic discrimination can be examined from several viewpoints: (1) in terms of level, individual discrimination and institutional discrimination; (2) in terms of intention, intentional discrimination and unintentional discrimination; and (3) in terms of expressed form, overt discrimination and covert discrimination.

Four categories of theories have been developed to account for ethnic discrimination: the prejudice hypothesis, gain/functional theories, class conflict theories, and social pressure theory.

The prejudice hypothesis attributes the main cause of ethnic discrimination to ethnic prejudice. Gain/functional theories emphasize the economic, political, and psychological benefits of discrimination, which motivate discriminatory actions. Class conflict theories treat discrimination as an outgrowth of class conflict between the capitalist class and the working class. Social pressure theory highlights certain social situations from which ethnic prejudice arises.

Ethnic prejudice and ethnic discrimination reinforce each other. Prejudice can cause discrimination, and vice versa. However, prejudice and discrimination are not always congruent. Ethnic prejudice may or may not lead to ethnic discrimination, and ethnic discrimination can occur with or without ethnic prejudice.

CHAPTER 9
RACISM

R acism is a buzzword in the lexicon of contemporary America and a hot topic in the ongoing race dialogue. It is also a term that is subject to different interpretations. Many people use racism interchangeably with prejudice and/or discrimination. In fact, these terms are entwined with one another, but they are not synonymous. It is imperative to understand their linkages and distinctions. This chapter reviews the changing meanings of racism in America, defines the concept of racism and its major dimensions, analyzes racism in the English language and social institutions, and, finally, discusses its effects on minorities as well as on white Americans.

THE EVOLUTION OF THE CONCEPT "RACISM"

Racism is a changing concept in America. According to Blauner (1994), the term *racism* did not enter the lexicon of social sciences and American public life until the 1960s. Gunnar Myrdal, a Swedish economist, did not use this term in his *An American Dilemma*, a classic study of American race relations in 1944 (Blauner 1994).

The term *racism* did surface occasionally before the 1960s. In the 1940s, racism was primarily understood as a set of beliefs assuming the superiority of a particular race (i.e., whites in the United States) over other races, a notion equivalent to what we call ideological racism today.

Webster's Fifth Collegiate Dictionary (1941, new words section) defined racism as "assumption of inherent racial superiority or the purity and superiority of certain races, and the consequent discrimination against other races; also, any doctrine or program of racial domination based on such an assumption." Racial prejudice and discrimination were not emphasized; rather, they were implied in the concept of racism or viewed as an extension of it. Ideological racism was originally developed to justify slavery. However, after World War II, the ideology of white supremacy lost legitimacy because of its association with Nazism.

In the pre-1960 period, the concepts of prejudice and discrimination were developed, paving the way for the widening notion of racism. Among the most notable were works of Gunnar Myrdal ([1944] 1962), Robert Merton (1949), and Gordon Allport (1954). During the 1950s and early 1960s, with racist ideology rejected, vicious racial attitudes and behaviors became the focal point of research, and the meaning of racism was widened to include racial prejudice and discrimination.

The emergence of the "Black Power," "Brown Power," "Red Power," and "Yellow Power" movements in the 1960s led to the recognition that racial inequality and injustice were not simply the product of prejudice and that discrimination is not merely a matter of individuals' actions. By the mid-1960s, the terms *prejudice* and *discrimination* were considered inadequate to capture an important component of racism, that is, its institutional dimension. Far from manifesting only in individual actions, discrimination is embedded in social institutions in the forms of laws, policies, and practices. Hence, a new concept—*institutional racism* or *institutional discrimination*—was coined. This concept emphasizes the social structure of racism. Racism moved from subjective ideas to objective structures and results. This dimension was deemed even more important than individual racism.

In 1970, the U.S. Commission on Civil Rights published a report entitled "Racism in America and How to Combat It," which reflected and synthesized the understanding of racism in American society up to that point. In that report, the concept "racism" was a combination of racist ideology, racial prejudice, racial discrimination, and institutional discrimination. The notion of racism commonly used in American society today is largely based on the understanding of racism in that report.

THE DEFINITION AND DIMENSIONS OF RACISM

Based on the foregoing review, *racism* can be broadly defined as any attitude, belief, behavior, or institutional arrangement that favors one racial group over another (Farley 1995). This broad definition of racism includes four specific dimensions:

1. *Ideological racism, or racist ideology.* Ideological racism is a system of beliefs that one racial group is biologically, intellectually, or culturally inferior or superior to another.

2. *Attitudinal racism, or racial prejudice.* Racial prejudice usually refers to negative attitudes or beliefs about a racial group and its members that are based on faulty or inadequate information.

3. *Behavioral racism, or racial discrimination.* Racial discrimination refers to discriminatory actions taken by individuals and groups.

4. *Institutional racism, or institutional discrimination.* Institutional discrimination refers to laws, policies, or practices of social institutions and organizations which favor one racial group over another.

Institutional racism is an important advancement of the early concept of racism, which emphasized individual belief, attitude, or behavior. As an extension of the "institutional racism" notion, came the notion of "racism atmosphere," which means that an organization or an environment might be racist because its implicit, unconscious structures favor one racial group over another. Another dimension is "racism as result," meaning that an organization is racist simply because racial minorities are underrepresented in numbers or in positions of prestige and authority. An institutional arrangement might appear race-neutral, but it could have discriminatory effects on members of minority groups. Hence, the emphasis of institutional racism analysis is on the effects that an institutional arrangement has on a racial group, rather than on the motivations of the majority group (Yetman 1991).

The narrow definition of racism as an ideology is still preferred by many. For instance, most sociology textbooks adopt this definition (see, for example, Macionis 1995; Robertson 1989). One important reason is that the broad definition is imprecise and ambiguous. Robert Miles (1989), for instance, contended that the inflation of the concept of racism may render it to the point of losing its precision. Others believe that it is important to include nonideological dimensions of racism, especially behavioral and institutional, in order not to ignore the external constraints and socially imposed disabilities.

Among those who accept the broad definition, there is disagreement on whether racism is primarily an ideological or structural phenomenon. Advocates of the former position argue that racism is first and foremost a matter of beliefs and attitudes, doctrine and discourse, which give rise to practices and structure. On the other hand, proponents of the latter view see racism as primarily a matter of institutional inequality, which gives rise to ideologies of privilege. It might be more beneficial to see both components as parts of the whole that interact with each other (Omi and Winant 1994). Ideological racism has structural consequences, and social structures give rise to racist ideology. Racist ideology and social structure interact to configure the nature of racism in a complex, dialectical manner.

RACISM IN THE ENGLISH LANGUAGE

Language is an integral part of a culture. As a transmitter of culture, language reflects the attitudes and thinking of a society. Language not only conveys but also shapes ideas or thoughts. As Moore (1976) discussed, racism in the English language is reflected in its terminology, symbolism, use of vocabulary, use of syntax, and context of expression.

The most conspicuous racist terminology in the English language is found in such disdainful terms as *nigger* and *spook* for black Americans; *spic* or *spik* for Hispanic Americans; *Jap* for Japanese Americans; *chink* and *Chinaman* for Chinese Americans; *Oriental* for Asian Americans; *redskin* for American Indians; *kike* for Jewish Americans; *mick* for Irish Americans; *wop* for Italian or other southern European Americans; and *honky* for white Americans. Whether or not a term is derogatory varies over time. For instance, nigger and Oriental were not given denigrating meanings in an earlier period, but they are not acceptable today. Although more educated people tend to reject these derogatory terms, they are certainly not extinct, especially among uneducated or less educated people. The rule is to use terms that a group feels comfortable with. In addition, idioms such as "The pot calling the kettle black" and "Call a spade a spade" have negative racial connotations but are still in common usage.

From the standpoint of language origins, some black-white words also reflect a racist view in the English language. In general, the word "black" is often associated with the negative while the word "white" is often linked with the positive. For example, while a "blacklist" refers to a list of undesirable people, groups, countries, etc., a "whitelist" is a list of legal persons or organizations. It may be excusable to tell a "white lie" (a lie not intended to cause harm), whereas one should never utter a "black lie" (a harmful, inexcusable lie). A "white day" (lucky day) is certainly a merry day, but a "black day" (hapless day) is not. "White magic" is a magic used to make good things happen, whereas "black magic" is magic believed to be done with the help of evil or evil spirits. One may have a "black outlook" (pessimistic or dismal outlook), be in a "black mood" (depressed mood), give someone a "black look" (angry look), get caught in a "black market" (illegal market), make a "black mark" (dirty mark) on his history, and therefore have a "black future" (dark future). On the other hand, "white hope" is a person who is expected to bring great success for a group or organization; and a "white witch" is a witch who does good things.

In addition to black/white words, black and white also symbolize different ideals and moralities. White often symbolizes purity, chastity, immaculacy, spotlessness, innocence, and virtue, whereas black represents evil, sin, wickedness, disgrace, and immorality. For instance, angels are white while devils are black. Good guys wear white hats and ride white horses, whereas bad guys wear black hats and ride black horses (Moore 1976).

Some authors argue that the use of certain common words or phrases may reflect a particular perspective and convey distorted information to the reader or audience. The terms *slave* and *master* are a good example in point. David Burgest (1973) argued that the psychological effect of the statement "The *master* raped his *slave*" differs from the effect of the same statement when different nouns are used. "The white *captor* raped a black female *captive*" has the same meaning but a much different effect, since the "master-slave" notion implies the ownership of the "slave" by the "master" and therefore waters down and legitimizes the atrocity committed by the slave holder against a black woman. Similarly, the use of *tribe* rather than *nation* or *people* to refer to American Indians may imply a view that Indians are primitive or backward.

The use of syntax, such as the passive voice, is another means to conceal the achievements of minorities or to downplay the inglorious actions of the actor. For example, the statement, "The continental railroad *was built*," conveniently deletes the contribution of Chinese laborers to its construction and the hardship they suffered. The sentence, "African slaves *were brought* to America," cloaks the roles of northern slave traders and southern slave holders in the slave trade. While the passive voice per se is not racist, the use of the voice can convey a biased perspective.

Racism is also reflected in the context of expression. For instance, the issue of the qualifications of black people to hold public office was often raised in the 1960s while it was never raised for white candidates. "*Qualified* minority and/or women candidates are especially welcomed to apply" is too familiar in current job advertisements. The statement conveys a connotation that qualification is not an issue for white candidates but qualified minority and/or female candidates are lacking.

It is important to realize that racist components are embedded in the English language and that conscious actions ought to be taken to reduce the negative effects of racism in the language. We may not be able to alter the language, but we can certainly change our usage of it. We can avoid using degrading or demeaning words for people; we can consciously use terminology that reflects a progressive perspective; and we can learn terminology that is positive and reflective of human values.

RACISM IN AMERICAN INSTITUTIONS

Not only is racism embedded in American culture, but it is ingrained in American institutions as well. This section reviews laws, policies, and practices of economic, political, educational, and legal systems that are racist in nature. The emphasis here is not the effects of racism, but institutionalized practices of racism.

In the Economic System

Economic freedom is supposed to be the hallmark of the American economic system. This means that everyone, regardless of race, has an equal opportunity to own capital and labor and the right to invest in profit-making enterprises. Largely in the name of free enterprise, many of the institutional forms of racism originated. For instance, the black slavery system—a typical representation of institutional racism in the history of America—began with the slave trade of indentured servants and later permanent slaves from Africa. Wall Street started to exchange stocks for the slave trade in the latter half of the seventeenth century. During more than two hundred years of slavery, black Americans were systematically denied entry to the free enterprise system, so that even today they are less likely than whites to own private land.

In the case of American Indians, some laws and government policies tremendously affected their economic life and opportunities. The government's land policies are a good example. The Dawes Act of 1887 stipulated that reservation lands be divided among individual families. The main purposes of the act were to turn Indians into farmers through small individual apportionments of forty to 160 acres and to provide opportunities for whites to buy unallocated leftover lands. The outcome of this federal policy was the large-scale sale of reservation lands to white Americans. The growth of industrial capitalism and urbanization in the late nineteenth century led to further encroachment upon Indian lands by white lumbering, ranching, and railroad interests. By the 1930s, only fifty million acres of Indian lands remained in their hands. The Indian Reorganization Act of 1934 partly halted overt land theft, but the termination of federal supervision of Indians in the 1950s rejected the reorganization policy and returned to the policy of forced conformity to individual land ownership. During the period of termination experiments, some tribes had no choice but to sell their lands to pay taxes, and trapped themselves deeper into poverty. In the early 1990s, only 3 percent of the land on the U.S. mainland was controlled by Indians.

Certain government practices have continued to impact the well-being of Indians. For example, according to Tinker and Bush (1991), the unemployment rate of Native Americans was sometimes almost twenty times higher than what was reported by government agencies since the federal government did not count "discouraged workers" (i.e., those who have given up looking for work because they feel that no jobs are available) as the unemployed. As a result of such undercounts, inadequate government funding is allocated to alleviate the high unemployment. Hence, the underreporting of Native American unemployment reflects institutional racism that prevents Native Americans from obtaining the resources necessary to improve their well-being. Together with other government attempts such as the 1887 Dawes Act, the 1934 Indian Reorganization Act, and the destructive relocation policy, underreporting represents overt as well as subtle racist institutional practices of the federal government to "solve" the Indian "problem."

Not only was the capitalist economic system historically established and controlled by whites in their own favor, but white male dominance in corporate America has remained a reality. Although flagrant racism is rare today, there are informal practices in corporate America that impede the upward job mobility of minority groups. For example, a pioneer and comprehensive report by the U.S. Department of Labor (1991) about the "glass ceiling" facing women and minorities in corporations uncovered several subtle practices of discrimination: First, minorities and women are more likely to be placed in highly technical or staff positions, such as human resources, research, or public relations, that are either slow on the career track to the top or off it altogether, as opposed to the fast-track positions in marketing, sales, or production. Second, minorities are often excluded from mentor programs; management training; opportunities for career development, tailored training, and rotational job assignments to revenue-producing positions; access to informal communication networks; and memberships on highly visible task forces and committees that provide interaction with senior managers. Third, they encounter special or different standards for performance evaluation and biased rating and testing systems. Fourth, recruitment practices at the executive level often do not reach out to or recruit minorities and women. Informal networks and discussions largely influence recruitment decisions. These practices, together with conscious or unconscious stereotyping and prejudice and the lack of government enforcement efforts, prevent minorities and women from moving up the corporate ladder.

In the Political System

As part of the machine that distributes power and resources, U.S. political institutions, even though democratic, were traditionally manipulated by white America to protect its privilege. Inequitable and racist practices of the political system are especially conspicuous in the arenas of citizenship and political participation.

The political institutions of the United States were long racist in terms of granting citizenship, which bestows basic political and civil rights. As proclaimed in the Nationality Act of 1790, prior to 1870 only "free white persons" were eligible for U.S. citizenship, and persons of African descent and Indian descent were excluded. African Americans did not gain their citizenship rights until 1870, when a new naturalization law based on the Fourteenth Amendment was passed. American Indians obtained their citizenship rights as late as 1924, when Congress enacted the Indian Citizenship Act. However, reservation Indians did not gain their voting rights until the 1940s. Although they arrived as early as the 1820s, Chinese were ineligible for U.S. citizenship until 1943 when the Chinese Exclusion Act was finally repealed. Other major Asian groups did not acquire their citizenship rights until the mid-1940s or early 1950s (e.g., Asian Indians, 1946; Filipinos, 1946; Japanese, 1952).

Due to the lack of citizenship, minority groups were disenfranchised for many decades, and political participation was almost impossible. Eventually, the Voting Rights Act of 1965 and its subsequent amendments constitutionally guaranteed minority access to voting. Voting and registration restrictions based on race were declared illegal. However, this was not the end of racism in U.S. political institutions. More sophisticated methods have been invented to hamper minorities' access to the ballot box. In periods following the Voting Rights Act of 1965, unjust practices in voter registration, such as poll taxes, literacy tests, Constitution tests, and Grandfather clauses, were widely used, and they were later outlawed by the federal government in response to complaints. The most familiar practice of subtle racism is known as gerrymandering or reapportionment—the redrawing of voting district lines in order to dilute the power base of a minority group. This has occurred historically in black, Latino, and Asian communities (Knowles and Prewitt 1969; Wei 1993). Some label this practice "minority voting dilution."

In addition to indirect dilution, there exist other types of racism that prevent equal opportunities for voting. Failure to provide bilingual ballots is an example. This has especially negative effects on Latino and Asian American voters since many are immigrants. This problem was not addressed until the 1975 amendments to the 1965 Voting Rights Act, which "broadened the 1965 law to include the issue of discrimination against 'citizens of language minorities' and banned practices denying the right of any citizen of the United States to vote" because of his/her language minority status. Despite the changes, studies have found that many foreign-born naturalized citizens who are not fluent in English are discouraged from voting because of lack of bilingual ballots and other native language election materials. Hence, de facto racism explains the political disengagement of Asians and Latinos. Significant progress notwithstanding, the U.S. political system is still far away from the eradication of racism.

In the Educational System

Inevitably, racism was manifest in the origin and development of the American educational system. The public school movement started in earnest in the early nineteenth century. The school was viewed not only as a transmitter of knowledge, but more importantly as a medium of social control. Early public schools were dominated by British settlers. British American industrialists and educators founded most public schools, shaped curricula, and controlled operations. Anglicization was an important goal of public schools, which emphasized the socialization of non-British immigrants into Anglo-Protestant norms, values, work habits, and manners.

As the ethnic composition of American society diversified, the Anglocentric curriculum and cultural representation gradually evolved into a Eurocentric one. For a long time, schools were controlled by whites. Textbooks and procedures were developed by whites and for whites and had little relevance to minorities. Policy decisions were mostly made by whites. The histories and cultures of minority groups were seldom taught before the 1960s. Even though, occasionally, "Negro history" was taught, it was taught by white-authority-picked teachers from the white perspective. Minorities had little say in school curricula. In addition, minority students were relegated to lower-status teaching groups through such practices as IQ testing, tracking, and classroom ability grouping.

Education policy on Indian children provides a good example. Formal education of Indian children began during the reservation period (1790 to the Civil War). From the 1890s to the 1930s, a high proportion of Indian children were forced to attend boarding schools run by the BIA or religious groups. The mission of these schools was to transform "wild Indians" into Anglo-civilized citizens. The schools made intensive efforts to destroy the tribal ways of life, and they punished students for speaking Indian languages. Starting in the 1930s, some boarding schools were superseded by public schools. However, Indian pupils still experienced forced acculturation. Little was taught about their ethnic culture and histories, and teachers tried to make their pupils "less Indian."

Another example is the subtle discrimination Asian American students have faced in contemporary times. In the 1980s, because of growing Asian student enrollment on university campuses, some elite schools devised subtle policies or measures to restrict their admissions. For instance, as mentioned in chapter 8, during the 1984 admissions cycle, UC

Berkeley raised the minimum high school GPA from 3.75 to 3.9 and would no longer exempt Asian Students from "redirection" (Chan 1990, 180). These two changes reduced Asian student enrollments, since Asian American students tended to have higher GPAs than standardized test scores and the possible redirection of the San Francisco Bay area's students to other UC campuses discouraged them from applying to UC Berkeley. A third change—mandating a minimum score of 400 on the verbal part of the SAT—was proposed for immigrant applicants but was not implemented. Since many recent immigrant students did less well on the SAT verbal test, this would have also cut down the admissions of Asian students. UC Berkeley and some other schools used informal quotas or criteria such as personal essays, extracurricular activities, and extra European foreign language courses to reduce Asian student enrollment in the name of diversity (Takagi 1990).

In the Legal System

Racism in the legal system can be seen in laws, legal structure, and informal practices that treat different racial groups differently. Over time, progress has been made, but problems still remain.

Historically, laws have protected and favored whites. The structure of the legal system has reflected white dominance. Judges, from the Supreme Court, to federal courts, to state courts, to local courts, were all white in early periods and remain primarily white today. The majority of lawyers are white, and minority attorneys are underrepresented. White dominance is also reflected in the personnel composition of law enforcement agencies. During the Segregation Era (1890s–1960s), southern cities had no black presence in their police departments, and northern cities also discriminated against blacks. A report by the U.S. Commission on Civil Rights in 1963 found that in the 1960s, "law enforcement agencies throughout most of the Nation are staffed exclusively or overwhelmingly by whites." While whites accounted for 65 percent of the population in major cities, they made up 95 percent of the police departments on average. Since the 1960s, the representation of blacks and Latinos in the nation's police forces has increased significantly. For example, the percentage of black police officers increased from 3.6 percent in 1960 to 10.5 percent in 1990. However, they are still far behind their representation in the general population. "Good old boy" friendship networks exclude minorities from the most sought-after assignments, especially criminal investigation, and therefore reduce their opportunities for promotion. Minorities are also underrepresented in law enforcement supervisory positions.

There are practices that place minorities in a disadvantageous position in court with regard to bail, jury selection, and provision of counsel. A seldom-discussed dimension of racism in the judicial system is bail practice. The severity of the alleged crime and the risk of flight posed by the defendant are probably the most important determinants of the amount of bail, but a judge has discretion to set that amount. An early study (Bing and Rosenfeld 1970) showed that in Boston courts black defendants were less likely to receive bail than white defendants, regardless of income level, and further, that those who were not bailed out before trial were more likely to be found guilty than those who were freed. A more recent study (Ayres and Waldfogel 1994) found that, holding constant the severity of the crime and risk of flight, the bail set for black men was 35 percent higher than for whites and the bail for Hispanic men was 19 percent higher than for white men. In addition, compared to that for white men, the bond rate was 16.5 percent higher for blacks and about 5 percent higher for Hispanics.

The selection of juries also mirrors subtle racism and therefore affects the outcome. Historically, minority groups could not serve on juries or testify against whites. Racism in jury selection was first addressed by the U.S. Supreme Court in its 1880 *Strauder v. West Virginia* decision. The Court ruled that a West Virginia statute limiting jury service to white males was unconstitutional. This ruling, however, did not preclude states from developing techniques designed to maintain all-white juries. Since the mid-1930s, the Supreme Court has consistently struck down techniques used to exclude or limit the selection of minorities for the jury pool. Despite the Court's decisions, many states, at one point or another, still used some seemingly objective methods in the selection of jury. Such methods included the requirements that jurors be registered voters or freeholders, own automobiles or other taxable property, or pass literacy tests. Since blacks were less likely than whites to register to vote, to own automobiles or taxable property, or to have acceptable literacy levels, they were more likely to be excluded from the jury pool. The financial hardship of absence from work that jury service entails further reduced their chance of selection to the jury pool (Fukurai, Butler, and Krooth 1993). Furthermore, the Supreme Court's requirements that the jury should be representative of the community and that race is not a valid qualification for jury service apply only to the selection of the *jury pool*, but not the selection of individual jurors for a particular case (Walker, Spohn, and DeLone 1996). Prosecutors and defense attorneys can use peremptory challenges—challenges without cause, without explanation, and without judicial scrutiny—if appropriate. The Supreme Court's 1965 *Swain v. Alabama* decision, which allowed prosecutors to use peremptory challenges to dismiss jurors on the basis of race was not overturned until its 1986 *Batson v. Kentucky* decision. The *Batson* decision notwithstanding, prosecutors continue to use peremptory challenges in the jury selection process, which remains a barrier to justice.

According to the Sixth Amendment to the U.S. Constitution, "In all criminal prosecutions, the accused shall enjoy the right to have the assistance of counsel for his defense." However, as late as the early 1930s the majority of defendants, especially minority defendants, were often tried without adequate counsel to represent them because they were too poor to hire their own attorneys. Progress has been made over time. The 1932 Supreme Court *Powell v. Alabama* ruling required states to provide attorneys for indigent defendants charged with capital crimes. Again, the Court's decision in a 1938 case, *John v. Zerbst*, required the appointment of counsel for *all* indigent defendants in all federal criminal cases; and in the Court's 1963 *Gideon v. Wainwright* decision, this requirement was extended to the state courts. In subsequent decisions, the right to counsel has been extended from trial to all critical stages of the criminal justice process including arraignment, preliminary hearing, entry of a plea, trial, sentencing, and the first appeal. In the effort to enforce Court decisions, public defender systems have grown rapidly and served more than two-thirds of the U.S. population. However, the quality of legal services to indigent defendants remains a major concern.

EFFECTS OF RACISM

Racism is a social problem, a social disease, and a social waste. Racism affects not only minorities but white Americans as well. This section examines the effects of racism on minorities and whites. Environmental racism—an issue garnering growing attention—and the distinction between white racism and minority racism are also discussed.

Effects of Racism on Minorities

It has been well documented that racism has a severe impact on ethnic minorities in employment, income, education, housing, and criminal justice, as well as psychological well-being. Ample evidence attests that racism negatively affects the employment opportunities and mobility of minorities. For instance, a 1991 Urban Institute study of job discrimination found that black Americans were less likely to be hired than white Americans. A total of 476 pairs of black and white male job auditors were sent to interviews for the jobs advertised in major newspapers in Washington, D.C., and Chicago, and they were matched on many demographic and socioeconomic variables. The study found that 15 percent of white applicants were offered jobs as opposed to only 5 percent of the black applicants (Turner et al. 1991). During the job selection process, white men were 13 percent more likely than black candidates to advance to the next round. In addition, black applicants were 23 percent more likely than white applicants to encounter rude or unfavorable treatment.

In 1990, the Urban Institute conducted an auditing study of discrimination against Hispanic jobseekers in San Diego and Chicago, using matched Hispanic-Anglo pairs. The study found that the white auditors advanced further in the hiring process in 31 percent of the cases, as compared to the Hispanic auditors in 11 percent of the cases (Cross et al. 1990). Twenty-two percent of the Anglos were offered jobs in contrast to 8 percent of the Hispanics (Cross et al. 1990). In terms of both hiring advance rates and job offer rates, the Hispanic-Anglo differences were greater than the black-white differences found in the 1991 audit.

Because of racism, it is difficult for minorities to move up the occupational ladder, especially the white-collar corporate ladder, and minorities are less likely to enter managerial and executive positions. For instance, the "glass ceiling" report by the U.S. Department of Labor (1991) found that, partly as a result of racial prejudice and informal institutional discriminatory practices, 97 percent of the senior managers of Fortune 1000 industrial and Fortune 500 companies were white; 95 to 97 percent were male. In Fortune 2000 industrial and service companies, 5 percent of the senior managers were women, all of whom were white.

The effect of racism on the income of minority groups is evident. The 1990 U.S. census data show that the per capita income of whites was much higher than all minority groups, even $2000 more than that of Asian Americans, although Asians had higher levels of educational attainment and occupational status than whites. A recent study of Asian Americans in the Los Angeles area (Cheng and Yang 1996) found that, controlling for other important demographic and socioeconomic factors, white males earned significantly higher salaries than Asian men despite the higher levels of education and occupational status of the Asians.

Minority groups suffer discrimination in schooling. In the case of black Americans, many southern states passed laws during the slavery era that prohibited the formal education of black slaves because of the concern that knowledge might cause a rebellious spirit (Weinberg 1977). In the North, school segregation between blacks and whites was imposed by codes, due to the belief in black inferiority and black incompetency to compete with white children in schools. In the mid-nineteenth century, African Americans were excluded from public schools in the North. Education discrimination against blacks continued into the twentieth century. In the southern states, a "separate but equal" rule provided African Americans with educational facilities that were grossly substandard compared to those of whites. School desegregation did not begin until 1957. Today, 70 percent of black students still attend segregated schools due to residential segregation patterns.

In the nineteenth century, Chinese children in California were not allowed to attend public schools. In the early twentieth century, Japanese children were pressured to attend segregated schools established by the Chinese. This attempt was temporarily foiled when President Theodore Roosevelt intervened. In the 1980s, some informal restrictive measures led to the restriction of the opportunity for Asian American students to enroll in elite schools such as UC Berkeley, UCLA, Harvard, Princeton, Brown, and others.

Early in this century, housing segregation, local ordinances, and gerrymandering of school and district lines caused school segregation of Mexican children. Mexican students were under constant pressures to become "Americanized" and to reject their own culture and identity. Education officials designated education a low priority for children of Mexican immigrants. Based on IQ tests given in English, children of Mexican Americans were often placed on slower tracks that prepared them for low-level jobs requiring little formal education. Even in the 1970s and 1980s, teachers, administrators, and counselors of Mexican descent were still severely underrepresented in school systems. The curriculum and practices of the public school system tended to alienate Mexican students from their culture. Housing discrimination, coupled with their lower economic status, also led many Puerto Rican children to attend de facto segregated schools where they were the majority (Fitzpatrick 1987).

Despite progress over time, Indian children have registered a very high school dropout rate, and they fall below national average on standardized test scores. The deprivation of their cultural, linguistic, and social identity has marked the history of formal education for Native Americans. Boarding schools took away their languages, religions, belief systems, and ways of life. Higher education has not created the same opportunities for self-realization and mobility available to white Americans and other minority groups.

Racism affects residential patterns of minorities. Residential segregation between minorities and whites has been a perpetual phenomenon in contemporary American life (Massey and Denton 1987). Many studies have documented that prejudice and discrimination against minority groups are a major factor contributing to residential segregation. Chapter 10 will further discuss how racism causes residential segregation.

Minorities, especially African Americans, are disproportionately represented in the criminal justice system. Blacks are more likely to be arrested, held, charged, sentenced, and jailed than whites. For instance, a study using a representative sample of adolescents aged 11–17 found that for serious offenses (e.g., felony assault, robbery, fraud, hard drug use, felony theft), the arrest rate for blacks was two to three times that for whites, controlling for history of delinquencies, extent of physical injury, and use of guns (Huizinga and Elliot 1987). Another study of thirty-nine states found that blacks normally received longer sentences than whites for robbery, rape, and murder (Hacker 1988). In the case of murder involving a white victim and a black offender, prosecutors and juries are more likely to demand the death penalty than in any other possible racial combination—white offender/black victim, black offender/black victim, and white offender/white victim (Amsterdam 1988; Ekland-Olson 1988; Jaynes and Williams 1989; Keil and Vito 1989). Bohm (1994) found that in Georgia the death penalty was sought in about 51 percent of the felony murder cases involving white victims but only in about 21 percent of the cases involving black victims.

The disproportionate representation of minorities in the judicial system is an inevitable consequence of a system designed to enforce laws made by whites and operating through a structure created and staffed by whites. Blatant racism in prosecution and sentencing, and unconscious and indirect racism acting through cultural and economic channels, explain differences in judicial and prison statistics between blacks and whites. The cultural myopia of white society permeates our judicial system, making it inherently incapable of delivering justice to minorities.

Racism has psychological effects on minority groups as well. It results in feelings of humiliation, isolation, and self-hatred, thereby causing doubts about self-worth and identity. The psychological damage of racial stigmatization is most evident in children (Goodman 1964). For instance, a black child hated her skin color so intensely that she "vigorously lathered her arms and face with soap in an effort to wash away the dirt"; when asked to describe dolls that had the physical characteristics of black people, young children chose such adjectives as "rough, funny, stupid, silly, smelly, stinky, dirty"; three-fourths of a group of four-year-old black children preferred white playmates and more than half felt themselves inferior to whites. Furthermore, racism can cause mental illness and psychosomatic diseases, as the affected persons react to it by seeking retreat into alcohol, drugs, or other kinds of antisocial behavior. Racism severely handicaps its victim's interest in and pursuit of a career. An early experiment found that among blacks and whites of similar aptitudes and abilities in a competitive situation, the blacks displayed defeatism, half-hearted competitiveness, and a high expectancy of failure (Allport 1954).

Effects of Racism on Whites

Earlier studies of the effects of racism exclusively focused on its impact on minority groups and the benefits whites gain from racism, although a few studies implicitly touched upon the effects of racism on whites (Katz 1976; Saenger 1965; Simpson and Yinger 1965). During the 1970s, however, researchers began to deal explicitly with the negative effects of racism on whites (e.g., Pettigrew 1973; Reynolds 1973; Szymanski 1976). The most closely focused analysis of the negative effects of racism on whites has been provided in a volume edited by Benjamin Bowser and Raymond Hunt (1981, 1996), now in its second edition. The main arguments and findings of these studies may be summarized as follows:

Psychological effects
Several writers have contended that racism has deluded some whites into a false sense of superiority that has left them in a pathological and schizophrenic state. It distorts their personality. For instance, Saenger

(1965) argued that prejudice results in a "coarsening of the emotions" on the part of the prejudiced person. Pettigrew (1973, 1981) treated racism as a psychological and mental health problem of whites. He argued that non-racists are mentally healthier than racists. Racism aggravates psychiatric disturbances, and it causes uncertainty about one's feelings and beliefs about self, others, and the world.

Economic effects

From an economic perspective, racism causes an insufficient use of labor (including white labor), a lack of real competition between whites and minorities, and decreased economic gains and bargaining power of white workers. A few available historical or empirical analyses have demonstrated the economic effects of racism on whites. For example, Reynolds (1973) and Szymanski (1976) both concluded that whites did not benefit from economic discrimination against minorities. Kushnick (1981) demonstrated that by obscuring class differences, racism was used to exploit both white and nonwhite workers. He showed that poor whites in the south received wages much lower than those in other regions, lower levels of public services than in other regions, and the contempt of the white capitalist class who treated them in much the same way as they treated the blacks. He further argued that domestic racism is partly re-sponsible for movement of U.S. capital to other parts of the world (Kushnick 1996). Mason (1996) complemented Kushnick's thesis by maintaining that the strategic loss of white labor's collective bargaining advantage is much more significant than their trivial income gain from racism against minorities.

Social effects

The main argument is that racism creates a racially divided soci-ety that bears a tremendous social cost. Specifically, racism isolates white Americans from people of color and divides them from one another; it pro-motes an ignorance and disdain of other races and cultures; from time to time it leads to racial conflicts and violence for which the whole society pays a high price. In addition, for white individuals, racism causes per-sonal and racial insecurity. Whites experience a sense of suffocation. Racism is as dehumanizing for whites as it is for people of color (Kovel 1970).

Educational effects

Racism in schools leads to miseducation of white children about the truth of history, the contributions of people of color, and the role of white people in American society and culture. The biased curricula and materials inculcate into white children false notions of superiority over minorities by presenting a distorted view of historical and contemporary roles of whites and nonwhites (Knowles and Prewitt 1969). They lead white children to believe that the current American system is fair for all people, and that no fundamental changes in American institutions are needed in order to achieve liberty, equality, and justice for all.

Effects on international relations

The impact of racism is not limited to the domestic terrain; it affects U.S. relations with other parts of the world. The assumption of white supremacy often leads to distorted images of the Third World nations and racist U.S. policies toward them. Racism justifies the economic exploitation of African, Asian, and Latin American countries in natural resources, such as petroleum, and the imposition of America's political will on those "inferior" countries. Racist distortions in U.S. foreign policy have fostered arrogant assumptions about international order, stability, and U.S. capability to manipulate international events. The solidarity and alliance of African-Asian countries are viewed as threats to American security. The racist ideology often prevents white American foreign policy makers and experts from understanding the causes of revolutionary movements in Africa, Asia, and Latin America and from devising appropriate policy to deal with them. The revolutionary movements are often viewed as illegitimate or communist inspired. Hence, the United States has not played a progressive role in the civilization and advancement of the world.

Racist ideology and foreign policy will negatively affect the survival and growth of America as a nation. America's survival in the world may depend on how it resolves its racial dilemma and rectifies its supremacist view of itself (Baldwin 1963). The existence of domestic racism and its extension to international relations may eventually isolate the United States from the bulk of African, Asian, and Latin American countries (Bowser and Hunt 1996). Other nations will respond with growing resistance and resentment, as evidenced in the current treatment of Americans in the Third World countries. Racism certainly affects the tone and character of U.S. military posture toward other countries. In short, racism breeds distortions about self and others, about control and security, and about threats, either real or perceived.

Environmental Racism

Before 1990, environmental justice was not a major concern of the Environmental Protection Agency or any other federal agencies or departments (Gaylord and Bell 1995). Since 1990 this issue has loomed large. Environmental racism is a major obstacle that endangers environmental justice.

Environmental racism can be defined as any policy or practice that intentionally or unintentionally places people of color, especially poor, working-class communities of minorities, at greater health and environmental risk than the rest of society. Put differently, different racial or ethnic groups encounter differential environmental consequences because of government policies or practices. Certainly, environmental pollution such as toxic chemicals, air and water pollution, and waste disposal affects the entire society. However, the communities of minorities are forced to bear its brunt due to certain policies and practices and their own disadvantaged position.

While both class and race contribute to the disproportionate distribution of environmental hazards, there is abundant evidence that race is a powerful predictor of environmental hazards, such as air pollution, the location of municipal solid waste facilities, the location of abandoned toxic waste sites, toxic fish consumption, and lead poisoning (Bullard 1994). For instance, lead poisoning plagues three to four million children, most of whom are African Americans and Latinos in urban areas. According to a study by the federal Agency for Toxic Substances and Disease Registry, among children aged five or younger living in urban areas with more than one million residents, African Americans far surpassed white Americans in the percentage of excessive levels of lead in their blood. Among families earning less than $6,000 per year, 68 percent of black children suffered lead poisoning, compared with only 36 percent of white children. In families with an annual income of over $15,000, 38 percent of black children had lead poisoning as compared to 12 percent of white children. Lead poisoning is preventable. However, little has been done to prevent it because minorities are underrepresented in the decision-making bodies of public and private institutions. Hence, they remain vulnerable to decisions affecting their likelihood of exposure to environmental toxins.

Minority residential communities have often been targets for location of toxic facilities such as garbage dumps, landfills, incinerators, sewer treatment plants, hazardous waste disposal sites, lead smelters, and other risky technologies. For example, a 1983 GAO study found that African Americans accounted for the majority of the population in three of four communities where off-site hazardous waste landfills were located, while they made up only about one-fifth of the region's population.[1] In 1992, African Americans were still concentrated in two of the four communities although they accounted for only one-fifth of Region IV's population. Few unwanted toxics are dumped in suburbs where middle-class, white families are concentrated because white homeowners have repeatedly mobilized to defeat proposals of dumping waste in their neighborhoods. In contrast, it has been difficult for millions of African Americans to say no since many do not even own homes. For more examples, see Phillips (1995), Westra (1995), and Wigley and Shrader-Frechette (1995).

Indian reservations have increasingly become primary targets of waste disposal locations since few reservations are subject to stringent environmental regulations or have a waste management infrastructure equivalent to those of state or federal governments. Across the nation, more than three dozens reservations have been targeted for landfills and incinerators. Economic conditions on reservations such as high poverty, unemployment, and few business development opportunities, have made reservations vulnerable, especially when government and industry promote the building of a waste facility as economic development.

In brief, environmental racism has a disproportionate effect on racial and ethnic minorities and the poor; affluence, residential patterns, land use planning, and institutional racism all contribute to environmental inequalities. Greater efforts must be made to achieve equal environmental protection for all communities regardless of their race, ethnicity, culture, and income.

White Racism and Minority Racism

Racism is not singular. There are different kinds of racism, such as white racism and minority racism. Some minority scholars view racism as a prob-

---

1. The four off-site hazardous waste landfills were located in the eight states (Alabama, Florida, Georgia, Kentucky, Mississippi, North Carolina, South Carolina, and Tennessee) that constitute the EPA's Region IV.

lem of power imbalance; they argue that racism does not apply to minorities because of their powerless position. This argument may be tenable in the case of institutional racism, but it does not hold up in the ideological, attitudinal, and behavioral dimensions of racism.

Racism is a white problem as well as a problem for people of color. Whites can at times be victims of racism by other whites or nonwhites as is the case of antisemitism and anti-Arab prejudice. Black supremacy, as well as other kinds of group supremacy, is as erroneous as white supremacy.

However, there is a distinction between white racism and minority racism. The effects of different kinds of racism are not the same. For example, the impact of white supremacy far surpasses that of black supremacy because of the dominant position of whites in American society and social institutions. Black supremacy can hardly constitute the threat that white supremacy does, nor can it be so easily absorbed and rearticulated in the dominant discourse. Nonetheless, the powerful effect of white racism does not justify the development of racism against other minority groups or against whites. The proliferation of single group superiority through university-based academic programs and student organizations will not help achieve ethnic equality in any way.

SUMMARY

Racism is not static. The concept "racism" first appeared in the 1940s, but it was not widely acknowledged until the 1960s. The meaning of racism has expanded over time. Racism as a concept commonly used today in American society is a very broad notion. It encompasses ideological, attitudinal, behavioral, and institutional dimensions. Some scholars prefer the narrow definition, namely, ideological racism, while others prefer the broad definition.

Racism is an integral part of American cultural fabric. The use of terminology, symbolism, vocabulary, syntax, and context in the English language mirrors racism. We should consciously avoid derogatory terms for ethnic groups and use progressive expressions.

Racism has permeated the economic, political, legal, educational, and other social institutions in America. Not only does racism affect minority groups but it also has negative effects on white Americans in psychological, educational, economic, social, environmental, and international spheres.

Racism is multifarious. There are white racism and minority racism, but the effects of white racism are much more severe than those of minority racism. Racism is a major social malady that deeply affects the stability of the nation.

CHAPTER 10
ETHNIC SEGREGATION

Ethnic segregation is in many ways entwined with other ethnic issues. It is a form of ethnic interaction; it is a cause of ethnic inequality; it shapes, and is partly shaped by, ethnic prejudice and discrimination; it can foster ethnic conflict. Ethnic segregation takes several forms as outlined below. This chapter highlights the most common form of ethnic segregation in America—residential segregation. It discusses the measures, status, causes, and consequences of residential segregation. The chapter also briefly examines school segregation—another existing form of segregation in America society today—focusing on school desegregation and re-segregation.

CONCEPT AND DIMENSIONS OF
ETHNIC SEGREGATION

"Segregation" is often used interchangeably with "residential segregation." In actuality, residential segregation is only one dimension of segregation, and segregation is a much broader concept than residential segregation.

Ethnic segregation refers to the separation of members of different ethnic groups in residential, economic, political, and social life. In other words, different groups have very little interaction with one another residentially, economically, politically, and socially. An antonym of ethnic segregation is *ethnic integration,* which refers to the intermingling and interaction of different ethnic groups. *Desegregation* is the process of transformation from separation to integration, especially in school.

Ethnic segregation includes several dimensions. The most common types of segregation include the following:

1. *Residential segregation*—members of different ethnic groups are separated into different residential neighborhoods.

2. *School segregation*—members of different ethnic groups attend different schools.

3. *Occupational segregation*—members of different ethnic groups are concentrated in different occupations.

4. *Public segregation*—separation of the members of different ethnic groups in public places such as buses, trains, stores, ticket counters, entertainment or recreation centers, and so on.

5. *Military segregation*—soldiers of different ethnic groups are trained on different bases and assigned to separate combat units.

In American society, public segregation between whites and blacks was very common before the Civil Rights movement, and it no longer exists today. During World War II, black soldiers and Asian soldiers were separated from white soldiers in training, living quarters, and combat. Executive Order 9981, issued by President Truman in 1948, began the process of desegregating the U.S. military, and today military segregation is history. School segregation still exists to some extent, and so does occupational segregation. In particular, residential segregation has remained pervasive, and it has captured immense scholarly attention. The remainder of this chapter will focus on residential segregation and will also discuss school segregation.

MEASURES OF RESIDENTIAL SEGREGATION

The "eyeball" method may be able to tell us whether there is residential segregation in a community. However, determining the degree of residential segregation requires more sophisticated methods. To gauge the degree of residential segregation between two groups in a community, scholars have developed several measures of residential segregation. The most widely used measure is the index of dissimilarity (or D index), initially developed by Taeuber and Taeuber (1965).

This index measures the degree of the evenness of groups' distribution among subareas (e.g., census tracts), or to what extent members of two groups are spread out in similar or different proportions throughout the subareas of a community. One often-used formula for the computation of this index is

$$D = \tfrac{1}{2} \sum | (x_i / X_t) - (y_i / Y_t) |$$

where D is the index of dissimilarity, and x and y could be any two groups. Suppose x stands for blacks and y stands for whites; x_i is the number of blacks in neighborhood i (e.g., a census block or a census tract); X_t is the total number of blacks in the whole community (e.g., a city); therefore, (x_i / X_t) is the proportion of blacks living in neighborhood i. Similarly, y_i is the number of whites in the neighborhood i; Y_t is the total number of whites in the whole community; (y_i / Y_t) is the proportion of whites living in the neighborhood i. Sizes of groups do not affect D in any way.

The scores of D vary from 0 to 1.00, or 0 to 100 if multiplied by 100. A score of 0 indicates no ethnic residential segregation between the two groups. If residents of two groups live evenly across different neighborhoods in a community, D will be equal to 0. A score of 1.00 or 100 means complete ethnic residential segregation between the two groups. If two groups are totally separated in different neighborhoods of a community, D will equal 1 or 100. The greater the D score, the higher the degree of residential segregation; conversely, the smaller the D, the lower the degree of segregation.

The D score can be interpreted as the percentage of an ethnic group that would have to move to other neighborhoods in order to completely eliminate intergroup segregation (i.e., bring D down to 0). For example, if the D score for black-white segregation in Los Angeles is 80, that means 80 percent of the blacks would have to change residence in order to produce residential integration.

There are other measures of residential segregation. For instance, the Gini coefficient, the entropy index, and the Atkinson index also measure residential evenness. There are also two indices of residential exposure—the interaction index and the isolation index. Conceptually, both measure the degree of potential contact, or the probability of interaction between two groups within subareas of a residential community. In addition, there are measures of residential concentration, centralization, and clustering. For detailed explanations and applications of the above residential segregation measures, see Massey and Denton (1988). Having introduced the measures of residential segregation, we now turn to empirical evidence on levels and trends in ethnic residential segregation.

LEVELS AND TRENDS IN ETHNIC RESIDENTIAL SEGREGATION

How serious is residential segregation in America? Which group is most segregated from whites, and which group is more likely to live with whites in the same residential neighborhood? How has residential segregation changed in America over time? Empirical evidence based on the D index from 1970 to 1990 can shed some light on these questions. Table 10.1 shows the average residential dissimilarity of three minority groups from whites in the sixty Standard Metropolitan Statistical Areas (SMSAs) and the five key SMSAs in the period of 1970–1980. Recall that a higher D score indicates a higher degree of segregation or a lower likelihood for two groups to live in the same neighborhood. As shown in the table, for the averages of the sixty SMSAs in both 1970 and 1980 the levels of segregation were the highest between blacks and whites (.792 and .694, respectively), followed by Latino-white segregation (.444 and .434), and finally by Asian-white segregation (.437 and .342). Between 1970 and 1980, the levels of segregation between the three minority groups and whites all declined, and particularly black-white segregation and Asian-white segregation registered an almost 10 percent drop.

Table 10.1 also shows the D scores for key SMSAs. Black-white segregation was the highest in these SMSAs, and Asian-white segregation was the lowest except for San Francisco-Oakland. With a few exceptions, segregation in the key SMSAs was higher than that of the sixty SMSA averages. Black-white segregation decreased significantly except for New York, and Asian-white segregation declined in all key SMSAs. However, Latino-white segregation increased in all areas, especially in the Los Angeles-Long Beach metropolitan area, partly due to the large influx of Latino immigrants.

There are a number of studies using the 1990 census data, but they are not neatly comparable with the measures shown above. Nevertheless,

Table 10.1 Average Residential Dissimilarity between Three Minority Groups and Whites in 60 SMSAs and Key SMSAs, 1970–1980

SMSA	Black			Latino			Asian		
	1970	1980	change	1970	1980	change	1970	1980	change
60 SMSA average	.792	.694	-.098	.444	.434	-.010	.437	.342	-.095
Chicago	.919	.878	-.041	.584	.635	.051	.558	.439	-.120
Los Angeles-Long Beach	.910	.811	-.099	.468	.570	.102	.531	.431	-.100
Miami	.851	.778	-.073	.504	.519	.015	.392	.298	-.094
New York	.810	.820	.010	.649	.656	.007	.561	.481	-.080
San Francisco-Oakland	.801	.717	-.084	.347	.402	.055	.486	.444	-.042

Source: Douglas Massey and Nancy Denton, "Trends in the Residential Segregation of Blacks, Hispanics, and Asians: 1970–1980." *American Sociological Review* 89 (1987), Tables 3 and 4.

they show similar patterns and trends in segregation. For instance, demographers Reynolds Farley and William Frey (1994) found that between 1980 and 1990 the D score for black-nonblack segregation declined from 68.8 in 1980 to 64.3 in 1990 in 232 metropolitan areas; Hispanic/non-Hispanic segregation remained virtually unchanged (42.2 in 1980 and 42.7 in 1990) in 153 metropolitan areas; and Asian/non-Asian segregation increased slightly from 40.7 in 1980 to 43 in 1990 in sixty-six metropolitan areas. However, black-nonblack segregation remained the highest. In another study, Frey and Farley (1996) also found that in multiethnic metropolitan areas with large black populations, segregation between blacks and whites, Latinos, and Asians was quite high.

What about the residential segregation of American Indians? Some may anticipate a high level of segregation for Indians due to their residence on reservations. In fact, available research indicates that the assimilation programs and urban policies of the federal government have resulted in a dispersed Indian population. About half of the Indians scatter in urban areas, and even among reservation Indians many spent a significant portion of their lives outside reservations. In a study of eleven cities in the Southwest in 1970 and 1980, Bohland (1982) reported that Indians were much less segregated than blacks and somewhat less segregated than Hispanics, and that the level of segregation for Indians declined between 1970 and 1980.

CAUSES OF ETHNIC RESIDENTIAL SEGREGATION

The persistence of residential segregation, especially the high level of black-white segregation, demands answers to the question of what causes it. There are at least four major explanations for ethnic residential segregation: (1) the group-preference explanation; (2) the economic-status explanation; (3) the housing-discrimination explanation; and (4) the historical and structural explanation. Let us briefly review the ideas of these four explanations and examine available empirical data to determine their validity.

The Group-Preference Explanation

The group-preference explanation asserts that the preference of people to live with members of their own ethnic group in the same neighborhood causes ethnic residential segregation. Put differently, like "birds of a feather flocking together," people feel more comfortable living with their own kind; hence, they tend to choose their houses or apartments close to members of their own groups. As a result, different groups are concentrated in different neighborhoods.

The group-preference explanation seems to be a common-sense argument. To prove this theory, one has to document that all groups have an in-group preference for neighborhood location and that people's behavior is consistent with their preference.

Is there any evidence that supports this argument? Studies have demonstrated that it is not true that all people prefer to live with members of their own groups in the same neighborhood. No studies have found that blacks prefer totally black neighborhoods. For instance, two well-cited Detroit Area Surveys (Farley et al. 1978; Farley, Bianchi, and Colasanto 1979) showed that 63 percent of the black respondents chose 50 percent black/50 percent nonblack neighborhoods as their first choice of residency, and only 12 percent of the black respondents selected 100 percent black neighborhoods as their first choice. For many blacks, the 70 percent black neighborhood was their second choice. On the other hand, whites did not prefer living with blacks in the same neighborhood. Seventy-two percent of the white respondents reported that they would feel uncomfortable living in the same neighborhood with blacks. The smaller the percentage of blacks in their neighborhood, the more comfortable they would feel. The 1992 follow-up study by Farley and Fred (1994) found that negative attitudes of whites toward blacks declined but significant proportions of whites still felt uneasy living with blacks and would avoid sharing neighborhoods with blacks.

In a more recent study using data from telephone surveys in Omaha, Kansas City, Milwaukee, Cincinnati, and Los Angeles, UCLA geographer William Clark (1991) found that in all these cities blacks preferred to live in racially integrated neighborhoods with 50 percent blacks and 50 percent others. In contrast, whites had a slight tendency to prefer white neighborhoods. As the percentage of blacks increased, the percentage of whites who preferred whiter neighborhoods decreased. Although there was a significant increase in white preference when the black percentage reached 50 percent, few whites preferred to live in high percent black areas.

Another study conducted by William Clark (1992) in the Los Angeles School District in 1987 reported that blacks preferred 50 percent black-50 percent white or Latino neighborhoods. Similarly, Hispanics preferred half Hispanic-half white neighborhoods. For the Hispanic-black combination, Hispanics preferred predominantly Hispanic neighborhoods; more than 60 percent of them preferred to live in all-Hispanic neighborhoods. Asians preferred 50 percent Asian-50 percent white neighborhoods; Asians also preferred half Asian-half black neighborhoods more than other types of neighborhoods, but significant percentages of them also preferred to live in predominantly Asian neighborhoods. Whites had a tendency to prefer neighborhoods with a higher percentage of whites.

Furthermore, based on migration patterns in the previous six years, Clark (1992) found that 96 percent of whites who preferred 80–100 percent white neighborhoods actually ended up living in those kinds of neighborhoods. Of whites who preferred 50 percent white and 50 percent black neighborhoods, all of them actually migrated to 80–100 percent white neighborhoods. Seventy-five percent of Hispanics who preferred 50 percent white-50 percent Hispanic neighborhoods selected 80–100 percent Hispanic neighborhoods. About 67 percent of Asians who preferred half Asian-half non-Asian neighborhoods selected 80–100 percent Asian neighborhoods. The pattern for blacks was somewhat different. Among those who preferred 50/50 black neighborhoods, 39 percent moved into an 80–100 percent black neighborhood; 31 percent relocated to a 51–79 percent black neighborhood; only .07 percent actually chose a racially mixed neighborhood. This may be due to the fact that there were very few 50/50 neighborhoods or that they were not available to blacks.

Eighty-nine percent of blacks who preferred 80–100 percent black neighborhoods actually chose such neighborhoods.

In sum, both supporting evidence and counterevidence exist. In terms of preference, there is little evidence to support the group-preference explanation except for a slight tendency toward white in-group preference. However, in terms of actual migration behavior, almost all groups including those preferring racially integrated neighborhoods, tend to select neighborhoods dominated by their own groups. This outcome may be due to other involuntary factors such as lack of financial resources to move into desired neighborhoods, housing discrimination, or unavailability of desired housing.

The Economic-Status Explanation

The economic-status explanation attributes ethnic residential segregation to group differences in economic status. The line of reasoning is as follows: Ethnic groups differ in average economic status and have unequal purchasing power in the housing market. Given that housing units with similar prices are clustered together in particular neighborhoods, ethnic groups with adequate financial resources are able to afford and live in high-priced neighborhoods, while poor groups with lower purchasing power are compelled to live in lower-priced neighborhoods or even slums. Hence, ethnic residential segregation is a result of the differential economic status of groups, and what appears to be ethnic segregation is essentially class-based segregation.

Empirical evidence for this economic argument is mixed. For nonblack groups, economic differences to varying degrees explain group differences in residential segregation. For example, Guest and Weed (1976) reported that more than half of the variation in residential segregation among European groups in Cleveland, Boston, and Seattle could be explained by group differences in income. Denton and Massey (1988) found that economic status did affect Hispanic-white segregation and Asian-white segregation. As income level increases, Hispanic-white segregation and Asian-white segregation decline steadily.

However, many studies have found that economic status does not have much effect on black-white segregation. Studies made during the 1970s and 1980s usually found that blacks and whites with similar income and occupational status did not live in the same residential neighborhoods, and economic differences explain very little variation in black-white segregation (e.g., Darden 1987; Farley, Bianchi, and Colasanto 1979; Schwab 1982). Denton and Massey (1988) reported that black-white segregation remained unvarying regardless of income. At least until 1980, money did not buy entry for blacks into white neighborhoods (Massey and Denton 1993). Not everyone agrees with these conclusions, though. For instance, Zelder (1970) and Clark (1986) argued that economic differences between black and white households account for much of black-white segregation. Moreover, although race overshadowed class in earlier periods, economic status may have gained more importance in explaining black-white segregation in recent periods. A recent study using the 1990 census data (Farley and Frey 1994) seems to support this view, as Farley and Frey found that income differences between blacks and whites do correlate with the degrees of black-white segregation in different metropolitan areas.

To recapitulate, the effects of economic status on residential segregation appear to be largely interactive, and economic status affects the residential segregation of different groups in different ways. A systematic comparison of its effects on different groups at various times will advance our knowledge of this dimension. Regardless of how incongruous the research findings regarding the effect of class on residential segregation might be, race is still undeniably a factor in the equation of segregation. Housing discrimination embodies the effect of race on segregation.

The Housing-Discrimination Explanation

The housing-discrimination explanation claims that the main cause of residential segregation is not preference or income, but discrimination in the housing market. That is, housing discrimination against certain ethnic groups prevents them from moving into their preferred neighborhoods or restricts their access to those neighborhoods, thereby leading to residential segregation.

Perhaps no one would deny that housing discrimination can result in residential segregation, but not every one would agree that housing discrimination is still pervasive and has a great effect on residential segregation. Hence, the linchpin to test the validity of this argument is to document the existence of housing discrimination.

Few people have doubts about the existence of housing discrimination before the 1960s because housing discrimination was to a large extent legal at that time. Housing discrimination used to be the law of this land.

For instance, the Jim Crow Laws, approved by the Supreme Court in its 1896 *Plessy v. Ferguson* ruling, allowed segregation between blacks and whites in all aspects of life, including residence and public facilities throughout the South. The Supreme Court decision was not reversed until 1954 in the case of *Brown v. Board of Education of Topeka*. Between 1910 and 1917, fifteen state courts upheld the right of local governments to enact zoning ordinances that explicitly prohibited blacks or other minority groups from entering white-zoned neighborhoods. These ordinances were struck down by the Supreme Court in the 1917 *Buchanan v. Warley* decision. After racial zoning was outlawed, the real estate community turned to race-restrictive covenants, which were agreements among property owners stating that they would not allow minorities to own, occupy, or lease their property at any time in the future. These covenants were widespread. Between 1917 and 1948, nineteen state courts upheld their legality. The racially restrictive covenant was not banned until 1948 when the Supreme Court's *Shelly v. Kraemer* decision declared it unconstitutional. The federal government's public housing policies also encouraged preserving racially homogeneous neighborhoods. For instance, in the 1930s the Federal Housing Administration encouraged local authorities to draw color-coded maps indicating the creditworthiness of neighborhoods. In short, overt discrimination against minorities in the housing market was prevalent prior to the 1960s. All major studies of housing segregation between blacks and whites before 1968 identified racial discrimination as a main cause of residential segregation (DuBois 1899; Myrdal [1944] 1962; U.S. Commission on Civil Rights 1961; U.S. Commission on Race and Housing 1958; Weaver 1948).

However, the 1960s saw the abolition of discriminatory housing laws. Title VI of the Civil Rights Act of 1964 banned discrimination in housing subsidized by the federal government. In 1968 Congress passed The Fair Housing Act (Title VIII of the Civil Rights Act of 1968), which explicitly outlawed discrimination in the sale and rental of private housing on the basis of race, color, religion, or country of origin. Since then, few people have openly refused to rent apartments or sell their houses to minorities for fear that blatant discrimination will lead to lawsuits and indictments.

Has housing discrimination continued since the Fair Housing Act of 1968? To what extent is housing discrimination still a problem in American society? During the late 1970s and the 1980s, at least seventy-one audit studies of housing discrimination based on a random sample of advertisements or housing agencies at the regional or local levels were conducted (for a detailed review of these studies, see Galster 1990; see also Pearce 1979; Saltman 1979). Varying in quality and sample size (ranging from twelve to 280 audits), these studies covered all regions of the country, both sales and rental markets, and primarily African and Hispanic Americans. These studies have overwhelmingly documented widespread housing discrimination against minority home seekers.

However, none of these audit studies are comparable in scope to the housing discrimination studies conducted by the Department of Housing and Urban Development (HUD). HUD conducted two national studies of housing discrimination: One was the 1977 Housing Market Practices Survey (HMPS), and the other the 1989 Housing Discrimination Study (HDS). The 1977 HMPS, using matched pairs of black-white auditors, studied discrimination against blacks, and it found that whites were favored in 48 percent of housing sales transactions and in 39 percent of housing rental transactions (Wienk et al. 1979).

The 1989 HDS expanded the scope of study to include housing discrimination against both blacks and Hispanics. The following are the main procedures and findings of this study (for further details, see the Urban Institute 1991; Yinger 1995). Researchers first randomly selected twenty-five metropolitan areas with significant minority populations (i.e., central city populations greater than 100,000 and consisting of more than 12 percent blacks or 7 percent Hispanics—the average percentages of black and Hispanic populations overall in 1980). In those metropolitan areas, 3,800 advertisements for housing rentals and sales units were randomly selected from the major Sunday newspapers. A pair of minority (black or Hispanic) and white auditors were sent to each of the 3,800 realtors who had placed the advertisements. Each pair of auditors matched each other in many demographic and socioeconomic characteristics, such as sex, age, general appearance, income, occupation, marital status, number of children, and assets available for down payment. In fact, minority auditors were always assigned slightly higher incomes to make sure they were not treated less favorably. Both auditors visited the same realtor within a short period of time, and who went first was randomly decided. After each visit, the auditors independently recorded their treatment by the realtor on a standardized form, and the results were tallied and analyzed.

The findings of the 1989 study revealed that during both the inquiry stage and the transaction stage, the whites were systematically favored over the minority auditors in both housing sales and housing rentals in terms of housing availability, courtesy, terms and conditions, information requested, information volunteered, and financing service. During the inquiry stage, minority auditors were more likely to be told that the unit had been sold or rented, to be shown the advertised unit but not other units, or to be recommended fewer rental units. During the transaction stage of the housing rental audits, minority auditors were more likely to be required to pay application fees, offered less incentives, and quoted a higher rent and higher security deposit; and realtors were less likely to show friendly attitudes when inquiring about income, reasons for moving, etc. In the sales audits, minority home buyers were less likely to get financing assistance. Moreover, minority home buyers were more likely to be steered to neighborhoods with a high percentage of minorities, low-income residents, and lower house values (so-called racial steering). Overall, the estimated incidence of discrimination against blacks was 53 percent in the rental market and 59 percent in the sales market; and the estimated incidence of discrimination against Hispanics was 46 percent in the rental market and 56 percent in the sales market (Urban Institute 1991, vi–vii, 42–43). Although the 1989 HUD audit study does not provide conclusive evidence on the rise or decline of housing discrimination against the 1977 HUD audit study, both studies showed that minority home seekers continued to face prevailing housing discrimination.[1]

Minorities, especially blacks and Hispanics, were not only discriminated against by realtors but by biased practices of financial institutions. For instance, one of the biased practices is so-called red-lining, which is a practice of banks or insurance companies to provide no loans or coverage for people, property, or businesses located in neighborhoods that are declining or deemed too risky for financial commitment. These so-called red-line areas tend to have relatively high percentages of minorities, although white working class areas have frequently been red-lined as well (Taggart 1974; Wrobel 1979). Jackson (1985) showed that areas with significant minority presence were systematically denied mortgage and home improvement loans. Dedman (1988) found that middle-class white areas received home loans from banks at a rate four or five times higher than middle-income black areas; and even low-income white areas obtained higher rates of home loans than middle-income black areas. Studies have also found that equally qualified minority customers are less

1. Changes in the measurements of housing discrimination in the 1989 HDS rendered a determination in the degree of housing discrimination over the two periods unattainable. For further details, see the Urban Institute (1991).

likely to receive mortgage loans than white customers; they are offered less favorable loan conditions, are required to pay application fees, or receive little attention and assistance from agents in filling out forms. For instance, in 1990, conventional mortgage loan rejection rates for blacks and Hispanics were 33.9 percent and 21.4 percent, respectively, compared to 14.4 percent for whites (Canner and Smith 1991). Even among the highest income groups, black applicants were more than twice as likely as white applicants to get rejected, and Hispanic applicants were almost twice as likely as whites to be turned down. In follow-up analyses (Canner, Passmore, and Smith 1994; Canner and Smith 1992), the patterns of home loan denials for home purchase, refinancing, and home improvement remained basically unchanged; and, holding median family income levels constant, blacks and Hispanics were much more likely to be denied a loan than whites. A survey of mortgage lending practices in Washington, D.C., for 1985 and 1991 conducted by *The Washington Post* (1993) found an inverse relationship between the percentage of the black population in a neighborhood and mortgage lending rates, controlling for relevant factors such as income and number of salable properties. That is, the higher the percentage of blacks in the neighborhood, the smaller the number of mortgages granted per one thousand properties. In addition, minorities have more difficulty selling their houses in order to move to other areas.

In sum, the available evidence on discrimination in the housing sales, rental, and mortgage markets indicates that housing discrimination is still a problem in America, and it explains a significant (if not major) portion of residential segregation.

The Historical and Structural Explanation

Unlike the foregoing explanations that account for residential segregation by focusing on attitudes, behavior, and economic status, the structural argument contends that ethnic residential segregation cannot be completely explained without taking into account the larger historical and structural processes.

The important role of historical and structural factors in causing residential segregation has been documented. The most important factors associated with residential segregation include, but are not limited to:

1. History and structure of cities. In general, old cities tend to have higher degrees of residential segregation than new cities. Massey

and Denton (1987, 818) observed that cities built prior to World War II have ecological structures that are more conducive to residential segregation, including high population densities and the concentration of working-class neighborhoods in inner city areas. Frey and Spear (1988) and Schnore (1965) reported a positive correlation between the age of a city and the level of segregation.

2. Suburbanization. Especially after World War II, many white families moved to suburban areas while many blacks remained in urban centers. Although suburbanization also occurred among blacks, whites suburbanized much faster. Suburban areas where whites predominate tend to have lower levels of segregation (Golant and Jocobson 1978).

3. Immigration. Immigration increases the degree of segregation because new immigrants are more likely to live with members of their own backgrounds.

4. New housing construction. In the 1940s, new housing construction in a city increased segregation since it enabled whites to distance themselves from blacks (Taeuber and Taeuber 1965). However, since 1968, new housing construction has reduced residential segregation, and areas with new housing construction tend to have a lower level of residential segregation (Farley and Frey 1994).

5. Functional specialization of cities. For instance, retirement communities and communities with a concentration of durable goods manufacturing industries tend to have high levels of segregation; segregation is moderate in government communities and college towns; and segregation is lowest in military communities because soldiers are assigned to integrated quarters on base or integrated apartment complexes (Farley and Frey 1994).

Other factors such as work location, housing supply, and form of transportation also affect residential segregation.

Certainly, no one of the foregoing theories alone suffices to account for ethnic residential segregation; but all of them together can provide a fuller explanation. Group preference, economic status, housing discrimination, and historical and structural factors all play roles. The importance of these factors varies across different ethnic groups and time periods. For instance, racial prejudice and discrimination may well be dominant determinants of black-white segregation, but they might not be critical for Asian-white segregation. Housing discrimination was surely the most prominent factor in segregation between minorities and whites prior to the 1960s, but its role has attenuated over time. It may be more fruitful to treat all of these factors as an interrelated system of causation. The effect of interactions among these factors merits further investigation.

EFFECTS OF ETHNIC RESIDENTIAL SEGREGATION

The pioneers of contemporary research on residential segregation, W. E. B. DuBois and Robert Park, showed ambivalence about segregated ethnic enclaves, or ghettos. On the one hand, they saw the enclave as a site of such social pathology as poverty, divorce, alcoholism, crime, juvenile delinquency, and ignorance. On the other hand, Park, and to a lesser extent DuBois, found some positive signs in ethnic enclaves, such as group solidarity, mutual aid organizations, sources of social control, and opportunities for economic mobility. In the 1930s and 1940s, there appeared to be a consensus among social scientists that residential segregation is primarily negative, as shown in the works of Charles Johnson (1943), Gunnar Myrdal (1944), Amos Hawley (1944), John Dollard (1937), among others. The post–World War II period saw the emergence of residential segregation as a prominent public issue. Since then, the literature on the effects of residential segregation has proceeded in two currents, one emphasizing its negative effects and the other acknowledging some of its positive effects. The key arguments of both are summarized below.

Scholars have identified several negative consequences of ethnic residential segregation. First, residential segregation helps maintain ethnic inequality. Since minority concentrated areas often have lower-quality schools, fewer employment opportunities, and fewer resources and facilities, continuing residential segregation means persistent educational, occupational, and employment inequalities. Much empirical evidence has supported this claim (e.g., Galster and Keeney 1988; Kain 1968; Roof 1972).

Second, residential segregation preserves poverty. Studies have shown that growing up in a ghetto neighborhood increases the chance of dropping out of high school, decreases the likelihood of attending college, reduces the probability of employment, lowers the level of income earned as adults, and increases the likelihood of unwed pregnancy and teenage childbearing. All of these increase poverty. Massey and Denton (1993) cogently demonstrated that racial segregation, as well as its institutional form, the black ghetto, is responsible for the creation of the black underclass and the perpetuation of black poverty.

Third, residential segregation reinforces prejudice toward other groups due to a lack of intergroup interaction. Segregation is the key nexus for the vicious circle of self-perpetuating prejudice and inequality (DeMarco and Galster 1993). Segregation, often initiated by whites on the claim of black inferiority, is a stigma for blacks, and it lowers their self-esteem and self-respect.

Finally, residential segregation hinders minority groups' integration into American society and their full participation in American life. It sows the seeds of interracial hostility and conflict (Pettigrew 1971). By heightening the tendency to think in terms of "us" versus "them," it leads to a divided and troubled society.

While social scientists questioned the desirability of assimilation and embraced cultural pluralism and other models, they also began to ponder over some of the positive effects of ethnic residential segregation.[2] One often-mentioned function of residential segregation is the maintenance of ethnic cultures, ethnic communities, and ethnic solidarity. By creating a critical mass, an ethnically concentrated location provides a geographical base for preserving ethnic cultural traditions, promoting ethnic identity and unity, and strengthening ethnic community (see, for example, Fischer 1976; Rodriguez 1975).

Another function of residential segregation is social-psychological protection. Namely, an ethnically concentrated location provides a supportive and accepting environment and shields group members from racial prejudice and discrimination. For example, Rodriguez (1975) found that Puerto Ricans in the ethnic enclave had a support network and felt the impact of discrimination less than those outside the enclave. Historical and contemporary Chinatowns are another example.

A third benefit of residential segregation suggested by the ethnic enclave hypothesis is that the ethnic enclave provides minority groups with opportunities and advantages for economic survival and mobility, such as earnings equivalent to those in the primary labor market, chances for up-

---

2. While residential segregation appears to carry a negative connotation, researchers who emphasize the positive side of this phenomenon prefer such terms as "ethnic residential concentration" or "ethnic enclave."

ward mobility, and entrepreneurial opportunities. Supporting evidence comes from the studies of Wilson and Portes (1980), Portes and Stepick (1985), Portes and Manning (1986), and Zhou (1992). In contrast, Jimy Sanders and Victor Nee (1987) maintained that segregation retards assimilation and socioeconomic achievement. They found that the ethnic enclave is a disadvantage for workers, although it may benefit employers and entrepreneurs. Kwong (1996) echoed the latter conclusion.

Finally, ethnic residential segregation/concentration increases the political power of minorities. Minority-concentrated areas are more likely to elect minority candidates to public offices. In 1985, for instance, 70 percent of black congressional representatives and some 40 percent of black big-city mayors were elected from districts where blacks constituted the majority of voters (Joint Center for Political Studies 1985). However, some scholars contend that segregation has political consequences. For example, Massey and Denton (1993) argued that segregation reduces blacks' chances of forming political coalitions, prevents them from participating in pluralist politics, and therefore limits their political influence. Today, whether residential segregation has positive effects or negative effects remains a moot issue.

SCHOOL SEGREGATION, DESEGREGATION, AND RESEGREGATION

While school segregation is not as prevalent as residential segregation today, it remains salient. The segregation of minority students from white students had been a long-lasting reality in America before the Civil Rights movement began. The *Brown v. Board of Education* decision of the Supreme Court in 1954, which required the desegregation of public schools, marked the beginning of de jure school desegregation in the United States. In spite of widespread resistance, legal school segregation began to be dismantled in the border states in the late 1950s and early 1960s, and later in the deep South. By the mid-1970s, roughly two-thirds of the nation's school districts had made some attempts to desegregate their schools through such measures as busing, school choice, magnet schools, use of ratios, redrawn school district boundaries, mandatary and voluntary intra- and interdistrict transfers, and consolidation of city districts with suburban districts (U.S. Commission on Civil Rights 1976). Largely as a result of court-mandated orders, school segregation gradually decreased. In 1965, 65 percent of black students were enrolled in schools with over 90 percent minorities. The percentage of black students in such schools decreased to almost 39 percent in 1972 and 33 percent in 1980 (Orfield 1993).

Since 1980, federal and state courts have eased their pressure on school desegregation. Especially in the 1990s, the courts have released school districts from court supervision of their desegregation efforts and transferred considerable desegregation supervisory power to local school boards. Consequently, the late 1980s and 1990s have witnessed a trend of quiet school *resegregation*, or a return to the previous status of segregated schools (Orfield 1996). Not only has school segregation decreased little but it has actually somewhat increased. For instance, the percentage of black students attending schools with more than 90 percent minorities was 32.5 percent in 1986 and rose to almost 34 percent in 1991; the percentage of black students attending schools with more than 50 percent minorities rose from about 63 percent in 1980 to 66 percent in 1992, which was higher than any time after 1968 (Orfield 1993). Furthermore, nationwide the increasing level of school segregation has been most evident for Latino students. The percentage of Latino students enrolled in schools with more than 90 percent minorities steadily increased from 23 percent in 1968 to 28 percent in 1980 and further to 34 percent in 1991; the percentage of Latino students attending schools with more than 50 percent minorities climbed from nearly 55 percent in 1968 to 68 percent in 1980 and to 73 percent in 1991 (Orfield 1993). These trends should alert us to the growing separation between minorities and whites in schools.

There are urban/rural, regional, and group variations in the level of school segregation. School segregation is most serious in cities, especially large central cities. Farley (1984) found that black-white school segregation was highest in the Midwest and Northeast and lowest in the South and West. The low level of segregation in the South can be largely attributed to court mandate while the high level of segregation in the Northeast was mainly due to de facto segregation. Latinos were most segregated in the Northeast and least segregated in the Midwest (Orfield 1996). Native Americans were most segregated in the Midwest (U.S. Commission on Civil Rights 1976).

Why has school segregation persisted and even increased? The retreat of the Supreme Court from desegregation largely explains the lack of progress and resegregation in the past two decades. Starting in 1974, a series of Supreme Court decisions made the implementation of desegregation orders much more difficult. For example, the 1974 *Milliken v. Bradley* decision ruled that a school district in an inner city area cannot cross school districts to include the suburban area that surrounds the district in its desegregation plan. This means that minority children who are concentrated in inner city areas cannot attend the same schools as white children who are concentrated in suburban areas. In several other decisions during the Reagan administration, the Court decreed that once a school system has been declared partially desegregated, it can dismantle all its desegregation programs.

Residential segregation also contributes to school segregation. Since children attend schools in their residential districts, highly segregated schools are an inevitable outcome of highly segregated residence. On the other hand, school segregation in turn affects residential segregation since the choice of school determines the choice of residence for many families. Realtors often sell homes by selling schools. The relationship between residential segregation and school segregation is reciprocal and they reinforce each other (Orfield 1980).

Another important factor is the continuing institutional practice of de facto segregation. A subtle method is the drawing of school districts based on de facto racial homogeneity. Although this method is illegal today, the preexistence of racially homogeneous school districts has continued to sustain present school segregation. Large metropolitan areas maintain school segregation through having smaller school districts with relatively high racial homogeneity, and this is most evident in New York, Illinois, Michigan, and New Jersey where school segregation for African American students is most severe (Orfield 1996).

The tremendous growth of white suburbs and the expansion of inner city black and Latino neighborhoods in large urban areas have also made desegregation more difficult than before. It should also be noted that there are concerns about whether desegregation (e.g., busing) programs are desirable to minority parents and whether other alternatives can achieve quality education for minority children.

There is also a problem of *within-school segregation*, or the separation of students by race or ethnicity within a desegregated school. This problem is extensive and pervasive. For instance, Morgan and McPartland (1981) found that the majority of white desegregated schools were likely to display a pattern of extreme classroom segregation, and that this pattern was most evident in the South and at the secondary level.

Within-school segregation results from sorting and assigning racially/

ethnically mixed students into homogeneous groups for instruction. Practices associated with sorting and assignment include tracking and ability grouping; remedial programs for poor and low-achieving children; special education programs for handicapped students; and bilingual education programs for students with limited English proficiency. These segregative practices may be well intentioned and based on the dominant educational philosophy of helping students to attain the highest possible levels of achievement. The practices can also be caused by cultural insensitivity and racism among school personnel, and by student and parent choice.

Within-school segregation has consequences. It undermines the possibility of interracial or interethnic contact and denies students from different ethnic groups exposure to similar educational expectations and experiences. It maintains racial stereotypes and hinders the minority achievement. It is a major menace to desegregation because it establishes de facto racial isolation, which school desegregation seeks to eliminate.

SUMMARY

Ethnic segregation or separation still permeates American life, especially in the form of residential segregation and to a lesser extent school segregation. Residential segregation has been the object of grave scholarly concern. Many measures have been developed by researchers to gauge residential segregation, the most common one being the index of dissimilarity, which measures the degree of evenness in the distribution of any two ethnic groups in different neighborhoods of a community. There are other measures of residential segregation that gauge the dimensions of residential exposure, concentration, centralization, and clustering.

Much of the research indicates the perpetuation of residential segregation between whites and minorities, particularly black-white segregation. Although black-white residential segregation has declined significantly in the past several decades, it remains very high, as compared to Hispanic-white segregation and Asian-white segregation. Overall, there were also some declines in Hispanic-white segregation and Asian-white segregation between 1970 and 1980, but Hispanic/non-Hispanic segregation and Asian/non-Asian segregation increased slightly between 1980 and 1990.

Four major theories attempt to explain ethnic residential segregation:

the group-preference explanation, the economic-status explanation, the housing-discrimination explanation, and the historical and structural explanation. Each of these theories emphasizes the prime role of a particular determinant or a particular set of determinants, as suggested by their labels. Empirical support for these theories varies. Probably, an integration of these theories can provide the best answer to the question of what causes ethnic residential segregation.

Ethnic residential segregation has consequences. Early research tended to focus on such negative effects as the maintenance of ethnic inequality, the preservation of poverty among minority groups, the reinforcement of ethnic stereotypes, the hinderance of group integration, and the engendering of ethnic hostility and conflict. On the other hand, recent studies have examined a mixture of negative effects along with such positive effects as cultural preservation, social-psychological protection, the provision of economic opportunities, and political empowerment.

As a result of judicial mandate beginning in the 1950s, school segregation in America had declined over time, but since the late 1980s public schools have been resegregated to some extent. Segregation has risen slightly in the case of black students and considerably in the case of Latino students. An array of factors, such as the retrogression of the Supreme Court from advancing desegregation, the persistence of housing segregation, the continuing institutional acceptance of de facto segregation practices such as school district fragmentation, the growth of both white suburbs and inner city minority neighborhoods, and concerns about the efficiency and desirability of desegregation programs is responsible for the tenacity of school segregation and resegregation. The effects of school segregation and residential segregation are reciprocal. Even *within* desegregated schools, the classroom segregation of students along racial lines through sorting and assignment practices looms large. Within-school segregation threatens to undermine the effects of past desegregation. Both racial prejudice and discrimination against some groups of minority students and the notion that teaching efficiency might be increased by grouping students with similar academic ability and educational needs are among the causes of within-school segregation.

CHAPTER 11
ETHNIC CONFLICT

Ethnic conflict is both a force that shapes human affairs and a social phenomenon that begs understanding. As worldwide ethnic friction heightens, information on the subject cannot keep pace with reality. In particular, what has yet to emerge is a comprehensive set of generalizations that fit the materials and within which newly observed phenomena can be situated. The gulf between the available information and the need for understanding calls for further scholarly examination of this facet of ethnic interaction. The present chapter is an attempt to address this underdeveloped issue.

This chapter first defines the concept of ethnic conflict and outlines its various forms. It then critically examines several major theories that seek to explain the emergence of ethnic conflict. The ensuing discussion of Korean-black antagonism aims at exploring the causes of interminority conflict. Based on the above discussions, the chapter then outlines a more inclusive theory of ethnic conflict. Finally, the scope, trends, and causes of "hate crime" are discussed.

DEFINITION AND FORMS OF ETHNIC CONFLICT

The existing literature seldom provides a clear definition of ethnic conflict. In this book, I define *ethnic conflict* as any expressed sentiments or actions between ethnic groups that are hostile or antagonistic. Similar terms are *ethnic confrontation*, and *ethnic antagonism*. While some see ethnic conflict as consisting of volatile collective actions between ethnic populations (Ozalk 1986, 29), others broaden the scope of conflict to include the venting of confrontational emotions and irreconcilable disagreements among beliefs and opinions. I incline to take a middle-of-the-road approach. I exclude mere differences of opinion or belief from ethnic conflict but include inimical sentiments that are expressed verbally, in written form, or in any other form. The inclusion of ideological or opinion-based disagreements will inflate the scope of ethnic conflict in a society. On the other hand, the inclusion of only confrontational actions will underestimate the problem of societal antagonism. Nonviolent but antagonistic behavior and hostile sentiments such as resentment and hatred should be considered part of ethnic conflict.

There are three basic categories of ethnic conflict: nonviolent confrontation, violent confrontation, and expressed hostile sentiments. *Nonviolent confrontation* comprises antagonistic actions that do not take violent forms. It includes such nonviolent actions as a boycott against another ethnic group, or a peaceful protest, sit-in, march, or demonstration directed toward another ethnic group.[1] An example of the former is African Americans' boycotts of Korean businesses in the black neighborhoods of New York City. Min (1996, 73–78) documented five black boycotts against Korean merchants in New York since 1981. One example of peaceful protest is the Indians' nonviolent protests against the celebration of the Columbus Quincentenary. As Indian activist Suzan Harjo (1991) put it, "As Native American peoples . . . we have no reason to celebrate an invasion that caused the demise of so many of our people and is still causing destruction today. The European stole our land and killed our people."

Another type of ethnic conflict is *violent confrontation*. Lynching is a form of violent confrontation, which was once practiced in the United States. After the Civil War (1861–1865) and Reconstruction, the lynching of black people by white mobs occurred from time to time.[2] Another form

1. Ethnic protest may not target another ethnic group, and it may be directed at the general public or some offices of government, seeking to present a grievance to this audience on behalf of its own ethnic group (Olzak 1992, 9).

2. Before the Civil War, lunching was often carried out by white mobs against whites, and seldom occurred to blacks because they were white property. If blacks were killed, the killer or killers had to pay the white owners of black slaves.

of violent confrontation is riot against members of another ethnic group. The most serious race riot in U.S. history in terms of casualties was the Draft Riot, which occurred in 1863 in New York City, during the Civil War. White workers, many of them Irish, were angry at being drafted to fight a war to which they were not committed, and they were also angry that black workers were used as their replacements and as strikebreakers. They lynched black people on sight, mutilated them, and even burned down an orphanage for black children. Another form of violent confrontation is ethnic fighting. Examples include fighting that has historically occurred between the Irish and Germans, Italians, and Jews in various cities. It should be noted that in reality, nonviolent confrontation and violent confrontation often go together, and the former often precedes the latter.

A third type of ethnic conflict is *expressed hostile sentiments* through verbal, written, or symbolic forms. Examples include hate speeches made by Ku Klux Klan leaders such as David Duke against black people; remarks by Nation of Islam leader Louis Farrakhan on Jews; and sentiments expressed in publications and graffiti. There have been many documented incidents of hate speech on college campuses (see Ehrlich 1990; Pinkow et al. 1990). For example, at the University of Michigan, racist leaflets were distributed in dorms, and white students painted themselves black and placed rings in their noses at "jungle parties." At Northwest Missouri State University, white supremacists distributed flyers stating: "The knights of the Ku Klux Klan are watching you." At California Polytechnic State University, a female Japanese American student collided with a white male on a skateboard as she was walking to her car. The skateboarder shouted, "You Asians are taking all the jobs away from Americans. Why don't you go back to Taiwan, Korea or Vietnam—wherever you came from—you nigger lover!" At Smith College, a black student found a note slipped under her dormitory room door reading, "African Nigger do you want some bananas? Go back to the Jungle." At Michigan State University, "Die Nigger" was scrawled over a collage of personal photographs on the dormitory door of a female student. At UC Davis, an Asian American professor found a swastika scratched onto his office door.

Ethnic conflict has always been a characteristic of American society, and Americans are creatures of conflict. From its very inception, American society has been characterized by social divisions, inequalities, and intolerance. Today, ethnic conflict still constitutes a pervasive feature of American society.

THEORIES OF ETHNIC CONFLICT

Why does ethnic conflict occur? There exist several approaches to this question. One often asserted but not systematically formulated theory of ethnic conflict is the *cultural-clash explanation* (for some early formulations of the role of cultural clash in engendering ethnic conflict, see Furnivall 1948; Smith 1965). Ethnic conflicts are often termed cultural conflicts since cultural differences are among the differences that divide ethnic groups. Cultural-clash theory attributes ethnic conflict to cultural strife. In other words, differences in language, religion, customs, norms, values, beliefs, and behavior generate confrontation among different ethnic groups. According to this theory, immigration increases ethnic conflict because it heightens the awareness of differences between groups; however, ethnic conflict will subside as new groups become assimilated into the culture and institutions of the host society and cultural differences between them, as well as inequality in socioeconomic status, diminish (Gordon 1964; Williams 1964).

Cultural differences in ancestry, language, religion, and nationality bear the potential for ethnic collision but the differences per se are not intrinsically related to the clash. There must be other mechanisms that spark the conflict. Moreover, as Smith (1965) suggested, value dissensus may cause conflict if one group transgresses the precious norms of another, but value dissensus may also reduce conflict as groups shift attention to alternative gratification.

An early sociological explanation of ethnic conflict is *human ecology theory*. In an early study that borrowed the biological concepts of invasion and succession, Robert Park and Ernest Burgess (1921) envisaged ethnic conflict as part of a universal and natural process. They maintained that the invasion of new ethnic groups induces group competition, which in turn causes ethnic conflict. They believed that as an intermediate stage of ethnic relations, competition and conflict will eventually subside, and accommodation and assimilation will ensue, creating a new equilibrium. A key drawback of human ecology theory is that competition does not always lead to ethnic conflict and it does so only under certain conditions. Human ecology theory does not specify the conditions under which competition engenders ethnic conflict.

Competition theory is an attempt to refine human ecology theory along the same line of reasoning. This theory treats ethnic conflict as an outcome of ethnic competition, but it specifies the mechanisms that link competition with conflict. For Barth (1956, 1969), a key mechanism through which competition is transformed into active conflict is "niche overlap"—the exploitation and occupation of the same resources coveted by other competitors. This is the essence of contemporary competition theory, that competition between two or more ethnic groups for the *same* economic and political resources produces ethnic conflict. Ethnic conflict occurs when ethnic groups struggle to control limited resources in the presence of other competitors, and competition encourages exclusion of competitors (Olzak 1992). Niche overlap increases ethnic competition. A niche is an environment occupied by a group in the absence of competitors. If different ethnic groups do not occupy overlapping environment, ethnic conflict is not likely to result. Olzak (1992, 3) also argued that ethnic conflicts occur when ethnic inequalities and racial hierarchy begin to break down.

Competition for the same scarce resources is certainly an important determinant of ethnic conflict. However, the imbalanced power and resources between groups may be as crucial in explaining why conflict is most likely to arise between the powerful group and the weak group. Researchers observe that ethnic conflict often occurs between the dominant group and the subordinate group, and therefore the reason for conflict must be sought in the unequal relations between the dominant group and the subordinate group. The fundamental source of ethnic conflict lies in ethnic inequalities and subordination. In other words, minority groups are economically exploited, culturally deprived, and politically disenfranchised by the dominant group, and this domination and its resistance unavoidably breed ethnic conflict. I label this thesis the *ethnic inequality/subordination argument*. A number of theories can be included under this rubric. For instance, the internal colonialism perspective emphasizes the internal colonization of minority groups by the dominant group as the major source of ethnic conflict (Blauner 1972). The theory of cultural division of labor stresses that the cultural division of labor or economic inequality between the dominant group and the subordinate group causes ethnic conflicts (Hechter 1975). Although the ethnic inequality argument captures the essence of ethnic conflict and explains the bulk of ethnic conflicts, it lacks the potency to account for conflicts between minority groups. Another limitation of this argument is that it neglects the intersecting role of class in engendering ethnic conflict.

Unlike the ethnic inequality argument, which emphasizes the ethnic dimension, the *class theory* of ethnic conflict underscores the role of class.

Advocates of early class theories attribute the root of ethnic conflict to competing economic interests between classes (see, for instance, Cox 1948). A major problem with the class theory is that class interests do not always match ethnic interests, and hence ethnic conflicts often do not occur along class lines. A modern class theory, the *split labor market perspective* formulated by Edna Bonacich, attempts to address the confounding effects of class and ethnicity on ethnic conflict while still underpinning the central role of class in ethnic conflict. Bonacich (1972) argued that the fundamental cause of ethnic antagonism is capitalists' desire to maximize profit. In order to make profit, capitalists bring in the cheap labor of minority groups and create a split labor market—the high-paid labor of the dominant group on the one hand and the cheap labor of subordinate groups on the other. The split labor market generates a three-way conflict between capitalists and the two groups of labor. Capitalists must confront both high-paid labor and cheap labor. High-paid workers could either prevent the physical presence of minority workers or restrict them to certain types of low-paid jobs. Suffering from both class exploitation and racial discrimination, minority workers are forced to resist from time to time. Hence, class, rather than just ethnicity, plays a critical role in this process. The economic factor is most important, and ethnic conflict is an expression of class conflict (Bonacich 1972, 553). Still, it may be too simplistic to assume that all ethnic conflicts are economically based.

INTERMINORITY CONFLICT: THE CASE OF KOREAN-BLACK ANTAGONISM

Until very recently, analyses of ethnic conflicts had mainly focused on the conflict between dominant and minority groups. However, growing evidence indicates that ethnic conflict also frequently occurs between minority groups (for descriptions of incidents, see chapter 10 of Levin and McDevitt 1993). One such example, which has captivated media attention in recent years, is Korean-black conflict. Let us review some of the evidence and then try to understand its causes.

There have been many incidents of black-Korean conflict. For instance, as mentioned earlier in this chapter, black Americans in New York have boycotted Korean businesses at least five times since 1981. The lengths of time of these boycotts ranged from more than one month to sixteen months (from January 1990 to May 1991) in a black Brooklyn neighborhood (for detailed descriptions, see Min 1996). There were also physical attacks, robbery, arson, etc.

In Los Angeles, despite several small-scale conflicts between Korean merchants and black customers, the Korean community had no major problems with the black community in the 1980s. However, in the 1990s the hostility and tension between Korean Americans and black Americans escalated. The most publicized event was the Latasha Harlins incident. In March 1991, Soon Ja Du, a female Korean storekeeper, gunned down a fifteen-year-old black girl, Latasha Harlins, while struggling with her over an unpaid bottle of orange juice. Two days later, Danny Bakewell, president of the Brotherhood Crusade, and the Reverend Edgar Boyd, pastor of the Bethel African Methodist Episcopal Church, organized about 150 African Americans to demonstrate in front of the store. Du was convicted of voluntary manslaughter and sentenced to five years of probation and a $500 fine by Los Angeles Superior Court Judge Joyce Karlin. This lenient sentence gave African Americans the impression that Koreans were protected by a white institution. They strongly protested. This sentence was linked to the targeting of Korean stores in the 1992 Los Angeles riots.

During the 1992 riots, about 2,300 Korean-owned stores located in South Central Los Angeles and Koreatown were looted and/or burned down by black and Latino rioters. One Korean was killed and forty-six Koreans were injured. Property damages were estimated at more than $350 million. A recent study by Min (1996) showed that although both black and Latino rioters were involved in targeting Korean stores, black rioters selectively targeted Korean stores and were more likely to burn them down, while Latino rioters were more likely simply to loot the stores to acquire merchandise. These different motives evince the hostility of African Americans toward Korean merchants.

What factors have caused the Korean-black conflicts? Early analyses mainly sought explanations of this phenomenon from sociopsychological factors such as cultural differences, mutual prejudice, and language barriers. One of these sociopsychological factors is mutual prejudice and stereotyping. On the one hand, many Korean immigrants hold stereotypes of black Americans. Empirical evidence supports this. For instance, Min's recent study (1996, 121) found that high percentages of Korean merchants agreed that compared to white people, black people are generally less intelligent (61 percent), less honest (61 percent), more criminally oriented (70 percent), and lazier (45 percent). Korean merchants' stereotypes of African Americans may have stemmed from several sources: first,

Koreans' learning about stereotypes of African Americans before immigrating to the United States, due to a pervasive U.S. cultural influence in Korea through movies, TV, radio, and other media; second, Koreans' lack of knowledge of the history of black Americans; third, Koreans' unpreparedness to live in a multicultural society because of their own cultural homogeneity and a resulting intolerance; fourth, Koreans' positive view of America as a "land of opportunity" and their attribution of black socioeconomic failure to cultural deficiency; fifth, class differences between college-educated, middle-class Korean merchants and usually less educated, unemployed black customers; and sixth, conflicting economic interests and stressful economic contacts between Korean merchants and black customers. On the other hand, black Americans also had stereotypes of Korean entrepreneurs. Min's study (1996) found that significant proportions of black Americans accepted such statements as "Koreans are overly concerned about making money," "Koreans do not try to learn English and American customs," "Koreans care about only other Koreans," and "Koreans are in general rude and nasty people." Hence, both groups are victims of racial prejudice and stereotypes in American society.

Another sociopsychological factor is cultural differences. For instance, by custom Koreans in stores often do not smile at customers and avoid direct eye contact with them. Many Korean female cashiers drop change on the counter rather than place it in a male customer's hand because Korean customs teach them to avoid physical contact with men. These culturally induced behaviors are usually interpreted by black Americans as rude and uncaring.

A third factor is the language barrier. Many Korean immigrant merchants lack the English proficiency to effectively communicate with their customers. Often they cannot answer complex questions about their products posed by customers and cannot express their feelings accurately. Their inability to communicate with customers may lead to misunderstanding and may be construed as impoliteness.

Other researchers, such as Nancy Abelmann and John Lie (1995), have pinpointed the role of the media in exacerbating the conflict. To them, Korean-black conflict was mainly a product of media fabrication. To be sure, the significant role of biased media coverage in aggravating Korean-black conflict cannot be denied. The media sensationalized events and exaggerated the conflict by portraying Koreans as gun-holding vigilantes protecting their community and blacks as vandals and hoodlums during the Los Angeles riots. By doing this, the media victimized both Koreans and African Americans.

In his recent book, Min (1996) has argued that in addition to the foregoing individual-level sociopsychological factors, a number of structural factors are largely responsible for Korean-black conflict. One such factor is the poor economic conditions of inner city neighborhoods which cause the economic frustration of black residents in the inner city. Frustrated by the deteriorating economic conditions and their inability to improve their economic position, blacks in inner city neighborhoods vent their frustration and aggression upon their local Korean merchants—the most convenient and politically powerless target. A second factor is Korean merchants' vulnerable position as middlemen, who distribute the products of white corporations to black consumers. In that role, Korean immigrants are scapegoated by both the ruling class and frustrated black residents, although the American social system is largely responsible for blacks' unemployment and poverty. The third factor is the role of black nationalist leaders and black nationalist ideology. Black nationalist leaders played a leading role in organizing anti-Korean boycotts and demonstrations and transformed black frustration into concerted actions; and black nationalism provided a needed ideology by emphasizing black economic autonomy and the need for economic control of the community by blacks.

It seems that minority conflict, as well as ethnic conflict in general, is a product of multilevels of forces: both structural forces and individual social and psychological factors. Structural conditions provide the underlying context in which ethnic conflict arises. Individual-level factors often serve as a fuse, as in the cases of Korean-black boycotts. The primary source of interethnic conflict is fundamentally economic and structural. Conflicting economic interests and competition for political power and other resources are often a critical dimension, but cultural variation cannot be ignored.

TOWARD A MORE INCLUSIVE THEORY

From the foregoing review of theoretical approaches and the empirical analysis of Korean-black conflict, it seems imperative to develop a more inclusive theory of ethnic conflict. In what follows, I outline such a theory, which attempts to incorporate structural conditions with individual psychological, behavioral, and organizational factors in an organic fashion and to account for conflicts between dominant and minority groups and between minority groups themselves.

In this more inclusive theory of ethnic conflict, ethnic conflict can be seen as a social outcome of specific structural conditions and various levels of human interaction. The initial and underlying condition of ethnic conflict is the unequal ethnic structure in a society. That is, ethnic groups are cast in hierarchical social positions. This structural arrangement is maintained by laws, customs, and institutional practices. The structure is fairly stable and changes little over time. Competing ethnic groups under this structural arrangement can be seen as opposing actors with opposing interests and differences in power and resources.

The direct outcome of this ethnic structure is the status inferiority, material deprivation, and disenfranchisement of lower-status groups, especially those at the bottom of the social hierarchy. This manifests in the form of poverty; lower levels of education, occupational status, and income; poor housing conditions; residential segregation; poor health; and political powerlessness. The effects of suffering from these long-lasting conditions on low-status groups are intensive feelings of frustration, resentment, and hostility.

Hence, structural conditions pave the way for the rise of intergroup conflict as groups in different positions develop separate and conflicting interests, position themselves for struggle as the offender and the defender, and transform ethnic interest groups into conflict groups. The structural conditions are most likely to beget conflict between the dominant group and the subordinate group because of the large gap between them. These structural conditions are also a basis for interminority group conflict especially when there are significant differences in group status and direct competition for resources and opportunities.

In addition to the ethnic structure, several other conditions are required in order for ethnic conflict to arise. One factor is sufficient motivation. Heightened frustration and resentment are decisive components of motivation. The belief that change can be reached through contention, the rising level of aspirations among group members, the forging of unifying common interests, an ideology that legitimizes conflict actions, and the willingness to accept the risks of conflict are also salient elements of motivation.

However, motivation alone is not sufficient to spark ethnic conflict without available power resources. Hence, another factor is the access to usable power resources, which can include withheld purchasing power, focused voting power, the use of the mass media, and the use of laws and courts.

Ethnic organizations are also very important in the conflict-generating process. Established ethnic organizations serve to concentrate, mobilize, and utilize available power resources. Ethnic organizations can largely affect the goals, agendas, strategies, tactics, and outcomes of conflict.

Finally, the manipulation and delivery of power resources require tactical devices. Such tactics include legal redress; direct action (e.g., boycott, strike); confrontation (e.g., interruption of ordinary institutional operation); calculated intimidation; and calculated and controlled violence against persons or property.

When all of these conditions have been met, ethnic conflict seems inevitable. In brief, this structural approach sees ethnic conflict as rooted in specific structural conditions and created by the dynamic between structural conditions and individual, group, and organizational interaction.

HATE CRIMES

Hate crimes against members of particular ethnic groups are part of ethnic conflict. However, the definition of hate crime exceeds simply ethnic violence. *Hate crime* can be defined as any criminal activities motivated by hatred for members of a particular group because of their race, ethnicity, religion, disability, or sexual orientation.

Hate crime normally takes the form of violence such as murder, attempted murder, assault, attempted assault, or rape, but it also includes threats of violence, harassment, vandalism, racist graffiti, and so on. Victims are typically minority group members, Jews, Arab Americans, or gays or lesbians. Ethnic violence is a major part of hate crimes. Hate crimes are often committed by certain types of organized groups such as the White Aryan Resistance (WAR), Church of the Creator (COTC), and some factions of the Ku Klux Klan.

The federal government did not collect hate crime statistics until 1979. Research has indicated that hate crimes have recently been on the rise (Levin and McDevitt 1993). According to the reports of the U.S. Commission on Civil Rights (1986, 1992), anti-Asian violence has been increasing since the early 1980s. Anti-Asian incidents have increased in

California, New York, and Massachusetts. The increase in California is especially evident. In Los Angeles County, where minorities make up almost half of the population, hate crimes increased by 25 percent from 1995 to 1996.

As the Internet penetrates American life, it also becomes a medium for hate crimes. Recently, cyberspace hate crime (or threats on the Internet) has captured national attention. A recent case against a former UC Irvine student is a good example (see Maharaj 1997a, 1997b). On September 20, 1996, Richard Machado, a nineteen-year-old ex-UCI student of El Salvadorian origin, sent an anonymous e-mail to fifty-nine mostly Asian students on UC Irvine campus, including his former roommate. In the e-mail, he declared, "I hate Asians. . . . You are responsible for ALL the crimes that occur on campus."[3] He ordered Asian students to leave the university; otherwise he would "hunt" them down and "kill" them, he warned. The message said, "I personally will make it my [life's work] to find and kill everyone of you personally. OK? That's how determined I am." The e-mail was signed "Asian hater." Some students first thought this was a joke, but when they discovered that many students had received the same message, they realized the real intent of the e-mail. Campus police also found that the suspect had issued a death threat against the school newspaper staff in 1995, warning that they were going to die. Machado was formally indicted by federal prosecutors on ten counts of civil rights violations on November 13, 1996. Machado's first trial ended in a mistrial in November 1997, with a jury deadlock of 9–3 favoring acquittal, because the majority of the jurors believed that he was merely a disturbed teenager. The retrial of this case in February 1998 found Machado guilty of violating the civil rights of Asian students at UC Irvine by sending e-mail threatening to kill them if they did not quit the school (Maharaj 1998). This was the first successful prosecution of a cyberspace hate crime. The government prosecutors vowed to continue to prosecute similar threats made via the Internet.

Several factors may explain why hate crimes have increased. The economic recession in the late 1980s and the early 1990s and growing economic inequality between the rich and the poor worsened economic conditions for most Americans, especially the white working class and poor whites, and increased their economic frustrations and anxiety. Some

---

3. Currently, about half of the UC Irvine's 17,000 students are Asian Americans, the largest percentage of any U.S. school.

whites blamed minorities and women for their economic difficulties and viewed them as a source of their job losses. This may help explain why support for hate groups has been strongest among working-class and poor whites. Perceived economic competition between Japan and the United States also contributed to violence against all Asian Americans because other Asians are often mistaken for Japanese.

Coupled with deteriorating economic conditions and fueled by opportunistic politicians, anti-immigrant sentiment also sparks hate crimes, especially those targeting Asians and Latinos, many of them immigrants. For instance, in many hate crime incidents against Asian Americans, perpetrators told victims to "go back to your country."

Hate crimes are also caused by lingering hostility dating back to past U.S. military involvement in foreign countries. For example, in 1989 two white men, Robert and Lloyd Piche, used a pistol to beat and kill a Chinese American Jim (Ming Hai) Loo in North Carolina. They mistook Loo for a Vietnamese and vented their hatred on him for the loss of their brother during the Vietnam war.

In addition, growing violence of all types in the United States in the early 1990s and the increasing presence of minority populations, especially Latinos and Asians, has increased the likelihood of hate crimes against minorities. Growing public awareness of hate crimes and tightening law enforcement efforts may also partly explain the rise of reported hate crimes in recent years.[4]

SUMMARY

Ethnic conflict has usually been treated as part of assimilation or adaptation. Until very recently, the existing scholarship had seldom singled out ethnic conflict as a topic of discussion. The result is an underdevelopment of theories of ethnic conflict. The tenacity of ethnicity and the apparent surge in ethnic conflict both in the United States and other parts of the world require a better understanding of this phenomenon.

Ethnic conflict is a form of hostility between ethnic groups. Hostility

4. President George Bush signed into law the Hate Crimes Statistics Act of 1990, which established hate crimes based on race, ethnicity, religion, and sexual orientation as a reportable category of crime statistics. By 1995, thirty-two states had enacted their own hate crime statutes.

can be expressed as actions or sentiments, and both are part of ethnic conflict. Ethnic conflict takes the form of nonviolent confrontation, violent confrontation, and hostile verbal, written, and symbolic expressions.

Different theories of ethnic conflict are premised on different assumptions. The cultural-clash explanation conceives of ethnic conflict as a result of the clash between incompatible cultural traits; human ecology theory and competition theory view ethnic conflict as struggle for scarce resources and opportunities; the ethnic inequality perspective highlights unequal power and position as the source of conflict between the dominant group and the subordinate group; and class theories see ethnic conflict as being both rooted in and the expression of class conflict.

Interminority group conflict has been a reality, but has not been a focus of scholarly inquiry. As a salient case of interminority conflict, Korean-black conflict has grabbed media and scholarly attention in recent years. Studies suggest that a constellation of individual-level and societal-level factors account for this conflict. The reliance on one specific factor is utterly inadequate in understanding either this complex phenomenon or ethnic conflict in general.

To better account for ethnic conflict, I have sketched the main ideas of a more comprehensive theory—the structural approach. In this approach, the underlying unequal ethnic structure interacts with psychological factors, motivation, power resources, organization, and tactics to generate ethnic conflict. Differential social positions embedded in the ethnic structure and competition between ethnic groups for resources play an important role, not only in majority-minority conflict but also in interminority conflict.

While the definition of hate crime encompasses criminal activities generated by hatred against religious and sexual-orientation groups, ethnic violence remains a major part of it. Hate crime has been on the rise in the 1980s and early 1990s. A legion of economic, demographic, and political factors are responsible for its ascension.

CHAPTER 12
ETHNICITY AND POLITICS

thnicity is an important determinant of the political process and out-come in the United States. Seldom has its role been systematically addressed, and information on this topic is scant. Based on available data, this chapter focuses on how ethnicity affects political party affiliation, political ideology, voting behavior, and political representation in government, and it also discusses factors that influence differential power across ethnic groups.

POLITICAL PARTY AFFILIATION

Two major political parties dominate in America: The Democratic Party, and the Republican Party, also known as the Grand Old Party (GOP). Other smaller political parties, such as the Reform Party, the Green Party, the American Independent Party, the Peace and Freedom Party, the Libertarian Party, and the Natural Law Party, exist as well, but they have much less impact on the political process and outcome in America than the two dominant parties.

Ethnic groups have demonstrated varying tendencies to affiliate with specific political parties. It is also important to note that the partisan identification of a group is changeable, and we need to place this issue in a historical perspective. Lay minds often assume that African Americans have always voted Democratic. In fact, the attachment of African Americans to the Democratic Party has only occurred since the 1960s. From the founding of the Republican Party in 1856 until 1877, blacks were primarily affiliated with the GOP. Prior to the end of Reconstruction, sixteen blacks, all Republicans, were elected to Congress. Numerous acts of denigration and perfidy toward black Republicans by white Republicans between 1877 and 1960, and the pull of the Democratic Party, led to a complete shift of black allegiance in the 1960 elections to the Democratic Party, where they have remained ever since. As shown in Table 12.1, in 1988 about 89 percent of blacks surveyed considered themselves Democrats or leaning toward Democrats as compared to about 6 percent Republicans and 3 percent Independents. Among the 89 percent, 57 percent identified themselves as strong Democrats. The favorable stance of the Democratic Party toward African Americans on many social issues such as affirmative action, social welfare, and social justice has played an important role in retaining their loyalty. There appears to be a gender split: black women are more likely to be strong Democrats than black men, who are more likely to be weak Democrats, Independents, or Republicans (Tate 1993). There exists a generational split as well: older blacks are more likely to identify strongly with the Democratic Party than younger blacks.

There is little documentation concerning the history of Latinos and the two political parties, partly because this group is more ethnically diverse than are African Americans. As shown in Table 12.1, the political party allegiance of the three largest Latino groups varies significantly. Mexican Americans (67 percent) and Puerto Rican Americans (71 percent) are mainly attached to the Democratic Party, while Cuban Americans (68 percent) are more likely to be affiliated with the Republican Party. In addition, Latinas are found to be more Democratic than Latinos (Welch and Sigelman 1992).

Early research on Asian American partisanship provided mixed results. For instance, several studies (Cain and Kiewiet, 1986; Cain, Kiewiet, and Uhlander 1991) concluded that Asian Americans were more Republican than Democratic. Based on a survey in Monterey Park, California, Nakanishi (1991), on the other hand, found that Asian Americans were somewhat more Democratic than Republican, with the exception of Chinese who were slightly more Republican. The 1994 Field Institute Poll in California largely confirmed Nakanishi's findings, reporting that as a whole, 48 percent of Asian Americans self-identified as Democrats; 32 percent as Republicans; and 20 percent as independents (Table 12.1). The most recent survey at the national level by *AsianWeek*

Table 12.1 Political Party Affiliation of Selected Minority Groups

Party Affiliation Group	Democrat	Republican	Independent	Other	Total
Black	88.8%	6.3%	2.9%	2.0%	100.0%
Latino					
Mexican	66.9%	21.5%	11.6%	NA	100.0%
Puerto Rican	70.9%	17.6%	11.5%	NA	100.0%
Cuban	25.6%	68.6%	5.8%	NA	100.0%
Asian[a]	48.0%	32.0%	20.0%	NA	100.0%

Sources: Figures for black partisanship were calculated on the basis of the 1988 National Black Election Study; Latino partisanship data were derived from the 1990 Latino National Political Survey; the data for Asians were taken from the 1994 Field Institute Poll in California.
[a] Including Pacific Islanders; California only.
NA—Not available.

(1996) reported that the party loyalty of Asian Americans was split evenly between Democratic (28 percent) and Republican (27 percent), whereas 41 percent were switch voters equally voting for either party. There are some variations among Asian groups. For example, according to the Monterey Park data, in 1989 Japanese Americans were significantly more likely to be Democrats, while Chinese Americans were somewhat more likely to be Republicans (Nakanishi 1991). A telephone survey of the Chinese in Southern California in May 1997 reported an even distribution of Chinese political party registration plus a large component of Independents. Twenty-one percent registered as Democrats, 22 percent Republicans, 20 percent Independents, and 6 percent other (Kang 1997).[1] A 1995 sampling survey of U.S. citizens of Filipino decent in Southern California found that 40 percent of Filipinos were Democrats, 38 percent Republicans, 17 percent Independents, and 5 percent other parties (Kang 1996).

Information on American Indians' political party affiliation is scant. Available studies suggest that they do not have strong bonds to either political party, but tend to lean toward the Democratic Party. However, there are significant differences across tribal groups. For instance, the Navajos shifted from the Republican to the Democratic Party and slightly back to

1. Only U.S. citizens were asked their party registration, and 31 percent were not registered to vote. The margin of sampling error for the entire sample was plus or minue four percentage points.

the Republican in national elections during the Reagan years. Since 1956, the Pagagos have consistently voted for the Democratic Party (McCool 1982). One important determinant of Indian partisanship at the national level has been the administration's stance on Indian issues. The Republican orientation of many Indians during Richard Nixon's administration was largely a result of Nixon's perceived strong stance on Indian policy, but many shifted to Jimmy Carter later because he was also viewed as "good for Indians." There are also differences between Indians on reservations and Indians outside reservations.

There is only limited information about the political party affiliation of some white ethnic groups such as Irish, Jews, and Italians. In general, Irish Americans have consistently supported the Democratic Party. Today, they remain substantially Democratic with a large proportion of liberal Democrats among them. Historically, Jewish Americans alternated their party allegiance between the Democratic and the Republican, depending upon which party supported issues of Jewish concern. However, since 1960 they have consistently voted for the Democratic Party (Heitzmann 1975; Isaacs 1974; Schneider 1985). The political party affiliation of Italian Americans has shifted over time. Before the 1980s, Italian Americans were more likely to vote for candidates of the Democratic Party. During the 1980s, many converted their allegiance to the Republican Party, as evidenced by the 53 percent of votes for George Bush, the Republican presidential candidate in 1988. By the early 1990s, Italians had become more Republican (49 percent) than Democratic (39 percent). The social conservatism in the 1980s and early 1990s, white ethnic discontent with affirmative action programs and similar programs, and long-standing Republican efforts to lure the Italian and other white ethnic votes appear to explain the shift.

What factors may be associated with ethnic differences in political party affiliation? From the available data, several generalizations may be made. (1) Minority or majority group status. All else being equal, minority groups are more likely to be affiliated with the Democratic Party than whites. (2) Group socioeconomic status. In general, ethnic groups with a higher socioeconomic status are more likely to support the Republican Party than groups with a lower status, holding other things constant. (3) Religious affiliation. In the United States, Protestants tend to be politically more conservative than Catholics, and consequently they are more likely to support the Republican Party (Wilson 1978). Protestant conservatism is probably due to the fact that Protestants have historically occupied a privileged social position in America. On the other hand, non-Protestant ethnic groups such as Catholics and Jews are generally more liberal than Protestants and are more likely to be affiliated with the Democratic Party than Protestant groups, all else being equal (Gallup 1982; Wilson 1978). The liberalism of Catholics and Jews is associated with their lower social standing. (4) Refugee status. Other things being equal, political refugee groups are more likely to be Republican than non-refugee groups. Cubans and Indochinese are good cases in point. (5) Stance of political parties on issues. Ethnic groups are more likely to support a party that sponsors policies that benefit them. The importance of issues has been ascending in American electoral politics. Other factors such as the experience of prejudice and discrimination, interethnic rivalry, and overseas loyalties may also impact political party affiliation.

POLITICAL IDEOLOGY

Associated with political party affiliation is the issue of political ideology. Political ideology refers to underlying beliefs, attitudes, and orientation about political issues. Table 12.2 shows the political ideology of selected minority groups based on the data sources of Table 12.1. Not surprisingly, black Americans tend to be more liberal, as 54 percent of them self-proclaimed as "liberal," 43 percent as "conservative," and only a tiny percentage as "moderate." In addition, the 1988 National Black Election Study revealed a generational difference: older blacks were more likely to label themselves liberal than were younger blacks. However, the effect of income seemed unclear, since both high-income blacks and low-income blacks identified themselves as conservative to a similar extent. Tate (1993) found that overall, blacks were generally quite liberal across a variety of policy issues, but with the exception of capital punishment, they were relatively conservative on a wide range of social issues.

Contrary to popular wisdom, the data in Table 12.2 indicate that all three largest Latino groups are more likely to self-describe as conservatives. This is not unexpected in the case of Cuban Americans since they are more likely to attach to the Republican Party. One would anticipate a more liberal orientation for Mexican Americans and Puerto Rican Americans, given their strong Democratic Party attachment. On the contrary, 47 percent of Puerto Rican Americans identified themselves as conservative as compared to 29 percent liberal; similarly, 38 percent of

Table 12.2 Political Ideology of Selected Minority Groups

| | Political Ideology | | | |
Group	Liberal	Moderate	Conservative	Total
Black	54.4%	1.8%	43.8%	100.0%
Latino				
Mexican	28.5%	35.4%	36.0%	99.9%
Puerto Rican	28.6%	24.7%	46.7%	100.0%
Cuban	22.8%	22.5%	54.7%	100.0%
Asian	38.0%	12.0%	50.0%	100.0%

Sources: Figures for black political ideology were calculated on the basis of the 1988 National Black Election Study; Latino political ideology data were derived from the 1990 Latino National Political Survey; the data for Asians were taken from the 1996 Gallup Poll conducted by *AsianWeek*.

Mexican Americans claimed to be conservative while only about 29 percent declared liberal.

The ideological orientation of Asian Americans resembles that of Latinos. The national survey conducted by *AsianWeek* (1996) reported that nearly half of Asian Americans self-proclaimed conservative or somewhat conservative while 38 percent identified themselves as liberal or somewhat liberal, and 12 percent said that they were middle-of-the-roaders. Because of their diversity, a lump-sum generalization misses the complexity of Asian American political ideology. For instance, Japanese Americans are more liberal than other Asian groups. A recent survey of the Chinese in Southern California indicated that they were evenly distributed between liberals (27 percent) and conservatives (25 percent), with 33 percent moderates and 15 percent "don't know" (Kang 1997). Furthermore, second-or-higher-generation Asians are more liberal than their first-generation counterparts. Homeland policies also influence different positions on U.S. foreign policy issues (Cain 1988).

The foregoing empirical evidence suggests that political ideology and party affiliation are not highly correlated. Being a Democrat doesn't necessarily mean liberal, and being a Republican doesn't necessarily mean conservative. The stereotypic labels of liberal and conservative may be problematic in assigning people to different categories of political ideology. One reason for the discrepancy between political ideology and political party affiliation is that the meanings of liberal and conservative are subject to interpretation. For example, according to popular notions of liberal and conservative, a liberal believes that the federal government should take an active role in reducing unemployment, providing services for the poor, and improving the socioeconomic status of minority groups; on the other hand, a conservative supports prayer in public school. However, many African Americans support both an active government role *and* prayer in school. Hence, the standard labels of liberal, moderate, and conservative based on national studies with samples of disproportionate white representation may not be applicable to minorities, and their meanings need to be clarified.

Information on the ideological inclination of Native Americans is scarce. A study by Ritt (1979), based on 151 Indian respondents, found that Indians were ideologically moderate. Overall, Irish Americans are generally more liberal than many white ethnic groups and have a progressive political tradition. Catholic Italian Americans also tend to be politically liberal. The 1990 National Jewish Population Survey found that liberals outnumbered conservatives among Jews (Kosmin et al. 1991).

The political ideology of broad ethnic groups spreads across a wide spectrum. These differing orientations will have important implications for the formation of intergroup coalitions.

VOTING BEHAVIOR

The way people vote in elections defines the term voting behavior. Historically, some minority groups were denied citizenship and voting rights. The Voting Rights Act of 1965 outlawed the denial or abridgement of any U.S. citizen's voting rights on account of race or color and granted equal voting rights for all Americans.

With equal voting opportunities, voter registration and turnout rates of minority groups have gradually risen, albeit with fluctuations. However, variations across ethnic groups in their voting behavior are still conspicuous, as evidenced in Table 12.3, which is based on data from the 1994 Current Population Survey (CPR). It is evident that as a whole, whites have a higher voter registration rate (69 percent) than other groups (African Americans, 61 percent; Latinos, 53 percent; Asians, 53 percent). The actual voter turnout rate of whites (73 percent) is significantly higher than that of African Americans (63 percent) and Latinos (64 percent).

Following general national trends, black registration rates increased

Table 12.3 Voter Registration and Turnout Rates by Ethnicity, 1994

Group	% Registered to Vote	% Voted in 1994 Elections
Non-Hispanic whites	69	73
African Americans	61	63
Latinos	53	64
Asian Pacific Americans	53	76

Source: Current Population Survey, 1994.

in the 1960s, dropped in the 1970s, and rose again in the 1980s (Williams 1987). Jesse Jackson's 1984 and 1988 presidential campaigns and the resulting voter registration drives obviously boosted black voter registration rates. The 1990s saw a return of declining black voter registration. The registration rate was 64 percent in 1992 and dropped to 61 percent in 1994, as shown in Table 12.3. However, black voting turnout rates rose from 54 percent in 1992 to 63 percent in 1994. Black women were more likely than black men to register and vote (Jennings 1993), probably because of their higher levels of education and occupational status relative to black men.

Latino voter registration rates have been lower than those of African Americans. The rates declined from 40 percent in 1984 to 35.5 percent in 1988 and further to 35.1 percent in 1992. The reasons for the lower Latino registration rates may include the composition of a disproportionately younger, poorer, and less educated general population; their unfamiliarity with the U.S. political system; and their lack of English proficiency (Hero 1992; Meier and Stewart 1991; Vigil 1987). Nonetheless, recent years have witnessed a surging Latino interest in electoral politics as reflected in their unprecedented 53 percent voter registration rate and 64 percent voter turnout rate in 1994. Although native-born Latinos and foreign-born Latinos had the same registration rate in 1994, the foreign-born were more likely to vote once they registered. Latinas were more likely to register but less likely to vote than Latino men (Jennings 1993).

For the first time, the Bureau of the Census included Asian Americans in the CPS in 1992. In that year, both the voter registration rate and voter turnout rate of Asian Americans were the lowest of all broad ethnic groups with 31 percent and 27 percent, respectively. As shown in

Table 12.3, 1994 saw substantial improvement in both rates. Despite their lower voter registration rate than those for whites and blacks (and a rate parallel to that of Latinos), Asian Americans registered the highest voter turnout rate among all ethnic groups in 1994. Furthermore, native-born Asians evinced higher levels of registration and voting than their foreign-born counterparts. Asian women were less likely than Asian men to register and to vote (Jennings 1993).

The Census Bureau has not garnered national statistics on the voting behavior of Native Americans. An available study of Indians in the Upper Midwest found lower rates of voter registration among Indians than among whites of comparable socioeconomic status (Doherty 1994). According to the limited data on six elections from 1982 to 1992, Indian turnout rates averaged 40 percent.

POLITICAL REPRESENTATION

How do groups differ in their political representation in government? This section presents some empirical evidence on this issue in the three branches of government at the national level: the legislative branch (Congress), the executive branch (the administration), and the judicial branch (the Supreme Court). It also explores possible reasons for these differences.

Congressional Representation

Table 12.4 summarizes the numbers and percentages of U.S. congressmen, Supreme Court justices, and cabinet members by ethnicity in 1995. Inspecting the number and percentage of congressmen in each group, we can see that whites garnered 476 congressional seats, or 89 percent. Since whites currently account for about 73 percent of the total U.S. population, this percentage indicates an overrepresentation. Representatives of white Protestant groups have taken the majority of the congressional seats. Some non-Protestant white ethnic groups also have significant political representation. For instance, in the early 1990s there were thirty-two congressmen of Italian ancestry, and forty-one U.S. congressmen of Jewish decent.

By contrast, minority groups were to varying degrees under-represented in Congress. While accounting for 12 percent of the total popula-

Table 12.4 Number and Percentage of U.S. Congressmen, Supreme Court Justices, and Cabinet Members by Ethnicity, 1995

		White	Black	Latino	Asian	Indian	Total
Congressmen:[a]	#	474.0	38.0	17.0	5.0	1.0	535.0
	%	88.6	7.1	3.2	0.9	0.2	100.0
Supreme Court Justices:	#	8.0	1.0	0	0	0	9.0
	%	88.9	11.1	0	0	0	100.0
Cabinet Members:	#	10.0	2.0	2.0	0	0	14.0
	%	71.4	14.3	14.3	0	0	100.0

Sources: Bowker (1995); Duncan and Lawrence (1996); Estell (1994); Kanellos (1993); and Zia and Gall (1995).

Note: Asians include Asians and Pacific Islanders.

[a] Voting members only.

tion, only 7.1 percent of the congressmen were blacks, although the number of black congressmen has steadily increased over time, especially in recent years. The underrepresentation of Latinos is even more severe (3.2 percent) since Latinos make up about 10.2 percent of the U.S. population.[2] The number of Latino legislators increased from ten to nineteen after the 1992 elections but dropped to seventeen as a result of the 1994 elections. Asian Americans share about 3.3 percent of the U.S. population, but only 0.9 percent of the congressmen. The number of Asian congressmen has remained unchanged since the 1970s.

Indians accounted for 0.7 percent of the total U.S. population, but represented 0.2 percent of the congressmen, an undeniable underrepresentation. There is only one Indian in Congress, namely, Senator Ben Nighthorse Campbell of Colorado. In fact, he is only half Indian, with a mother of Portuguese decent and a father of Northern Cheyenne. He is the only member of Congress who wears a ponytail and a bolo tie.

An array of demographic, socioeconomic, and political factors may explain ethnic differences in congressional representation.

---

2. The thirteen Latino congressmen with voting power included nine Mexican Americans, two Cuban Americans, and two Puerto Rican Americans.

1. Population size of an ethnic group. Large groups are more likely to have a higher political representation, all else being equal. In 1996, there were about 190 million whites, 30 million blacks, 23 million Latinos, 8.8 million Asians, and 2 million Indians in the United States. This may partly explain the differences.

2. Citizenship status. Since only U.S. citizens are eligible to vote, ethnic groups with a higher proportion of U.S. citizens are more likely to have a higher congressional representation. In 1994, 98 percent of adult whites were U.S. citizens, compared to 95 percent of blacks, 56 percent of Latinos, and only 45 percent of Asians. The underrepresentation of Asians and Latinos in Congress may be in part attributed to this factor.

3. Districting/redistricting. The ways in which boundaries of congressional voting districts are drawn influence the likelihood of electing a congressman from a particular group, due to the group's geographical concentration. A minority-concentrated voting district is more likely to elect a minority congressman, other things being equal. Empirical evidence is mixed. In 1992, for example, boundaries of several congressional districts were redrawn to create several largely ethnic minority districts, and several black congressmen were elected from those new districts. However, the results of the 1996 elections show that the effect of redistricting may not be as great as people have thought. The congressional voting districts of several black congressmen were redrawn so that blacks were no longer the majority in those districts, but the black congressmen still got reelected.

4. Voting behavior. The propensity to register and to actually vote is also partly responsible for ethnic differences in congressional representation. As discussed in the preceding section, some ethnic groups are less likely to vote, and therefore this will lower their congressional representation. Voting behavior can be further explained by such factors as discrimination, lack of interest in politics due to cultural tradition, lack of voting experience, lack of resources, and unfamiliarity with the political system.

5. Strong/weak political party affiliation. Strong group affiliation with a specific party can increase the chance of electing its repre-

sentatives because the votes of the supporting group are more likely to concentrate on the candidates from that party. For instance, since African Americans are predominantly Democrats, they are more likely to elect black Democratic candidates to Congress. On the other hand, the split of Asian American votes between candidates of different political parties because of their weak party affiliation may reduce their congressional representation.

6. Group solidarity. Groups that lack intragroup solidarity due to cultural, regional, or religious differences are less likely to elect their congressional representatives. Group solidarity increases the chance of electing representatives of an ethnic group.

In addition, group political organization, historical white dominance, social and political networks, financial ability, and quality of candidates may influence congressional representation. It is too simplistic to reduce the explanation to any single factor.

Representation in the Administration

It is of interest to examine the ethnicity of U.S. presidents. Table 12.5 exhibits the ancestry and religion of U.S. presidents. In terms of ancestry, throughout the nation's history, all the presidents have had western and northern European origins. As indicated in Table 12.5, among the forty-one presidents,[3] 36 (or 88 percent) have British and/or Irish ancestry, including eighteen with pure English ancestry (e.g., George Bush), one with pure Irish descent (i.e., John Kennedy), and seventeen with Scottish, Welsh, English-Scottish, English-Irish, Scottish-Irish, or English-Scottish-Irish ancestry. Three presidents (Van Buren, Theodore Roosevelt, and Franklin Roosevelt) have a Dutch lineage; and two presidents (Herbert Hoover, and Dwight Eisenhower) have a mixed Swiss-German origin. There have been no presidents of southern and eastern European descent; and none of Jewish, African, Latino, Asian, or Indian descent.

Theoretically, every U.S.-born citizen has an equal opportunity to be elected president. In reality, however, the opportunity is not equal be-

---

3. Grover Cleveland was elected in 1885 for his first term, then defeated by B. Harrison in 1889 and reelected in 1893.

Table 12.5 Ethnicity of U.S. Presidents, as of 1998

Ethnicity	#	%
Ancestry		
British and/or Irish	36	87.8
Dutch	3	7.3
Swiss-German	2	4.9
Other Europeans	0	0
Africans	0	0
Latinos	0	0
Asians	0	0
Indians	0	0
Religion		
Protestantism	40	97.6
Catholicism	1	2.4
Other religions	0	0
Total	41	100.0

Source: Adapted from Joseph Kane (1993). *Facts about the Presidents*, p.305.
Note: British include English, Scottish, and Welsh.

cause of ethnic backgrounds. Ethnicity has a strong impact on the likelihood of being elected president. A white, Anglo-Saxon, Protestant man would have a much greater chance of being elected than someone of southern or eastern European origin. Furthermore, the likelihood of electing a minority president is still distant although opinion polls showed an increasing inclination to vote for a qualified black candidate for president. Unless something is done, this situation is not going to change soon. Steps should be taken to ensure that every U.S.-born citizen has an equal opportunity to be elected president of the United States.

Religion is another important factor in determining the chance of a presidential bid. Table 12.5 shows that all but one president have been Protestants. John Kennedy has been the only president who was Catholic. Before the 1960 election, many predicted Kennedy's defeat. He won by the slimmest margin of popular votes (49.9 percent vs. 49.6 percent) in the history of American presidential elections, and he captured only twenty-three of the fifty states. His selection of Lyndon Johnson, a Protestant, as his vice-presidential running mate, played a critical role in his victory over Richard Nixon. Given the importance of religion, some presidential candidates have switched their religion to Protestantism in order to get elected.

Table 12.4 also shows ethnic differences in the number and percentage of cabinet members in the first Clinton administration. Ten out of the fourteen cabinet members were whites. There were two African Americans (Secretary of Energy Hazel O'Leary and Secretary of Veterans Affairs Jesse Brown),[4] two Hispanic Americans (Secretary of HUD Henry Cisneros and Secretary of Transportation Frederico Pena), and no Asian Americans or Indians. This ethnic distribution remains almost unchanged in the second Clinton administration.

Representation in the Supreme Court

The Supreme Court is not only the final authority on Constitutional issues, but it also shapes the policy-making process and establishes the legal framework within which all ethnic groups coexist and interact. The underrepresentation of minority groups in the judicial system, especially in the Supreme Court, is well known. Thurgood Marshall, nominated by President Lyndon Johnson in 1967, was the first black (and the first minority as well) who ever served on the high court. After his retirement in 1991, President George Bush nominated black conservative Clarence Thomas to fill the vacancy. Thomas was confirmed after bitter confirmation hearings, which included Anita Hill's sexual harassment accusations. Currently, he is the only minority Supreme Court justice, and all other justices are white (Table 12.4). Two of the justices are white females: Sandra Day O'Connor and Ruth Bader Ginsberg.

SUMMARY

Ethnicity is a key variable that influences the political process and outcome in America. Political party affiliation is more or less divided along ethnic lines. In general, minority groups are more likely to attach to the Democratic Party, but there are intragroup differences across them. Socioeconomic status, religion, refugee group status, and party policies

---

4. Two other African Americans among President Clinton's initial cabinet appointments included Secretary of Commerce Ronald Brown, who died of a plane accident in April 1996, and Secretary of Agriculture Michael Espy, who later resigned.

are also key dimensions that determine the political party alignment of different ethnic groups.

Survey data suggest that except for African Americans, all minority groups tend to self-proclaim as conservative more than as liberal. The correlation between political ideology and political party affiliation is not high, largely because of the ambiguous meanings of "liberalism" and "conservatism." Even with the entitlement of voting rights, minority groups are less likely to register to vote and turn out to vote than whites, but there has been significant progress in recent years.

In terms of political representation, minority groups are to varying degrees underrepresented in Congress. Population size, citizenship status, geographical concentration, voting behavior, strong/weak partisanship, group unity, historical reasons, and other social factors all contribute to ethnic disparity in congressional representation. Ethnicity also plays a key role in determining the chance of being elected U.S. president. So far, western and northern European origins, especially British descent, seem to be a "precondition" for the success of a presidential bid. Moreover, with one notable exception, Protestantism is almost a prerequisite for the qualification of successful presidential candidates. The administration and the Supreme Court are also primarily white, although some inroads have been made.

CHAPTER 13

RACE, CLASS, AND GENDER

In the past couple of decades, scholars have increasingly recognized the need to study the complex intersections and workings of race, class, and gender, because these three dimensions are the basic organizing principles of American life, the inseparable determinants of inequality, and the crux of many current issues.[1] The triplicity needs to be seen through a multiplicity of lenses. The phrase *race, class, and gender* has become a mantra, indicating that the study of race, class, and gender is moving from the margins to the center of scholarship.

This chapter reviews important theoretical approaches to the nexus of race, class, and gender and to their three-fold effect on people's lives. It also discusses how race, class, and gender intersect with work; how gender roles vary among racial and class groups; how race, class, and gender complicate power status and sexuality; and how social institutions and race, class, and gender interact with one another.

PERSPECTIVES ON THE INTERRELATIONS OF RACE, CLASS, AND GENDER

Race, class, and gender are by no means new concepts. Social scientists such as sociologists, anthropologists, and psychologists have long studied these phenomena, especially in the fields of social stratification, race and

---

1. Gender is analytically distinguished from sex. Sex emphasizes the biological dimension, whereas gender reflects a social dimension.

ethnic relations, and social psychology. What are the interrelations among race, class, and gender? Two basic approaches in scholarly treatment of this issue may be distinguished: the traditional approach and the newly emerging structural approach. The *traditional* approach treats race, class, and gender as parallel, independent variables and separate identities. The categories of these variables are viewed as fixed or relatively stable. Researchers normally analyze these variables separately. For instance, in social stratification research, class is examined as a social system sequestrable from race and gender. In social science research, race is often treated as independent of class and gender, and the importance of race or class has been an ongoing issue laden with many debates. In the early period of women's studies, gender was narrowly viewed as a women's issue. Although some earlier studies did examine the interaction and connection among these variables, race, class, and gender were often treated as independent variables rather than as interrelated social systems and processes, and in particular, the interrelations of these variables had never been made the center of scholarly inquiry.

In the last two decades, the so-called *structural* paradigm arising in both women's and ethnic studies is challenging the traditional approach. This new paradigm maintains that race, class, and gender are the interlocking dimensions of social structure and the simultaneous and intersecting systems of relationships that affect the experience of all people (Andersen and Collins 1995; Collins 1990). This new approach has several salient features. First, the new perspective highlights structural linkages and interconnections among the three systems. According to this approach, all three forces are embedded in the social structure and interrelated to one another. They are all bound up with the broader systems of social inequality, and social inequality is shaped and complicated by the intersections of the three. The interconnections of these dimensions overshadow their boundaries, boundaries that are unclear to begin with. Second, the new perspective underscores the ubiquity and simultaneity of race, class, and gender. In other words, race, class, and gender are viewed as the simultaneous processes that shape all social relations. These relations form the structural and symbolic bases for both objective conditions and subjective meanings of women's and men's lives. These social systems affect the experiences of all members of society in countless ways. Third, this new theoretical perspective stresses the dynamics of these systems and their configurations, which are socially constructed and constantly changing.

The new structural approach contributes to our knowledge of social systems and social relations by heightening the prominence of race, class, and gender over other social markers and by highlighting the interconnections and interdependency of these systems. However, emphasizing the "trinity" of these social identifiers does not preclude analyzing their relative autonomy; it does not mean that they have no independent effects. A more comprehensive alternative is to integrate the traditional approach and the structural approach and to examine both the independence *and* interdependency of the three systems. We need to study how each system originates, develops, and operates, and how they interrelate and intersect with one another.

In addition, research on race, class, and gender ought to consider variations in the importance of the three dimensions. Leith Mullings (1997) argued that among the three variables, class fundamentally prefigures the meaning and experience of both race and gender. A more reasonable approach is to consider their varying primacy in historical perspective. In a given historical moment, race may be predominant. For instance, slavery dictated the meaning of race for almost three hundred years. Race remains significant in America today. In another particular period, race may be outweighed by class or gender. Gender, for example, was critical in defining rights and privileges in America at least until the ratification of the nineteenth Amendment to the Constitution in 1920, which granted women suffrage in all federal, state, and local government elections.

How are people simultaneously "racialized," "classed," and "gendered"? At the microlevel, individuals inhabit many identities and experience race, class, and gender differently. The example of the U.S. Senate hearings on Clarence Thomas's nomination to the Supreme Court illustrates the dynamics of race, class, and gender all operating with one another. It made a difference to viewers that Clarence Thomas was a black *man* and that he was a *black* man. To the African American community, he was a black man raised in *poverty* (Bikel 1992). Each categorical dimension played off the others and off the comparable but quite different categorizations of Anita Hill. Most white women who watched the hearings identified gender and men's domination as the most salient aspects of the hearings, whether in making sense of the Judiciary Committee's handling of witnesses or understanding the relationship between Hill and Thomas (Bikel 1992). By contrast, most African American viewers saw racism as the most salient aspect of the hearings, including white men's prurient interest in black sexuality and the exposure of troubling divisions between black women and men (Bikel 1992; Morrison 1992). The Thomas hearings embodied a stellar case of the inseparable qualities of race, class, and gender.

EFFECTS OF RACE, CLASS, AND GENDER ON PEOPLE'S EXPERIENCES

Every individual or group is positioned in a structure of race, gender, and class relations in a specific time and place. How do race, class, and gender affect the experiences of the people who inhabit those groups? The two approaches to race, class, and gender discussed above offer contrasting answers to this question. The traditional approach sees the effects of race, class, and gender on human experience as additive, meaning that the total effect of the three variables is the sum of the individual effects of each variable (i.e., race + class + gender). Such terms as "double jeopardy," "triple jeopardy," or "triple disadvantages," which depict the disadvantageous positions of low-class, minority women, mirror this theoretical approach. Critics (e.g., Andersen and Collins 1995) contend that this additive model misses the "social structural connections between them and the particular ways that different configurations of race, class, and gender affect group experience"; it only examines the effects of these systems on the experience of their victims (e.g., women and people of color) rather than seeing them as an integral part of the social structure; and it dichotomizes people into either/or categories.

The structural perspective moves away from the single additive model to a multiplicative, interactive model. According to this interactive model, the relationships among race, class, and gender are not simply cumulative, but are interactive (i.e., race x class x gender), producing dissimilar results for different combinations of categories.[2] "They overlap, intersect, and fuse with each other in countless ways" (Omi and Winant 1994, 68). Race effect is gendered and classed; gender effect is racialized and classed; and class effect is gendered and racialized. Put differently, gender and class constrain the experience of different racial groups; race and class condition the experience of men and women; and gender and race shape the experience of different classes. There is no longer a universal law that applies to race, class, and gender separately. In short, the

---

2. I label this model "interactive" because interaction best characterizes the varying effects of race, class, and gender on people's experiences.

structural approach emphasizes race, class, and gender as interlocking systems and accentuates their interactive effects on the people who belong to different racial, class, and gender groups.

There are several advantages of emphasizing the effects of interaction and intersection of race, class, and gender on human experience. First, highlighting the interactive and intersective effect of the three dimensions forces researchers to recognize that race, sex, and class combine to produce race-specific, class-specific, and gender-specific effects. For instance, although most people of color experience racism, their real experience with racism varies depending on their intersected positions of class, gender, age, sexuality, and other social markers (Andersen and Collins 1995). Some people of color with class privileges can elude the entanglement of racism, while other people of color (e.g., blacks) cannot water down the effect of racism even with class privileges. In spite of similar experiences, women feel oppression differently because of their race and class positions. However disadvantaged by their gender, white women take advantage of their race, and some may enjoy class privileges as well (McIntosh 1995). In the same vein, men experience gender differently depending on their race and class. Not all men benefit equally from patriarchy. Because of the interactive and combining effect of race, class, and gender, lower-class, minority women encounter more than "triple constraints," whereas upper-class, white men reap more than "triple advantages."

Second, examining the interactive and intersective effect of the trio can help better understand the position of a particular race-class-gender group. For example, why do black men experience disadvantages in education, the labor market, and the criminal justice system, even though they have privileges as men? Why are Native American women at the bottom of the social hierarchy in terms of the combination of their race, class, and gender? And why don't all white Americans fare well to the same extent despite their privileges of race? The interactive approach better answers these questions than the traditional approach.

Third, focusing on the tripolar interactive and intersective effect helps capture the complexity of human experience, human actions and outcomes, and social structure and constraints. It is precisely the inseparable, interactive nature of race, class, and gender that shapes the differential social construction for diverse kinds of men and women in different historical and sociocultural contexts. It also produces tension, contradictions, and constraints for men and women; it creates opportunities for women to negotiate, cope with, and even resist various forms of structural domination and inequality; and it enhances and restricts features of culture and society, structure and process, institutions and individuals.

Having laid out the conceptual framework for the intersection and interaction of race, class, and gender, the balance of this chapter is devoted to showing how the three interlocking systems intersect with gender roles, work, power, sexuality, and social institutions.

RACIALIZED, CLASSED GENDER ROLES

Gender roles refer to the differential activities associated with men and women in a society. The traditional theoretical formulation of gender roles uses the experiences of white, middle-class men and women as the norm. As a result of industrialization, a clear gender-based division of labor gradually emerged in white, middle-class families; namely, the husband was expected to be the sole breadwinner in the public domain while the wife performed the role of homemaker or breadbaker in the private sphere, raising children and taking care of the family. This was the so-called "doctrine of separate spheres." Gender role division was justified because it protected women from dangers and arduous labor in the workplace. This white, middle-class model of gender roles was viewed as universal, and any practice different from this norm was considered aberrant. The normality of these roles went uncontested until the 1960s.

The new perspective on race, class, and gender transforms our knowledge and challenges the generalization of past gender role division to all races and all classes. This interactive approach maintains that there are no universalized gender roles and that gender roles vary across different racial and class groups. Studies along the lines of the new perspective found that while the doctrine of separate spheres partly applies to white, middle-class women, it is not universally true. For most women of color, lower-class women, immigrant women, and female heads of single-parent families, paid employment outside the home has been an integral, normative part of their roles (Glenn, 1980; Jones 1985; Seifer, 1973). Their typical gender role may be characterized as "co-breadwinner" or "sole-breadwinner," and they do not separate paid work and unpaid housework.

One important reason is that these women have never had the option of leaving the paid labor force to become housewives because the economic status of their households requires their paid employment to sus-

tain the family. For example, racial discrimination has produced high unemployment rates among black men or segregated them into low-paying
jobs, and hence black women have been forced to work outside their
homes to provide the family livelihood.

Another reason is that there are differences across racial groups and
classes in attitudes toward marriage and gender roles. For instance,
Joseph (1981) reported that white daughters were likely to receive messages with a more positive view of men and a more romanticized notion of
marriage and gender role division than their black counterparts. Other
studies (Hershey 1978; Ladner 1971) found that black women have negative attitudes toward the dependability of men and doubts about the desirability and security of marriage. Black women's conception of womanhood emphasizes self-reliance, strength, resourcefulness, autonomy, and
the responsibility to provide material and emotional support for the family (Ladner 1971). Dogger (1996) found that black women were more
likely to reject the norm of traditional gender roles than white women.
Black women do not see labor-force participation and the roles of wife and
mother as mutually exclusive. In black culture, employment is an integral, normative, and traditional component of gender roles (Gump 1980;
Malson et al. 1990), and so are unpaid domestic labor, child care, and
home maintenance. In fact, minority and working-class women are over-
burdened but undervalued producers in the public sphere and social re-
producers in the private sphere.

The new line of studies also rejects a false notion of fixed gender
roles. Housewife was the typical role of white, middle-class women prior
to the 1960s. However, the modern women's movement that began in the
1960s challenged this traditional gender role. Since then women have entered the labor force in record numbers and have transformed the composition of many professions. The notion of separate spheres has increasingly become inapplicable even to white women. The interpenetration of
the two spheres in most women's lives has rendered obsolete the traditional functional description of a gendered division of labor.

RACE, CLASS, GENDER, AND WORK

Race, class, and gender interlock and influence people's labor market experiences in employment, occupation, and job mobility. First, race and
gender intersect with class in the workplace. For example, the lower oc-

cupational status of poor African Americans can be understood from both a racialized context and a gendered context. Racial disadvantages partly account for their lower class status. However, black men's unemployment alone does not explain the lower status of poor blacks; and gender segmentation and the low wages of black women are central to their class inequality.

Second, division of labor by gender is overlaid with the effects of race and class. For instance, Brewer (1993) found that a disproportionate number of black women were at the bottom ranks of the division of labor, and they represented a significant portion of the new working class. Data also show that black women and white women tend to hold different kinds of jobs. Typically, white women take white-collar jobs such as clerical worker, teacher, health-related worker, and sales person, while a typical job for black women is a blue-collar job, especially private household worker, service worker, and machine/vehicle operator. Women's work is race divided.

Third, class and gender also intersect with race. For instance, race in the context of class and gender means that black women are quite vulnerable. Black women are more likely to be unemployed and to be paid less (Simms and Malveaux 1986). Although black women and white women do the same kinds of jobs, black women are more likely to be supervised and white women are more likely to supervise (Simms and Malveaux 1986). Black women's relationship to capital is different from that of white women. If one focuses only on the gender dimension, one finds the following order of labor hierarchy: white men, black men, white women, and black women. However, the simultaneous consideration of race and gender will generate a different kind of labor hierarchy: white men, white women, black men, and black women.

Hence, race, class, or gender alone cannot fully explain the race, class, and gender inequalities of African Americans. It is the dialectic intersection of the three factors that sheds the greatest light on the subject. The same logic may be used to analyze the inequalities of other groups and other issues.

The economic restructuring, uneven economic growth, and internationalization of the labor force further complicate the racial and gender divisions of labor. The capitalist class no longer needs to depend solely on the labor of people of color since sources of cheap labor can be found in Third World countries and among immigrants. In particular, minority or immigrant women are preferred workers for certain industries such as the garment, food service, and domestic industries while their male counterparts are preferred in agriculture, construction, and restaurant and hotel services. Minority and immigrant men and women are at the bottom of the racial and gender divisions of labor. Thus, race/gender hierarchies are shaped by existing arrangements of race/gender divisions of labor. Moreover, within the racial/gender divisions of labor, class intersects with racial constraints.

RACE, CLASS, GENDER, AND POWER

Race, class, and gender also intersect to produce differing power relations in society and in the family. People experience the "social trinity" in various combinations with a wide range of effects. In a racist and classist society, most men of color and immigrant men occupy the bottom economic positions in their gender group; they receive the lowest pay and endure the worst working conditions. Racism also leads to their lower public status. Their loss of control over economic and social resources is often accompanied by loss of power and status in the family. The result is a change in power relations in the family between men and women of color.

Changing power relations are most evident among immigrants of color. Immigrant men, especially those of color, often experience a loss of economic power and social status during the transition to a new life in the United States. Their public status is further eroded because of racism. On the one hand, the relegated position of immigrant men creates opportunities for greater equality between men and women here than in their home country. The elevated relative position of women erodes men's patriarchal authority in the family and empowers women to challenge the traditional authority. On the other hand, the lost or lowered status of immigrant men may prompt them to seek an outlet at home by abusing their wives and children, who are even more powerless.

The changing family relations of Japanese Americans during the internment of World War II provide a good example. Until the internment, the Issei (first generation) man had been the breadwinner and the family decision maker with undisputed authority over his wife and children (Espiritu 1997). The incarceration stripped men of their roles as breadwinners and protectors and thus their absolute power in the family. Some felt desperate, useless, hopeless, and frustrated; others tried to reassert their patriarchal authority by abusing their wives and children. Failure to support the family and reliance on their wives's earnings undermined their sense of worth and power. The Issei women, on the other hand, gained status relative to the Issei men as they found employment and more free time in the camps (Kitagawa 1967). The experiences of Issei men and women during the internment years illustrate how race and gender interacted to change the lives of the Issei men and their families.

Women of color experience both gains and losses of power. Women's wage employment gives them a greater degree of autonomy and brings a greater chance of equal gender relations to the family. However, this gain is accompanied by not only a heavier workload at home but also exposure to racial and gender exploitation in the workplace and thereby a sense of lost power in society. They are often employed in the most exploitative sectors of the economy such as sweatshops, fast-food service, domestic service, and cleaning service, and they perform physically strenuous, labor-intensive, and low-paying jobs. Furthermore, racism and classism may further lessen women's gains. The social-structural location of women in a male-dominant society may force women to accept certain elements of the traditional patriarchal system in order to have a strong and intact family and thus resist class and racial oppression. Hence, both gender inequality and male dominance are still the harsh reality for women of color.

RACE, CLASS, GENDER, AND SEXUALITY

Sexuality is racialized, classed, and gendered. In other words, sexual norms, behaviors, and orientation vary across racial, class, and gender groups. The upper class tends to be seemingly more strict about sexuality. This may be associated with the transmission of property, which depends on the determination of father-son relationship. Not only do sexual norms and behaviors vary across social classes, but they differ among races and sexes. For example, middle-class, white women's norms of marital sex are often based on male sexual standards and expectations, rather than their own. Although both sexual partners are expected to achieve orgasm, quite a few women admit that they have sometimes submitted to intercourse regardless of their own disinclinations (Gatlin 1987, 58–59). These women often respond to their husbands' initiatives and repress their own sexuality.

On the other hand, women of color and the white working class develop a more complex, ambivalent, and realistic set of expectations and practices than white middle-class women. Affection and pleasure are mollified by sexual bargain and criticism of male behavior. For example, Mirande and Enriquez (1979, 183) observed that "Chicana attitudes toward the Chicano decidedly contradict the long honored stereotype of the women as passive and the male as the dominant."

Oliva Espin (1984) observed that Latina women of all social classes believe that most men are not dependable and cannot be trusted, but they still endure a man's infidelities and abuses because "having a man around is an important source of a woman's sense of self-worth." For them, the enjoyment of sexual pleasure, even in marriage, may indicate lack of virtue while the denial of sexual pleasure and the consideration of sex solely as an unwelcome obligation toward her husband and an evil indispensable for reproduction may be seen as a manifestation of virtue. Some Latina women even express pride in their lack of sexual desire.

Black women's sexual norms appear to be less repressive than those of Hispanic cultures, but many black women also view men as untrustworthy and feel it is necessary to bargain with them. When these women seek sexual gratification, they require verbal and material signs that they are respected.

Even more contentious is the fissure between heterosexuality and homosexuality. American society (as well as almost all societies in the world) defines and enforces heterosexuality as the only normal and permissible form of sexual relationship. Heterosexuality pervades in society, and homophobia—the fear of homosexuality—is fostered. This norm is being challenged. Homosexuality is not just a private issue, but a political issue as well. Homosexuality is not just a white, middle-class, male problem, but a problem of people of color.

The structural perspective that emphasizes the intersection of race, class, and gender also helps explain common images of sexuality that are popularly applied to different groups. If one only examined this issue from a single dimension, say, gender, one would encounter simplified images of men and women: Men are independent, capable, and powerful, and are the protectors, while women are dependent, incompetent, and feeble, and are the protected. However, these gender-divided images are too simplistic. Adding the race dimension reveals the complexity of stereotypes regarding sexuality among different racial and gender groups. While whites may fit the foregoing images constructed by the media, people of color do not. Although white, middle-class women are presumed to deserve protection, women of color are characterized as oversexed and therefore do not warrant protection (Crenshaw 1989; Davis 1981). White men have been portrayed as macho protectors of women, but men of color are portrayed as "hypersexual," "asexual," or neuter. They are not women's protectors but aggressors or threats to white women (Davis 1981). There are further variations involving people of color. For example, black men have been cast as "oversexed." Images of black men as rapists, as menaces to society, have been sensational cultural currency for some time. On the other hand, Asian men are sometimes depicted as asexual, lacking sexual prowess and desirability, or considered to be both hypermasculine and effeminate. Asian women have been portrayed as both superfeminine and castrating. Overall, both sexes among Asians have been skewed toward the female side. Both feminization and masculinization of Asian men and women confirm the superiority of white men.

RACE, CLASS, GENDER, AND SOCIAL INSTITUTIONS

Social institutions are the stable structures of a society that have been organized to meet one or more of its basic needs. For instance, the family is a social institution that is organized to meet the needs of reproduction, child rearing, socialization, and personal lives. Education is a social institution that transmits knowledge and culture from one generation to another. The economy is a social institution that governs the production, distribution, and consumption of goods and services. The state is a social institution that protects citizens from one another and from foreign enemies. Each institution serves a specific purpose. Social institutions are supposed to be neutral in their treatment of different groups. However, in reality, institutions do separate and treat people differently based on race, class, and gender.

The relationships between social institutions and race, class, and gender are interactive and reciprocal. On the one hand, social institutions are structured by race, class, and gender. That is, institutions are built upon the cumulative patterns of race, class, and gender in society. On the other hand, it is precisely for that reason that institutions have differing and unequal effects on the lives of various race, class, and gender groups.

Take the state as an example. Consisting of the government, the police, the military, and the law, the state is presumed to protect all citizens regardless of their race, class, and gender, or any other characteristics. However, most representatives of the state, such as elected officials, judges, police, and military personnel are men. Hence, laws, policies, and practices tend to protect the interests of men. The state is a "gendered" institution (Acker 1992). In short, race, class, and gender shape the state and its policies, just as the state determines the privileges and penalties for these categories.

The economy is another example. The labor market is structured by race and gender: white males tend to work in the primary market characterized by high salary, high stability, and ample opportunity for promotion; and people of color and women tend to concentrate in the secondary labor market characterized by low wages, frequent turnover, and lack of advancement opportunities. The capitalist system of the U.S. economy has created classes such as upper class, middle class, working class, and underclass, and it benefits the capitalist class at the expense of working class. Hence, the economic system tends to favor white middle-and upper-class males while penalizing the working class, people of color, and females.

The family is also structured along gender lines. While women are socialized to take care of the household and children, men are taught to provide subsistence for the family. Men are the heads of family and principal decision makers whereas women are logistic supporters. Although family structures and gender roles vary among different races and classes, the white middle-class norm is treated as a universal one.

In sum, the interlocking of race, class, and gender creates a set of stratifying forces embedded in social institutions that legitimize social practices, reinforce power relationships, and create conditions that shape human interaction and everyday life experience. These institutions are highly gendered, race-specific, and class-relevant and serve as systems of control to maintain existing hierarchical orders and to determine differential opportunities, privileges, and resources for diverse groups of men and women.

SUMMARY

Emerging from women's and ethnic studies in recent decades, new research on race, class, and gender is transforming our knowledge and moving the intersection of the trinity to the center of inquiry. The traditional approach separates race, class, and gender in analysis, and sees the effects of the three dimensions as additive. In contrast, the new line of inquiry points to the interlocking nature of race, class, and gender and focuses on the interactive effects of the triplicity.

Having reviewed the theoretical approaches on race, class, and gender, this chapter shows that race, class, and gender intersect with gender roles, work experience, societal and family power, sexuality, and the larger social institutions in complex ways.

It may be imperative to emphasize the interlocking of the three dimensions at the current stage. However, from a long-term standpoint, it may be as important to balance our attention between the relative independence and intersection of the three dimensions. In any case, to ignore either the independent effects or the interlocking effects of the trio would be lopsided.

Corresponding to race, class, and gender are racism, classism, and sexism. As defined in chapter 9, racism is racist ideology, attitude, behavior, law, policy, and institutional practice. Classism refers to any discriminatory attitude, belief, action, or institutional arrangement that favors people with a higher class status over those with a lower status. Sexism is any belief, attitude, behavior, action, or institutional arrangement that assumes the superiority of one sex over the other and therefore justifies greater social power. To achieve genuine social equality, we must eliminate racism, sexism, and classism.

PART III
SOCIAL ACTION AGENDAS
AND THE FUTURE OF
ETHNIC STUDIES

CHAPTER 14
CURRENT ISSUES IN ETHNIC STUDIES

There are many current issues in ethnic studies in America that demand social action. This chapter focuses on several important and controversial issues being debated across the nation, such as affirmative action, illegal immigration and Proposition 187, the (legal) immigration debate, bilingual education, and the English-Only movement. The chapter provides historical backgrounds about the debates and presents the arguments of both sides of each issue in the hope that solutions and compromises to the controversies can be explored and worked out.

AFFIRMATIVE ACTION

Affirmative action is a very important and highly controversial issue dealing with ethnic equality as well as gender equality. Even though Proposition 209 was approved, this issue won't go away soon. This section defines affirmative action, outlines the historical backdrop of its creation and enforcement, summarizes the major pros and cons of this policy, depicts the battle over Proposition 209 (the California Civil Rights Initiative), and discusses possible solutions to the dilemma.

What Is Affirmative Action?

Affirmative action has come to mean different things in the public mind. Some see it as a means of equal opportunity, while others view it as apportionment or proportional representation. Even further, some view it as a special privilege given to minorities and women; as a system of reserved quotas of jobs, school openings, or government funds for minorities and women; or, even worse, as "government-mandated discrimination against white Americans." Hence, for both its advocates and its opponents it is useful to clarify the meaning of affirmative action.

According to presidential directives, government enforcement guidelines and regulations, laws, and court decisions on this subject, *affirmative action* may be defined as a government policy designed to end discrimination and to ensure equal opportunity for traditionally disadvantaged groups by giving preferential treatment to equally qualified minorities and women in employment, school admission, and government contracting. This definition specifies the goal (the elimination of discrimination and the guarantee of equal opportunity for minorities and women) and means (preferential treatment toward equally qualified minorities and women) of affirmative action. Literally, affirmative action means taking affirmative or positive steps to ensure equal opportunity for minorities and women. Affirmative action normally covers three areas: employment, university or college admission, and government contracting.

It should be noted that neither executive orders on affirmative action nor civil rights laws endorse the use of "reverse discrimination," "quotas," or even "preferential treatment." No laws or government policies or regulations state that unqualified or less qualified minorities or women can be hired, admitted, or given government contracts. In practice, however, some organizations have used quotas for minorities and women, lowered standards to admit or hire less qualified minority and woman applicants, or given contracts to less qualified firms owned by minorities or women. These practices violate the laws or regulations and are not what affirmative action was intended to be. Court rulings, however, did endorse, either explicitly or implicitly, the use of preferential treatment of minorities and women. For example, in the first significant case on affirmative action addressed by the Supreme Court—*Regents of the University of California v. Bakke (1978)*— the Court held that while race could not be used as a quota to set aside specific positions for minority candidates, it could be considered as a factor in admission. As Supreme Court Justice Harry Blackman put it, "In order to go beyond racism, we must first take account of race. There is no other way. And in order to treat some persons equally, we must treat them differently." Other rulings that have permitted temporary use of preferential treatment for redressing past discrimination include: *United Steelworkers of America v. Weber (1979)*, which allowed a union to favor minorities in special training programs; *Sheetmetal Workers v. New York City (1986)*, which approved a specific quota of minority workers for a union; *International Association of Firefighters v. City of Cleveland (1986)*, which gave the green light to the promotion of minorities over more senior whites; *United States v. Paradise (1987)*, which endorsed favorable treatment extended to minority state troopers in promotion decisions; *Johnson v. Transportation Agency, Santa Clara, CA (1987)*, which approved preference in hiring for minorities and women over equally-qualified men and whites; and *Metro Broadcasting v. FCC (1990)*, which supported federal programs aimed at increasing minority ownership of broadcasting licenses.

The Historical Background of Affirmative Action

Prior to the 1960s, discrimination against minorities and women ran rampant. In the 1940s and 1950s, there were conscious efforts by the federal government to curtail discrimination in employment. In the early 1940s, President Franklin Roosevelt issued executive orders to stop discrimination in the federal civil service and created the Fair Employment Practices Committee. Continuous endeavors were made in the ensuing decade. During the 1950s, President Truman issued two executive orders to establish fair employment procedures within the federal government structure, to abolish discrimination in the armed forces, and to set up compliance procedures for government contractors. The basic approach then was voluntary "nondiscrimination." However, the voluntary "good faith" approach proved to be ineffective and insufficient in terminating deep-rooted discriminatory behavior patterns.

Affirmative action policy emerged in the 1960s as an alternative to the early voluntary approach. It originated from a series of executive orders issued by Presidents John F. Kennedy and Lyndon B. Johnson and related to legislation passed during their successive presidencies in the 1960s. In March 1961, President Kennedy issued Executive Order 10925, where the phrase *affirmative action* first surfaced. The order required government contractors and subcontractors to take "affirmative action to ensure that applicants are employed, and that employees are treated during employment, without regard to their race, creed, color, or national origin." That order did, for the first time, "place the full prestige of the presidency behind the moral imperative of non-discrimination."

Meanwhile, the power of the Civil Rights movement reached its zenith in the mid-1960s, among escalating black protests, with the passage of the landmark Civil Rights Act of 1964. Title VII of the act prohibited discrimination "against any individual because of such individual's race, color, religion, sex or national origin" (Bureau of National Affairs 1964). Seeking to mollify fears of preferential treatment, Section 703(j) of Title VII stated that "Nothing contained in this title shall be interpreted to require any employer, employment agency, labor organization, or joint labor-management committee subject to this title to grant preferential treatment to any individual or to any group . . . on account of an imbalance which may exist with respect to the total number and percentage of persons of any race, color, religion, sex, or national origin" (Bureau of National Affairs 1964).

However, simply making discrimination illegal by law was not enough. The government had to find an effective way to enforce the 1964 Civil Rights Act, to monitor the progress, and to ensure equal opportunity for every citizen. In this context, President Lyndon Johnson issued Executive Order 11246 on September 24, 1965, which laid an important underpinning for affirmative action policy. This order was a continuation of Executive Order 10925, but it proposed specific requirements. It mandated contracts with the government to include a nondiscrimination clause and federal contractors with one hundred or more employees to take "affirmative action" to achieve the goal of nondiscrimination in "employment, upgrading, demotion and transfer; recruitment or recruitment advertising; layoff or termination; rates of pay or other forms of compensation; and selection for training, including apprenticeship." It required contractors and their subcontractors to submit compliance reports with information on the practices, policies, programs, and racial composition of their work force. It imposed penalties for noncompliance such as cancellation, termination or suspension of federal funds, and ineligibility for further federal contracts. To implement the executive orders and the Civil Rights Act of 1964, the Equal Employment Opportunity Commission (EEOC) and the Office of Federal Contract Compliance (OFCC), located in the Department of Labor, were founded.

In October 1967, President Johnson issued Executive Order 11375, which expanded affirmative action stipulations to include sex discrimination and required every federally funded organization with more than fifty employees and a contract in excess of $50,000 to submit a "written affirmative action compliance program" with goals and timetables. "Goals" were the expected percentages of new employees from various minority groups. Specifically, the ethnic or racial makeup of an organization was expected to roughly match the makeup of the general population. "Timetables" were timelines for achieving the goals.

The enforcement of affirmative action policy continued even during the Nixon and Ford administrations in the late 1960s and 1970s. Executive Order 11478 of August 1969, issued by President Nixon, listed affirmative action steps. During the Carter administration, the Office of Federal Contract Compliance Programs (OFCCP, formerly OFCC until 1975) published a *Construction Compliance Program Operations Manual* detailing the responsibilities of contractors, federal contract agencies, and the OFCCP. The regulations required contractors to include in affirmative action programs the utilization analysis of minorities and women in the work force and to increase their representation.

Although the executive orders and related regulations did not explicitly approve the use of preferential treatment, pressures to increase the representation of minorities and women resulted in the use of race, ethnicity, and gender in hiring, contracting, and college admissions. In various rulings, the Supreme Court ratified preferential treatment because the most important element of the 1964 act was to eliminate discrimination against minorities and women and to bring up equal opportunity, the so-called "benign race-conscious decision making."

It should be noted that affirmative action was never intended to be permanent. It was considered a temporary measure for offsetting the effects of past and present discrimination. Once discrimination was no longer a major problem and everybody had an equal opportunity, affirmative action would not be needed. In his 1978 *Bakke* decision, Supreme Court justice Harry Blackman speculated that race-conscious policy could be eliminated in ten years.

Pros and Cons of Affirmative Action

Since its emergence on the national scene, affirmative action policy has been surrounded by controversies and legal challenges.[1] Over time three major arguments supporting affirmative action have been developed. One

---

1. See Weiss (1997) for the history of affirmative action.

traditional argument is that affirmative action is needed to combat past and present discrimination, and it is a remedy or a compensatory measure for correcting historical and contemporary discrimination against minorities and women. The line of reasoning is: Historically, white males were given preferential treatment; minorities and women have suffered from historical and contemporary discrimination, which impedes their ability to fairly compete with white males since they start from a disadvantageous position; in order to make competition equitable, preferential treatment has to be given to minorities and women *temporarily* until everybody has the same starting point. The remedy is race-conscious, not color-blind.

In recent debates, a diversity argument has increasingly been emphasized by advocates of affirmative action policy. Proponents insist that affirmative action is necessary to increase the diversity of the student population and the work force (e.g., Jackson 1995). This new argument differs from the classic argument in that if diversity is a goal, affirmative action will not be a temporary measure but an open-ended commitment or a long-term task.

The third argument is that affirmative action is effective and beneficial to the whole society. It has significantly increased the representation of minorities and women in educational institutions and the work force; it has benefited not only minorities, but also white women and their families as a result of having two-wage earners in their households; and it has helped corporations to diversify their labor force and to reach out to consumers from different ethnic groups (e.g., Jackson 1995). In a 1985 survey by *Fortune*, nearly 90 percent of corporations polled claimed that they would retain hiring goals and targets even if they were not required to do so.

In the opposite camp, opponents have supplied several arguments against affirmative action. A chief objection is that affirmative action is tantamount to "reverse discrimination" against white males (Glazer 1975). Namely, while minorities and women reap the benefits of affirmative action, white males have become its victims. Opponents argue that reverse discrimination is just as unfair as discrimination against minorities or women. Two wrongs do not make one right. Some white males contest that since they have not discriminated against minorities or women, they should not be punished for past discrimination. Some argue that reverse discrimination has heightened racial division, resentment, and disharmony, and that it pits one group against another (Puddington 1995).

A second objection is that affirmative action disregards individual merit and lowers the quality of the labor force or student body by giving positions or admissions to less qualified persons, since set-aside quotas must be filled by less qualified candidates.

A third argument is that affirmative action is ineffective. Some opponents assert that affirmative action programs should be dismantled because they are costly but unsuccessful in advancing the positions of minorities and women (e.g., Smith and Welch 1984). Others contend that well-off minorities reap the benefits of affirmative action programs to the detriment of poor minorities such as the "underclass" since they are more likely to be preferred over those "truly disadvantaged" who lack job skills, educational preparation, and resources (e.g., Wilson 1987). Furthermore, some whites who are rejected might be the most disadvantaged in that their qualifications are marginal due to their disadvantages.

Another opposing argument is that affirmative action hurts the very minorities and women it intends to help. On the one hand, qualified and competent minority members and women may be viewed as less qualified and as having been granted favor by the government, and be stereotyped as people who cannot really make it on their own merit. On the other hand, it may create a feeling of inferiority or self-doubt among its beneficiaries and undermine their self-esteem (Murray 1984; Steele 1990). Along this line, some opponents (e.g., Sowell 1984) argue that affirmative action may discourage hard work and acquisition of skills since it encourages minorities to think that they can still get admitted or employed, even if they do not work at it.

Proposition 209

Proposition 209 was initiated by two Cal State professors, Glynn Custred and Thomas Wood, both of whom self-described as "angry white men." Although it did not mention affirmative action at all, Proposition 209 sought to repeal affirmative action. Below is the key paragraph from the proposition.

> The state shall not discriminate against, or grant preferential treatment to, any individual or group on the basis of race, sex, color, ethnicity, or national origin in the operation of public employment, public education, or public contracting.

Proposition 209 was passed by California voters on November 5, 1996, with 54 percent yeas and 46 percent nays. Upon its passage, some anti–

Proposition 209 groups immediately filed lawsuits. They contended that Proposition 209 contradicts federal civil rights laws, and that it violates the U.S. Constitution's equal protection clause because it singles out women and minorities, making it more difficult for them to win passage of laws and policies that benefit them. California Governor Pete Wilson asked U.S. District Judge Thelton Anderson, who handled the lawsuits, to delay the hearings until the State Superior Court ruled on the proposition.

On Nov. 27, 1996, Judge Anderson issued a ruling that temporarily blocked Governor Wilson and Attorney General Dan Lungren from enforcing Proposition 209 until at least December 16, because there was a strong probability that Proposition 209 would be shown to be unconstitutional.[2] On December 16, 1996, Judge Anderson granted the temporary order, blocking the enforcement of Proposition 209 pending a trial or a final ruling on its legality.

Lawyers for the state of California appealed to the U.S. Ninth Circuit Court of Appeals. On April 8, 1997, three federal appeals judges of the U.S. Ninth Circuit Court of Appeals overturned Judge Anderson's ruling. They decided that Proposition 209 is constitutional and can be enforced. With no appeal, the decision would have taken effect in twenty-one days. However, opponents of Proposition 209 appealed and asked the full Ninth Circuit Court for a broader review. The Ninth Circuit Court reaffirmed its support for Proposition 209 on August 21, 1997. Opponents appealed the case to the U.S. Supreme Court and meanwhile sought a continuing order blocking the referendum from becoming law. On September 4, 1997, the Supreme Court rejected the pleas from advocates of affirmative action to block the enforcement of Proposition 209. On November 3, 1997, the Supreme Court rejected, without comment, the appeal of the American Liberties Union, clearing the way for full enforcement of the nation's first across-the-board repeal of affirmative action in state and local government. The legal battle was over. However, there is still a long way to go before the full enforcement of this new law, since Proposition 209 does not change federal law and many local programs supported by federal affirmative action requirements.

Proposition 209 has generated ripple effects across the nation. Other

---

2. Anderson, who is black, had personal experience of being discriminated against in the 1960s in Mississippi. He was arrested for a traffic violation, assaulted, called a racial epithet, and nearly jailed before he had a chance to show that he was a lawyer for the U.S. Department of Justice. He said several years ago that he was "more acutely aware than many of the feeling of being powerless."

states and cities have initiated similar measures. Congress is considering a bill to end affirmative action in public hiring and contracts. However, in Houston, Proposition A, the second ballot measure in the nation to challenge the precepts of affirmative action, was defeated on November 5, 1997, by a 55 percent to 45 percent margin, partly because of the change in the proposition's wording from "no discrimination against anyone on the basis of race, sex, color, ethnicity or national origin" to the abolition of "affirmative action for women and minorities . . . including ending the current program and any similar programs in the future."

The full impact of Proposition 209 on employment, education, and government contracting is still too early to tell. What we do know from the data released by the University of California is that undergraduate students of African, Latino, and American Indian descent who intended to enroll in the UC system in the Fall 1998 (i.e., the first class assembled without any preference for race or ethnicity), dropped by 24 percent, 5.5 percent, and 4.8 percent, respectively, in comparison to the Fall of 1997 numbers. The declines were most drastic at UC Berkeley, UCLA, and UC San Diego. On the other hand, UC Irvine, UC Riverside, and UC Santa Cruz recorded significant increases in the percentages of African, Latino, and Indian students.

What Is the Way Out?

Both sides of the issue may have valid points. There are interests involved, and it is difficult to reconcile conflicting interests. It may be more useful to work out compromises or alternatives that could attain the same goals.

Since affirmative action was never intended to be permanent, the real question is: Is now the time to abolish this policy? There are currently two approaches to this question: "End it," represented by the conservative Republicans, and "Mend it," represented by President Clinton. To determine whether to end it or mend it, we need to have a comprehensive overhaul of affirmative action policy and programs. Specifically, we need to review whether the goals of affirmative action policy have been accomplished. If discrimination against minorities and women is no longer a major problem in society and everybody basically has equal opportunities for schools, jobs, and government contracts, it is the time to end affirmative action. Otherwise, we need to keep it for a while and make it work better. Opponents of affirmative action often claim that racial and gender discrimination is no longer a major obstacle in today's society, while its proponents assert that discrimination is not "an evil of the past," but "a very painful reality" (Jackson 1995). Systematic empirical evidence should be collected in order to make a credible assessment at the national level. We also need to review the means of affirmative action to evaluate whether preferential treatment toward minorities and women is the best way to achieve the goal of affirmative action. If not, we should either end it or use other means to attain the goals of affirmative action.

Moreover, we need to review existing affirmative action programs. There are different types of affirmative action programs, such as preference programs; target hiring; quota programs—programs that set specific numbers for minorities and women; and outreach programs—programs that attempt to recruit or reach out to underrepresented minorities and women. Some programs work and some do not. The Clinton administration did a comprehensive review of all federal affirmative action programs in 1996. Based on the review, President Clinton declared in July 1996 that "When affirmative action is done right, it is flexible, it is fair, and it works." He set forth four criteria for all affirmative action programs to comply with: (1) no quotas, in theory or in practice; (2) no illegal discrimination of any kind, including reverse discrimination; (3) no preference for unqualified individuals for jobs or other opportunities; and (4) termination of programs once the goals have been achieved. Most Americans agree that quota programs should be eliminated, but they tend to favor outreach programs. Other types of programs, such as target hiring and preference programs, should be further examined.

Outside the yes/no framework, an alternative to affirmative action based on race, ethnicity, or gender is affirmative action based on class or economic status, which is favored by many Americans of different races. The idea is to give preference to people who suffer economic disadvantage, regardless of their race, ethnicity, or gender. The rationale is that within each group or each gender, there are successful people who do not need extra help and there are also less successful people who do need help.

Another alternative is to create diversity programs or use diversity approaches. Opinion polls have found that most Americans favor diversity. If diversity is a goal, one way to achieve it is to devise diversity programs specifically for that purpose. One example in college admissions in California may be illustrative. A recent proposal suggested the admission of the top 12.5 percent of the graduates of each of California's 844 public high schools, including rich ones, poor ones, and racially mixed ones

(Weiss 1997). Proponents contended that this plan would help maintain ethnic diversity of the university system, increase the geographic distribution of UC students, encourage competition within high school, and reward disadvantaged students. A study of the effect of this proposal by the university found that there would be more black and Latino students eligible but fewer Asian and white students, and that the plan would also reduce the average academic index score based on GPA and SAT scores for UC candidates. Several other competing proposals have recommended lowering the percentage to the top 4 percent or top 6 percent or setting aside slots for the top two students of each high school. Other proposals include academic enrichment programs such as the Early Academic Outreach Program, and Berkeley's Break and Cycle Program, which dispatches university students to give individual math instruction to neighboring poor and minority students. These proposals are certainly not problem free, but they mark the initial efforts to explore other diversity-maintenance avenues. Another example is that in a bid to maintain student diversity, UC Berkeley's Boalt Hall Law School recently threw out a controversial admissions policy that gave greater weight to GPAs of applicants from elite colleges and universities (Woo 1997).

ILLEGAL IMMIGRATION AND PROPOSITION 187

Another volatile issue in recent years has been illegal immigration. The controversy originated in California in the early 1990s as a result of the deepening economic recession, rising nativist sentiment, and some politicians' needs for survival and gains. Proposition 187, the so-called Save Our State (S.O.S.) Initiative, was born of this context and passed by California voters in November 1994. It generated backlash in the nation and partly led to passage of the Illegal Immigration Act of 1996. This section first highlights the status of illegal immigration and then discusses the debate on Proposition 187.

Demographics of Illegal Immigrants

Illegal immigrants are foreign nationals who reside in the host country (i.e., the United States in our discussion) without proper documents. Immigration specialists sometimes prefer the term "undocumented immigrant" over "illegal alien" due to the sinister tang of the latter term.

Illegal immigrants enter this country through two major channels. One is to cross the border without undergoing inspection, including being smuggled in. The other is to come with legal entry documents (e.g., tourist visa, business visa, student visa) but later overstay them. Less frequently, some foreigners enter with fake documents at the ports of entry. Differing from an earlier INS estimate of a roughly 50/50 split, the latest INS estimates have indicated that nearly 60 percent of undocumented immigrants became illegal by crossing borders illegally, and about 40 percent through overstaying their visas (McDonnell 1997; Smith and Edmonston 1997).

Official estimates released by the INS on February 8, 1997, placed the total number of illegal immigrants in the United States at more than five million, which represented a significant increase from a low point reached after the Immigration Reform and Control Act (IRCA) of 1986 established an amnesty program (McDonnell 1997). In early 1987, the total number of illegal immigrants was estimated at six million, and over three million were legalized under the 1986 IRCA. The INS estimated that 275,000 illegal immigrants enter this country each year, which was somewhat down from an earlier INS estimate of 300,000 (McDonnell 1997).

Illegal immigrants come from many countries. According to the 1997 INS estimates, more than half (54.1 percent) came from Mexico, 6.7 percent from El Salvador, 3.3 percent from Guatemala, and 2.1 percent from Canada (McDonnell 1997). Significant numbers also came from Poland, the Philippines, Italy, and other Latin American countries such as Haiti, Bahamas, Nicaragua, Honduras, Columbia, Ecuador, Jamaica, and the Dominican Republic.

Undocumented immigrants are highly concentrated in seven states: California, New York, Texas, Florida, Illinois, New Jersey, and Arizona. The recent INS data showed that two million, or 40 percent of the national total resided in California, and they made up about 6.3 percent of the California population (McDonnell 1997). New York used to take the No. 2 spot and Texas No. 3 in terms of the total number of illegals. Today, Texas has moved up to the No. 2 place, and 3.7 percent of the Texas population is undocumented. Nationally, illegal immigrants account for 1.9 percent of the population.

Proposition 187

Since California shared the largest portion of the nation's undocumented population and suffered severe economic recession in the late 1980s and early 1990s, illegal immigration naturally became a hot source of contention and an issue utilizable by politicians for their own political survival and gain. That was why illegal immigration became the centerpiece of Governor Pete Wilson's 1994 reelection campaign. Against this backdrop, California voters passed Proposition 187 by a margin of 59-41 percent on November 8, 1994. Some important stipulations of Proposition 187, including several controversial ones, are listed below:

1. Exclude illegal immigrants and their foreign-born children from publicly funded nonemergency medical care and other health care. Once illegal status is determined, authorities are to deny such care.

2. Exclude foreign-born children of illegal immigrants from public elementary and secondary schools. School districts are required to report illegal status of parents, guardians or pupils to state agencies and INS.

3. Exclude illegal immigrants from public postsecondary educational institutions. Admissions officials are required to report any illegal immigrants to authorities.

4. Exclude illegal immigrants from welfare services. Once illegal status is determined, authorities are to deny such services.

5. Law enforcement agencies are required to verify the legal status of every arrestee and notify the attorney general for deportation of illegal immigrants.

6. The state attorney general is required to maintain records of all reports received from state agencies on illegal immigrants and send them to the INS.

7. Any person who manufactures, distributes or sells false documents shall be punished by imprisonment or a fine.

8. Any person who uses false documents shall be punished by imprisonment for five years or by a fine of up to $25,000.

There are pros and cons to Proposition 187. Its proponents argue: First, Proposition 187 will deter illegal immigrants from coming to the United States by making life difficult for the undocumented. Second, Proposition 187 will save money paid for services and benefits to illegal immigrants and help the economy. Governor Wilson (1994) argued that California was compelled by federal law to spend more than $3 billion each year (or nearly 10 percent of the state budget) to provide services to illegal immigrants, which hurt California's economy and limited its ability to serve its legal residents. Third, Proposition 187 is not racist; it is about responsibility and resources (Wilson 1994).

The opposition runs the whole gamut of arguments. Major counterarguments include: First, Proposition 187 is ineffective in reducing illegal immigration because it does not address the main cause of illegal immigration—job opportunities. That is, illegal immigrants come here primarily for jobs rather than for schools, health care service, or social services. The most effective measure to control illegal immigration is to eliminate job opportunities available for illegal immigrants. However, Proposition 187 does not address this source of illegal immigration. The latest INS estimates suggest that Proposition 187 has failed to daunt illegal immigrants from entry.

Second, some stipulations of Proposition 187 will have unintended consequences and will be more costly. For instance, the reluctance of illegal immigrants to see a doctor for health problems could eventually cost the U.S. government and taxpayers more money. Moreover, if their diseases are untreated and spread to the general population, the consequences are unthinkable. Another negative effect is that if children of illegal immigrants are not allowed to attend public schools, they are more likely to go to the street and become trapped into criminal activities, becoming problems for society.[3] In addition, these measures may increase discrimination against all immigrants and minorities who look or sound "foreign."

Third, Proposition 187 is racist and mean-spirited because it scapegoats illegal immigrants for California's economic problems, victimizes innocent immigrant children, and lets employers off the hook (Kadetsky 1994). Some politicians have used public sentiment to get elected or reelected by blaming illegal immigrants for California's budget crisis and exonerating themselves from their own responsibility.

In December 1995, U.S. District Judge, Mariana R. Pfaelzer issued an injunction that allowed measures 7 and 8 to stand but struck down or preempted by federal law major portions of Proposition 187, including all of

3. In fact, the exclusion of children of illegal immigrants from public schools violates several federal mandates as well as a Supreme Court decision which granted all children the right to free education.

the first six stipulations mentioned above. However, issues raised by Proposition 187 have moved onto the national stage. In March 1996, the House of Representatives passed an illegal immigration crackdown bill, which included a provision denying free public education to students illegally in this country. In August 1996, Congress enacted the Welfare Reform Bill (the Personal Responsibility and Work Opportunity Reconciliation Act of 1996), and President Clinton signed it into law on August 22, 1996. In November 1996, Judge Pfaelzer ruled that California can use the nation's new welfare law to implement its cuts in aid to illegal immigrants and to cut prenatal care for undocumented pregnant women, but other portions of her 1995 injunction against proposition 187 remained in effect. On November 14, 1997, Judge Pfaelzer ruled again that Proposition 187 was unconstitutional and violated the 1996 Welfare Reform law. She wrote that "California is powerless to enact its own legislative scheme to regulate immigration," and, "It is likewise powerless to enact its own legislative scheme to regulate alien access to public benefits."

Former California Governor Pete Wilson appealed Pfaelzer's decision to the U.S. Ninth Circuit Court of Appeals. New Governor Gray Davis inherited the appeal and decided in April 1999 to turn the proposition over to a mediator. As of this writing the major portions of Proposition 187 have not yet been put into effect in California. It is likely that this matter will eventually go to the Supreme Court.

THE IMMIGRATION DEBATE

As the tussle on illegal immigration turned red-hot, legal immigration became an issue of controversy as well. A rising tide of newcomers and the economic recession in the late 1980s and early 1990s also helped renew the debate over legal immigration. Immigration is an important issue in ethnic studies because of its impact on ethnic composition, ethnic relations, ethnic identity, and the socioeconomic status and cultural integration of ethnic groups. This issue was part of the 1996 presidential campaign. Congress is currently considering various proposals for immigration reform.

State of Legal Immigration

To understand the debate, we need some basic knowledge about the history and current status of legal immigration to the United States. Figure

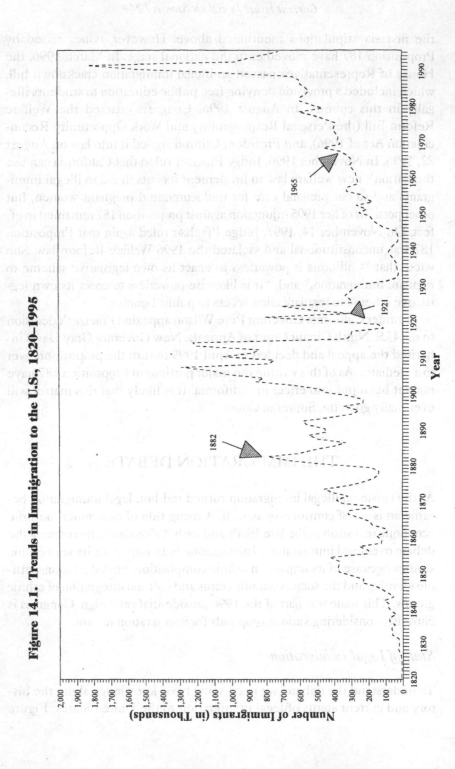

Figure 14.1. Trends in Immigration to the U.S., 1820–1995

14.1 shows the trends in legal immigration for fiscal years 1820 to 1995. Historically, the apex of immigration occurred in the early twentieth century as millions of new immigrants arrived on American soil. In 1907 alone, nearly 1.3 million newcomers came. We then see declines in immigration, with fluctuations around the two world wars. Legal immigration has steadily increased since 1965. In the 1990s, between 800,000 and about 1.8 million immigrants have been admitted each year.

The sudden leaps from 1988 to the early 1990s were largely due to the amnesty program established by the IRCA of 1986, which allowed illegal immigrants who had resided in the United States continuously since January 1, 1982, plus some unauthorized agricultural workers, to become legalized and to obtain permanent resident status after two years of temporary residency. More than three million illegal immigrants were legalized under this act. Starting in 1988, the former illegal immigrants were eligible to become permanent residents—legal immigrants—so the numbers soared after 1988 and then gradually decreased after 1991 as most former illegals obtained their permanent resident status. The record-breaking number of over 1.8 million immigrants in 1991 often cited by politicians and the media greatly inflated the normal level of legal immigration, since more than 1.1 million were former illegals amnestied under the IRCA of 1986. As a matter of fact, the number of admissions from abroad in 1991 was about 700,000.

In the post-1965 period, Latin America and Asia have become the major sources of legal immigration. In 1965 European and Latin American countries topped the list of immigrant suppliers. Thirty years later, Latin American and Asian countries became the main sending countries. Immigration from Europe decreased after 1965 because fewer Europeans are motivated to come here, although there has been a slight increase in European immigration in recent years, mainly due to the influx from Russia and eastern Europe.

The geographic distribution of new immigrants is very uneven. The bulk of the new immigrants are concentrated in six states: California, New York, Texas, Florida, Illinois, and New Jersey, and they are also disproportionately clustered in urban centers.

The immigration debate focuses on three aspects of concern about immigration: the economic impact of immigration, the social impact of immigration, and the environmental impact of immigration. Each of these issues is discussed below.

The Economic Impact of Immigration

Opponents of immigration argue that immigration harms the U.S. economy. Specifically, they assert that, first, immigrants take jobs away from native-born citizens; second, immigrants drive down wages since they are willing to work for less pay; and third, immigrants increase the burden on society because they are more likely to depend on welfare support.

In contrast, proponents of immigration contend that immigration benefits the U.S. economy. Specific arguments run tit for tat against those of immigration opponents. First, immigrants complement the native-born labor force since they tend to take unwanted or less desirable jobs such as agricultural workers, garbage collectors, cleanup workers, household workers, busboys, janitors, and so on. The basic assumption is that the labor market is segmented and that many immigrants and native-born citizens are not competing in the same market. Second, immigrants lower the prices of goods and services. Third, immigrants contribute more than they cost.

Does empirical evidence support or reject these arguments? There have been many studies of the economic effects of immigration in the past several years. Some of them are biased and untrustworthy because of their interest group sponsorships, selective presentation of results, and/or flawed methodologies. In order to assess the economic, fiscal, and demographic effects of immigration, Congress appointed a bipartisan U.S. Commission on Immigration Reform to provide policy advice. Directed by the Commission, the National Research Council (NRC) assembled a panel of twelve prestigious immigration experts to submit a report. After two years, the panel completed its report in May 1997. The major findings of this report may be summarized as follows (see Smith and Edmonston 1997).

With regard to job competition, the report concluded that (1) immigrants provide a crucial work force for many businesses, especially the agriculture and textile industries and the service sector, such as restaurants, hotels, and janitorial service; (2) at the national level, immigrants do not significantly reduce job opportunities of competing native-born groups, who can migrate out of the areas to which immigrants move; and (3) immigrants do compete with some low-skilled, native-born workers and earlier immigrants in areas where immigrants are concentrated. The report rejected the often-asserted assumption that African Americans suffer disproportionately from the inflow of low-skilled immigrants, because the majority of native-born blacks live away from areas where immigrants are concentrated.

As for wage depression, many of the typical local labor market studies summarized in the report found that immigration only has a weak (either positive or negative) effect on the wages of all types of native workers—black and white, male and female, and skilled and unskilled. The group that suffers significant negative effects from new immigrants is earlier immigrants, rather than natives. For certain groups of native-born workers, such as high school dropouts, competition from immigrants has depressed their wages by about 5 percent since the 1980s. In addition, immigrants lower prices quite uniformly for most domestic consumers, and in particular households with high levels of education and wealth reap more benefits from lower consumer prices.

Whether immigrants are a burden or an economic plus to society is the most contentious issue in the recent debate. Prior to the NRC panel report, quite a few studies showed conflicting results. For instance, the statistics released by the Los Angeles County Board of Supervisors in 1992 showed that while immigrants comprised 25 percent of the county's residents, they were responsible for 35 percent of its public costs, but paid just 10 percent of its taxes. In November 1993, a report written by Rice University economist Donald Huddle found that in 1992, the 7.2 million immigrants who had come to California since 1970—both legal and illegal immigrants—cost taxpayers $18 billion more than they paid in taxes. He estimated that when taxes paid by newcomers were subtracted from the value of benefits they received, the net cost for roughly twenty million legal, illegal, and amnestied aliens accepted into the United States since 1970 was $30.6 billion—an annual social welfare price tag of $1,585 per immigrant.

Contrary to the studies using state or county data, a study at the national level released by the National Immigration Forum (an immigration advocacy group) in December 1995 and authored by University of Maryland professor Julian Simon found that both legal and illegal immigrants use fewer government resources than native-born citizens. "As of the 1970s, immigrants contribute more to the public coffers in taxes than they drew out in welfare services." "The most recent data . . . show that each year an average immigrant family put about $2,500 into the pockets of natives from the excess of taxes over public costs." Simon concluded that government expenditures are lower for immigrants than for native-born Americans. According to the report, the average immigrant family received $1,404 in welfare services during its first five years in the country, compared to the $2,279 for native-born families. Jeffrey Passel (1994) found that immigrants admitted into the United States between 1970 and 1992 produced a surplus of $25 billion to $30 billion.

The NRC panel report reflects a compromise between the arguments of both sides. It shows that at the national level immigrants contribute up to $10 billion each year. The majority of the American people benefit from immigration since immigrants are concentrated in six states and their taxes mostly go to the federal government. However, the report estimates that in California, services (especially education and health care) for new legal and illegal immigrants cost each California household headed by a native-born citizen $1,178 each year because immigrant-headed households on average have more school-age children, are poorer, have lower incomes, and own less property than native households. Their taxes paid to the state and local governments are not enough to cover the costs of services for them, because only a small percentage of their taxes go to the state and local governments through sales, license, income, and property taxes. The federal government collects the bulk of their income taxes and all social security taxes. One solution may be that the federal government gives some tax money back to the state to pay for services for immigrants. A drawback to the report is that no distinction is made between legal immigration and illegal immigration. A better assessment of the costs and benefits of immigration must distinguish among legal immigrants, illegal immigrants, and refugees.

The Social Impact of Immigration

No less controversial than the economic effect of immigration is the concern about its social and cultural impact. Opponents of immigration contend that growing diversity caused by the influx of new immigrants from Latin America and Asia threatens American culture and society. They believe that immigration increases racial tensions and cultural fragmentation and imperils American culture and national unity. They see an identity crisis. Who are we as a nation, they ask, if people of different cultures do not have a common sense of Americanness? These anxieties are reflected in public opinion polls and political discourse. For instance, a 1993 Gallup poll found that 55 percent of the respondents agreed that the increasing diversity brought in by immigrants mostly threatens American culture. Patrick Buchanan (1993) lamented the decreasing proportion of whites in the U.S. population and its potential impact, which he saw as the dissolution of America. He worried that by 2050, whites will be a near-minority and "the United States will have become a veritable Brazil of North America." Since in the twentieth century all the great multinational empires have fallen apart and currently multinational states such as Canada, Czechoslovakia, India, Russia, Yugoslavia, South Africa, and Ethiopia are breaking up, the multinational state America would not be immune to this trend. His solution was a ten-year "time out" to allow immigrants to assimilate.

Proponents of immigration maintain that diversity is a good thing and that American culture should not be viewed as White Anglo-Saxon Protestant culture or European culture. The history of the United States has proven the vitality of America. As the most diverse nation, with no common origins and no apparent basis for unity, America has nevertheless endured as a unified nation for more than two centuries of tremendous transformation. What binds Americans together is not common ancestry, or common race/ethnicity, but common beliefs in freedom, equality, democracy, and justice. There is no evidence that large numbers of recent immigrants from Latin America, Asia, and the Middle East will jeopardize the unity and identity of the American nation (Neuhaus 1993). On the contrary, alienating those newcomers and minority populations sows the seed for social unrest and undermines efforts to unify a diverse nation like America.

There is also concern about whether the new immigrants can be assimilated into American society, since they have different physical attributes and cultural traditions. This disquietude is certainly not new. Historically, whenever a new immigrant group arrived there was such a concern. For instance, during the great wave of Irish immigration in the 1840s, there were doubts about the assimilability of Catholic Irish. History has proven such concern groundless. Several generations later, the Irish, a group who used to be considered as separatist and alien, have been successfully integrated into American culture and society; they have become congressmen and even president (Cole 1994). When the Chinese first arrived in large numbers in the mid-nineteenth century, they were considered "unassimilable aliens" and were made ineligible for U.S. citizenship in 1882. Today, the Chinese have not only become assimilated but have achieved great socioeconomic success. The experiences of many other groups such as Catholic Italians, Jews, and the Japanese have repeatedly refuted the unassimilability argument. History has proven the strength and absorbability of the American culture and social system. Whether the same generational progress will be duplicated for new immigrants and their descendants remains to be seen, although some recent immigrants and their children, especially Asian groups, have matched native-born whites in educational and occupational states fairly quickly.

Concerns also arise about whether immigration aggravates a range of social problems, especially crimes. Immigrants are often blamed for crime and random violence in cities. For instance, Peter Brimelow (1996, 182–186) claimed that immigration contributes to crime and violence and that immigrants are more likely to commit crime because disproportionately they are young men. He used fragmentary evidence to back up his claims. During the Republican Party's 1992 presidential campaign, Patrick Buchanan warned that "our cities are riven with gangs' wars among Asian, black, and Hispanic youth who grow up to run ethnic crime cartels" (Farrell 1992). In contrast, the NRC panel report (Smith and Edmonston 1997, 364) concluded that in terms of historical and current evidence, "immigrants are no more likely to participate in socially disapproved activities than are native-born Americans." Using the available records for federal and state prison inmates in 1991, the panel reported that noncitizens were overall less likely to commit crimes than citizens (the ratio of noncitizen to citizen crime rate was .80 for all offenses), except for drug offenses (Smith and Edmonston 1997, Table 8.6). By and large, due to scant research on the subject and scarce statistics on immigrant crime patterns, it is too soon to draw any firm conclusion about the impact of immigration on crime.

In addition, the NRC panel report recognizes the contributions of immigrants to the development of science, art, and other fields in America. For example, as of 1995 immigrants accounted for 26 percent to 32 percent of the U.S. Nobel laureates in chemistry, physics, economics, literature, and physiology or medicine. As of July 1996, the foreign-born represented 21 percent of the members of the National Academy of Sciences and 14 percent of the National Academy of Engineering's members. Among the ninety recipients of Kennedy Center honors who throughout their lifetimes had made significant contributions to American culture through performing arts from 1978 to 1994, twenty-two, or nearly one-fourth, were foreign-born.

The Environmental Impact of Immigration

More recently, opponents of immigration have argued that immigration causes excessive population growth and consequent environmental destruction (Beck 1996; Bouvier 1992; Stein 1992). Demographer Leon Bouvier (1992) predicted that largely because of immigration, the U.S. population is projected to grow from 254 million in 1990 to between 388 million and 454 million in 2050. He argued that the growth in U.S. population would increase global warming, air pollution, and waste production; decrease food production and water supply; and destroy wetlands and infrastructure. Hence, he called for restriction on legal immigration to a much lower level (350,000 per year). Similarly, Beck (1996, 31–32) asserted that immigration, combined with the much higher fertility rates of immigrants, has been the number one cause of population growth since 1970, which has been a substantial cause of environmental problems.

However, despite the important role of immigration in U.S. population growth during the past two to three decades, there are flaws with these arguments. First, to what extent environmental problems can be blamed on U.S. population growth is an indeterminate issue since many other factors may have even greater environmental impact. Among these are government environmental policies, industrial development, and population distribution. Second, to what extent these environmental effects could be directly attributed to immigration is even more debatable. Empirical evidence of immigrant-induced environmental destruction is usually missing. Third, although it is evident that, overall, immigrant women had higher fertility rates than native-born women, there are large variations among ethnic groups in fertility (Yip 1996). For instance, according to the 1990 census data the fertility rates of Thai, Korean, Asian Indian, and Chinese women were lower than the rate of white women. Thus, who immigrates does affect fertility and population growth. Who comes and how many come should be considered simultaneously. While goals of population size and growth should be an essential part of immigration policy consideration, passing the blame for environmental problems to immigration may not be fair.

BILINGUAL EDUCATION AND THE ENGLISH-ONLY MOVEMENT

The surge in immigration inevitably brings up the issue of language education for non-English-speaking children and the broader issue of national culture and identity. Bilingual education and the English-Only movement are two different but interrelated topics. This section first discusses bilingual education and then extends it to the English-Only movement and its countermovement—English-Plus.

Great confusion clouds public discourse on bilingual education. "Bilingual education" is a term that describes a number of educational approaches using both students' native language and English in instruction. The word *bilingual* means two languages; any program that does not involve two languages or does not include English as a second language component is not a bilingual education program. To understand bilingual education, we need to fathom its history, the types of bilingual education programs, and the debate over this issue.

Origin and Development of National Bilingual Education Policy

Bilingual education is not a new phenomenon in the United States. Bilingual education was common in the eighteenth and nineteenth centuries in communities where German, French, Spanish, and other minority language speakers were concentrated (e.g., New Mexico, California, Louisiana, northern New England, the Midwest, and the East).[4] Laws that required English to be the only language of instruction were enacted in California and New Mexico by the end of the nineteenth century. By 1923, thirty-four states had passed similar English-only instruction laws (Ambert and Melendez 1985). This linguistic xenophobia was checked in 1923, when the Supreme Court ruled in *Meyer v. Nebraska* that a Nebraska state law prohibiting the instruction of a foreign language to elementary students was unconstitutional. Nevertheless, the Court underscored the power of the state to "make reasonable regulations for all schools, including a requirement that they should give instruction in English." As a result of the *Meyer v. Nebraska* decision, the strict English-only instruction laws were generally abolished or ignored. However, thirty-five states still retained English-only instruction laws of some kind in 1971 (Laosa 1984). From the 1920s to the 1960s, the language needs of limited-English-proficiency (LEP) students received little attention.

In the 1960s, the Civil Rights movement pressed for cultural pluralism; the failure of English classrooms to teach LEP students called for effective solutions; and the success of an experimental bilingual education program in the Coral Way Elementary School of Dade County, Florida, in 1963 captured national attention. Against this historical backdrop,

4. For detailed discussions of bilingual education in the United States, see Malakoff and Hakuta (1990), and Crawford (1991, ch. 2).

Congress enacted the Bilingual Education Act (BEA) of 1968, which was the genesis of national bilingual education policy in the United States.[5] President Lyndon Johnson signed the bill into law on January 2, 1968. This act legitimized bilingual education programs at the national level and allocated funds for teaching LEP children of low-income families in their native languages while they were learning English. However, the BEA neither defined specific bilingual education programs nor mandated their creation. The amendment to the Bilingual Education Act in 1974 dropped the low-income requirement and for the first time required schools receiving grants to include instruction in children's native language and culture. The Equal Education Opportunities Act of 1974 required each school district to take "appropriate action to overcome language barriers that impede equal participation by its students in its instructional programs." That is, the failure to provide opportunity for LEP students to overcome language barriers was tantamount to denying their equal educational opportunities. Both laws significantly expanded bilingual education programs.

The Bilingual Education Act was reauthorized in 1978. The act permitted a child's language to be used "to the extent necessary to allow a child to achieve competence in the English language," but it prohibited language maintenance programs. Basically, all programs funded by Title VII were to be transitional.

In 1984, the reauthorized Bilingual Education Act clarified the goal of bilingual education programs as enabling LEP children to "achieve competence in the English language" and "to meet grade-promotion and graduation standards." For the first time, the act permitted the addition of developmental (maintenance) bilingual education programs, even though only a small portion of instructional grant funds could be used for this purpose.

The 1988 reauthorization of the Bilingual Education Act changed the formula for the allocation of funds and moved in the direction of flexibility. Specifically, the funds used for alternative bilingual approaches such as language maintenance programs and English as a second language (ESL) increased from 4 percent to 25 percent while the funds for transitional bilingual programs decreased from 96 percent before 1988 to 75 percent after 1988.

---

5. The BEA was introduced as Title VII of the Elementary and Secondary Education Act, rather than as a separate piece of legislation.

Types of Bilingual Education Programs

There are four basic types of bilingual education programs (August and Garcia 1988; Crawford 1991; and Malakoff and Hakuta 1990).

Transitional bilingual education (TBE)

In this model, children learn school subjects (e.g., math, literature, arts, science, and social studies) in their native language, while they study English in programs designed for second-language learners. The goal is to prepare students to enter mainstream English classrooms. In a typical program, students might begin attending art, music, and physical education classes in English, but learn other subjects such as math, science, reading, and social studies in their native language. As they learn English, they gradually move into English math classes and then other classes until they study all subjects in English. TBE students usually complete the transition from native language to English within three years. In the most extreme cases, it could take several years for students to move into mainstream classes. This is the most common model in U.S. public schools.

English immersion

The goal of this model is to assist students to achieve proficiency in English. English is the language of instruction in this type of program. Students are "immersed" in English. They learn school subjects in English, usually with simplified vocabulary and sentences, visual aids, and sometimes with support from a classroom aide fluent in their native language. This model is also very common in the United States.

Note that *submersion* programs differ from immersion programs in that in submersion programs, LEP children are placed in regular classrooms and receive *no* special language assistance. Since their native language is not used in instruction, students either sink or swim. In essence, submersion programs are not bilingual education programs because they do not involve two languages in instruction. Under the Supreme Court's *Lau v. Nichols* decision (1974), submersion is a violation of federal civil rights law.

Maintenance bilingual education, or two-way bilingual education

Its purpose is to help all students achieve proficiency in both English and their native language. Instruction is given in both languages. Normally, a school day is divided into two language periods: students learn school subjects in one language in the morning and in another language in the afternoon. Emphasis is not placed on leaving the program for English-only instruction, as is the case with the transitional and immersion programs. This is an enrichment model, but it is rare at the secondary level in the United States.

English as a second language (ESL)

This is really not a program as much as a combination of methods used to teach English to non-English speakers. When educators use special methods designed for non-English speakers in order to teach English in classrooms, they teach "English as a second language." For some schools, this is the only bilingual education program; for others, it is just part of a larger program.

As you can see, most of these programs are "subtractive" or are designed to produce monolinguals. Only maintenance bilingual education is "additive" since it aims at assisting students to maintain proficiency in two languages rather than one.

Pros and Cons of Bilingual Education

Bilingual education has been an issue of ongoing controversy. Arguments in favor of bilingual education include the following: First, bilingual education helps LEP students make the transition to the regular English program. Second, bilingual education programs give bilingual children advantages over monolingual children in cognitive skills, especially in the ability to analyze the form and content of language and knowledge (Hakuta 1986). The development of skills in cognitive-academic language proficiency is believed to be most effective when built upon the foundation of the native language, rather than English (Crowford 1991, 107). Third, bilingual education helps children develop certain language and literacy skills that are transferable for learning a second language, such as the organization of a paragraph or an argument (Snow 1990). Finally, bilingual education helps non-English speaking students to maintain their native language and culture.

There are at least three major arguments against bilingual education programs. First, the history argument contends that European immigrants of the late nineteenth and early twentieth centuries arrived with no English, but became successful and productive members of American society without federally sponsored bilingual education programs. Why can't today's immigrants learn English like previous generations of immigrants? Second, bilingual education programs slow down the transition of LEP students to the regular English program by totally or near-totally separating LEP students from other English-speaking children and by reducing the amount of time spent on learning English. In addition, teachers responsible for bilingual education frequently do not speak English as their mother tongue and therefore may not be ideal models for children's English learning. Hence, bilingual education programs create precisely the opposite effects than they are designed to produce. Third, bilingual education encourages ethnic separation and ethnic tribalism in schools and in society by reinforcing the loyalty of LEP students to their native languages and by delaying their integration into the English-speaking society.

There have been several studies concerning the effects of bilingual education programs. For instance, a longitudinal study conducted in the 1980s by the Office for Research and Evaluation of the El Paso Independent School District found that both the transitional bilingual program and dual language immersion (both English and Spanish were used as languages of instruction) were insufficient, but that the dual language program showed slightly higher student test scores (El Paso Independent School District 1989). A four-year study of about two thousand Spanish-speaking elementary school pupils in five states by the U.S. Department of Education in 1991 compared three bilingual approaches: (1) immersion with all or nearly all instruction in English, (2) four-year-exit bilingual programs, and (3) six-year-exit bilingual programs (Aguirre International 1991). This study concluded that children in all three groups outperformed their counterparts in the normal student population and that bilingual instruction did not hinder their learning of English or any other subjects. However, no conclusion can be made about the relative superiority of the three approaches.

Overall, available empirical evidence seems to provide some support for bilingual education as a proper education *option* for LEP students. Well-designed bilingual educational programs seem to be as effective as other methods in some learning settings, but there is no unambiguous evidence that they are more effective than other programs. The controversy over bilingual education has more to do with social and political concerns than with pedagogical concerns. Whether to participate in a bilingual education program should be the choice of parents and students. To achieve the maximum from bilingual education, educators ought to move in the direction of enrichment programs that make students truly "bilingual."

Proposition 227

In November 1997, California voters passed Proposition 227 (The English Language Education for Children in Public Schools Initiative) by a large margin (61 percent to 39 percent). The proposition sought to eliminate bilingual education in California public schools. It proposed the following key provisions: "All children in California public schools shall be taught English by being taught in English"; all children with limited English proficiency should be placed in sheltered English immersion programs for a temporary period of no more than one year; under parental waiver conditions (i.e., existing English proficiency; ages ten or older; special physical, emotional, psychological, or educational needs), parents could request their children to be transferred to classes where children are taught through bilingual education techniques permitted by law; and $50 million per year shall be allocated for ten years to fund programs of adult English language instruction.

Proposition 227 was an attempt to fix the problems of existing bilingual education in California. More than half of the 1.4 million LEP students in California's bilingual education program spent more time being taught in their native languages than in English; there was a lack of qualified bilingual teachers. As a result, students improved their English proficiency slowly and did not have the English skills needed to compete in college and the labor market. Recognizing these problems, the sponsors of Proposition 227, Silicon Valley millionaire Ron Unz and Latino teacher Gloria Tuchman, hoped that the proposition might be a cure.

However, there is no indication that the proposition's prescription will work. According to the preliminary data from California Department of Education, one month after the implementation of Proposition 227, high proportions of students returned to bilingual education classrooms at the request of their parents and in some school districts the return rates reached 80 percent or higher (e.g., San Francisco Unified, almost 100 percent; Oxnard Elementary, 81 percent; Pomona Unified, 64 percent; San Jose Unified, 58 percent). As mentioned in the previous section, English immersion works for some LEP students but not for all. In addition, one year of English immersion may not be sufficient for some LEP students to complete the transition from their native languages to English, especially in written language.

Furthermore, Proposition 227 is shortsighted. In an increasingly global economy, we need more bilinguals and multilinguals to engage in works pertaining to international transactions and technological transfers. The LEP students are most likely to become bilingual or multilingual and are potential assets to California. Nevertheless, by eliminating bilingual education, Proposition 227 sees these students merely as burdens and forces them to abandon their potential language skills.

In short, existing bilingual education programs in California need to be reformed, but Proposition 227 is not the answer to the problem. A better solution may be two-way bilingual education, through which both LEP students and English-speaking students can become bilingual. We do not need a legislative mandate for instructional programs. We should leave the choices open and let parents and children choose whatever is the best for them.

The English-Only Movement

Although English is the language of the U.S. Constitution, government, and laws, America, like Britain, does not have an official language. English is the principal or common language rather than the official language. The framers of the Constitution were silent on this issue, and the question of the national language probably never came up at the Federal Convention. Other languages are spoken at home by twenty-five million Americans. For instance, in 1990 about twenty million, or 8 percent of Americans, spoke Spanish at home.

While controversies over language issues in early periods were confined to local and state arenas, the national debate over language education in recent decades has pushed the language issue to the national stage, giving rise to the English-Only movement and its counterpart, the English-Plus campaign. The English-Only movement began in 1981 when the late U.S. Senator S. I. Hayakawa introduced a bill calling for an amendment to the U.S. Constitution to declare English the official language of the nation. The bill failed to pass. In 1983, Hayakawa and Dr. John Tanton, a Michigan ophthalmologist, environmentalist, and population-control activist, co-founded an organization called U.S. English, the principal force of opposition to bilingual education, as an offshoot of the Federation for American Immigration Reform (FAIR), a Washington-based lobby group. It later outgrew its parent organization and claimed more than four hundred thousand members as of 1992. The goals of the group are to pass legislation at the national, state, and local levels to declare English our official language, to eliminate or reduce bilingual education, to abolish multilingual ballots, and to prevent translation of road signs and government documents into other languages. The growing use of the Spanish language by newcomers is a particular concern to U.S. English.

Thus far, U.S. English and its allies have succeeded in getting English designated as the official language, either constitutionally or by law, in twenty-three states. Especially, in 1986 California voters passed Proposition 63 by a three to one margin, declaring English the official language of the state. Between 1987 and 1988, similar proposals were considered by voters and lawmakers in many states. Eight were passed, including one in Arkansas while Bill Clinton was governor, but thirteen states rejected similar proposals.[6] The effects of these laws are more symbolic than substantive. Bilingual education programs have remained intact in states where official English language legislation has been enacted. For example, a large number of bilingual education programs continue to exist in California.

Currently, English-only legislation is in the process of formation at the national level. On August 1, 1996, the House of Representatives passed the English Language Empowerment Act, by a 259 to 169 margin. This bill declared English the official language of the United States. According to this bill, all government documents (including income tax forms and instruction booklets) must be printed in English; government officials cannot conduct business in foreign languages; states cannot use bilingual ballots in elections in areas with significant immigrant population; and the INS cannot conduct citizenship ceremonies in foreign languages. However, the bill made some exceptions. For instance, the bill permits the use of foreign languages in the census, international trade and diplomatic relations, national security, public health and safety, criminal pro-

---

6. In chronological order, the states that have declared English the official language of their states are: Nebraska (constitutional amendment 1920); Illinois (statute 1969); Virginia (statute 1981); Indiana, Kentucky, and Tennessee (statutes 1984); California and Georgia (constitutional amendment and ceremonial resolution 1986); Arkansas, Mississippi, North Carolina, North Dakota, and South Carolina (statutes 1987); Arizona, Colorado, and Florida (constitutional amendments 1988); Alabama (constitutional amendment 1990). In 1978, Hawaii adopted a constitutional amendment recognizing both English and native Hawaiian as official languages.

ceedings, language education (including bilingual education), and oral communications with the public by federal employees, officials, and congressmen. The Senate introduced a similar measure, but sidestepped the repeal of bilingual education and bilingual ballots. As of now, English-only legislation has not yet become the law of the nation.

Advocates of English-only legislation have made several arguments in its behalf. First, such legislation is imperative to preserve English as our common language and bond. Second, it will encourage people to speak English, to succeed economically, and to fully participate in our democratic society. Third, and more importantly, it will help maintain national unity. Former House speaker Newt Gingrich argued that dual languages can lead to internal strife and separation, as in Quebec, Canada. He asked immigrants "to become American. And part of becoming American involves English."

Opponents of English-only legislation have supplied several counterarguments. First, English-only legislation is unnecessary. Currently, 97 percent of all Americans already speak English, and more than 99 percent of all government documents are printed in English. Opinion polls found that most Latinos agreed that it is essential for them to learn English as quickly as possible. Hence, the bill cites a threat that does not exist. English is not endangered. What is endangered is native languages. Studies have found that first-generation immigrants continue to speak their native languages; the second generation is less likely to speak native languages; and by the third generation, native languages almost extinguished. Second, such legislation has negative effects. It will deprive Americans with limited English ability of their essential rights to vote and free speech, encourage cutbacks in services for non-English-speaking newcomers, reduce resources for programs such as bilingual education, and destroy cultural heritage. Finally, English-only legislation is divisive. It will stimulate xenophobia and anti-immigrant sentiment and create a racially divided nation.

The English-Plus Campaign

To counter the English-Only movement, the English-Plus campaign was launched in 1985 by the League of United Latin American Citizens and the Spanish American League against Discrimination. Their goals were to encourage the mastery of English *plus* a second or multiple languages and to promote multilingualism and multiculturalism. These goals were supported by many professional associations such as the National Association for Bilingual Education, the National Council of English Teachers, the Modern Language Association, and the Linguistic Society of America.

In late 1987, a coalition of ethnic, educational, and civil rights organizations established the English-Plus Information Clearinghouse (EPIC), the first national effort to counterattack the English-Only movement (Crawford 1991). It contended that English-Plus policy would promote equal opportunities, increase cross-cultural understanding, guarantee minority language rights, and enhance the nation's position in world trade and diplomacy. Bilingual education is an important way to achieve the goals of English Plus.

We need to encourage the use of English in instruction and daily life but not by law or by force; for the best interest of the nation we also need to encourage people to acquire other languages, if possible. English Plus seems to be more positive than English only.

SUMMARY

As a government policy attempting to counter discrimination and ensure equal opportunity, affirmative action originated in the 1960s from Executive Orders 10925 and 11246 and the Civil Rights Act of 1964. As it evolved, controversy ensued. The pros of affirmative action include the compensation argument, the diversity argument, the effectiveness argument, and the beneficial argument, while the cons consist of the reverse discrimination argument, the nonmeritocracy and lower quality argument, the ineffectiveness argument, and the counterproductive argument.

Proposition 209 was the first ballot measure in the nation seeking to scrap affirmative action policy. Following its passage by California voters in November 1996, there was a one-year legal battle over the legality of the proposition. The battle finally ended in the Supreme Court's rejection of an appeal from the American Liberties Union in November 1997, clearing the way for the full implementation of this proposition in California. However, at the national level, affirmative action policy is still in place.

Options for resolving the controversy of affirmative action include: (1) review existing affirmative action policy and programs to decide whether to end it or mend it; (2) replace race or gender-based affirmative action by class-based affirmative action; and (3) create diversity programs or use other diversity instruments to achieve the goal of diversity without resorting to preference based on race, ethnicity, and gender.

The economic, political, and social contexts in California in the early 1990s brought the issue of illegal immigration to the forefront of controversy, resulting in the passage of Proposition 187 and inducing repercussions across the nation. Opponents attack the proposition's ineffectiveness, unintended consequences, and racist nature while proponents defend its necessity, its benefits for money saving and the economy, and its nonracist essence. Except for a few measures concerning violation penalties, the major portions of Proposition 187 were invalidated by federal District Judge Mariana Pfaelzer. Its final kismet will likely have to be decided by the Supreme Court.

Contention surrounding illegal immigration spills over to legal immigration. The debate has centered on the effects of legal immigration on the economy, culture and society, and the environment. Despite many charges, available empirical evidence seems to suggest that the positive effects of immigration on the economy outstrip its negative ones. Although cultural and social problems do accompany immigration, none appears to endanger the vitality of this nation. The environmental effects of immigration are nothing more than a unproven hypothesis.

Bilingual education is not new, but as a national policy it began in 1968 and has evolved over time. Key bilingual education programs include transitional bilingual programs, English immersion, two-way bilingual education programs, and ESL programs. Bilingual education is a political issue as much as it is an educational one—maybe even more so. Both sides of the issue debate about its necessity, effectiveness, and larger societal impacts. However, empirical evidence has not proven that bilingual education programs are either inferior or superior to regular education programs, nor has it substantiated the superiority of specific bilingual approaches.

The debate over whether English should be the official language of the nation is an outgrowth of the bilingual education controversy. U.S. English, English First, and other pro-English-only groups have pushed official-English legislation through many states and the House of Representatives. English-Plus is the countermovement to English-Only, and it champions the acquisition of strong English language proficiency plus the mastery of other languages as well as multiculturalism.

CHAPTER 15
LOOKING INTO THE FUTURE

W hat is the gist of this book? What messages does it seek to convey? What will be the fate of ethnic studies in the foreseeable future? What needs to be done to advance the discipline of ethnic studies? This final chapter addresses these questions.

The present chapter first recaps the key points and main themes of the book.* It then focuses on the pivotal issues that will determine the future course of ethnic studies as a discipline, such as institutionalization of ethnic studies, academization versus politicization of ethnic studies, multiculturalism and ethnic studies, the study of whiteness and ethnic studies, and ethnic studies and national unity. I contend that for its survival and future advancement, ethnic studies should continue to secure and expand its institutional basis; pursue academization in order to increase its scholarly recognition while continuing to promote the interests of minority groups and ethnic equality; take the initiative in turning the so-called "multiculturalism threat" to its advantage; incorporate the study of whiteness in ethnic studies; and balance concerns about ethnic diversity and national unity. Each of the foregoing issues is elaborated.

SUMMARY OF THE BOOK

In the United States, ethnic studies as a discipline emerged in the late 1960s as a direct result of the student movement at college campuses in-

*A portion of this chapter was presented at the Silver Anniversary Conference of the National Association for Ethnic Studies in La Crosse, Wisconsin, March 1997.

spired by the Civil Rights movement, women's movement, and other social movements. After more than three decades of struggle, ethnic studies has become a considerably fledged discipline and taken deep roots in American universities and colleges. Ethnic studies seeks to understand ethnic groups (including both culturally defined and racially defined groups) and their interrelations with an emphasis on historically neglected groups such as Native Americans, African Americans, Latinos, and Asian Americans. As the discipline grows increasingly comparative, the study of white Americans has also entered the realm of ethnic studies teaching and research. Notwithstanding the continuous use of disciplinary methodologies, interdisciplinarity, multidisciplinarity, and comparativeness constitute the overarching methodologies of ethnic studies.

In studies of ethnic groups and their interrelations, a number of key issues tirelessly recur, and there are also very different approaches to those recurring issues. This book has critically highlighted those key issues and influential approaches and often suggested alternative and/or integrated perspectives. One of the basic issues in ethnic studies is the nature and basis of ethnicity—an affiliation or identification with an ethnic group. What is the nature of ethnicity, why does ethnicity emerge and persist, and what determines people's ethnic affiliation or identification? Three paradigms exist to answer these questions: primordialism, which stresses the ascription of ethnic group membership, immutable ethnic boundaries, and the biological determination of ethnicity; constructionism, which underscores the social construction of ethnicity, mutable ethnic boundaries, and the importance of social environment; and instrumentalism, which highlights the utility of ethnicity and the rational choice of group membership. My synthesized approach suggests integrating the useful elements of the existing paradigms.

Another fundamental issue in ethnic studies is ethnic stratification or institutionalized inequality among ethnic groups. Ethnic stratification is almost omnipresent in multiethnic human societies. The eradication of ethnic stratification must begin with an understanding of its origins. The social Darwinian approach, the social psychological approach, the functionalist approach, the conflict approach, and Donald Noel's theory are the existing approaches to the origins of ethnic stratification. While Noel's theory is by far the most comprehensive, it needs to be refined by taking class into consideration. At the very least, the origin of the black slavery system appears to be a good example to justify such a refinement of his theory.

The processes and outcomes of ethnic adaptation or interaction dwell at the heart of ethnic relations. Assimilation theory, melting-pot theory, cultural pluralism theory, the ethnogenesis perspective, the internal colonialism perspective, and the class approaches offer descriptions of the processes and outcomes and in some cases prescriptions to this pivotal issue as well. Equality, diversity, and unity ought to be recognized as the main principles for dealing with future ethnic relations in America.

Why do ethnic groups differ substantially in socioeconomic achievement? This is a critical question related to ethnic equality and ethnic adaptation. The biological argument, the cultural argument, the social class approach, and the immigrant argument are the major internal explanations for group variation in achievement that emphasize the qualities and characteristics of ethnic groups themselves. On the other hand, the discrimination argument, the economic restructuring perspective, and the contextual perspective form the key external explanations that stress the importance of external or structural factors beyond the control of ethnic groups. I have offered a preliminary integration of the foregoing theories.

Ethnic prejudice, ethnic discrimination, and racism are pervasive concepts and intertwined issues in ethnic studies. The development and perpetuation of ethnic prejudice are currently explained by biological theories, psychological theories, and sociological theories (e.g., social learning theory, and conflict theory). The integration of the sociological and psychological theories provides a better solution to this issue. Current explanations of ethnic discrimination include the prejudice hypothesis, functional/gain theory, class conflict theory, and social pressure theory. Interaction and reciprocity best characterize the relationship between ethnic prejudice and ethnic discrimination. The concept "racism" has been broadened over time. Today, although some scholars still prefer the narrow definition of racism as an ideology, American society tends to use a broad definition of racism which includes racist ideology, racial prejudice, racial discrimination, and institutional racism. Racism is reflected in American culture (e.g., the English language) and in American economic, political, legal, educational, and other social institutions. Racism adversely affects both ethnic minorities and white Americans in many spheres.

Ethnic segregation is still part of American life today. In particular, residential segregation, especially black-white segregation, remains pervasive. The group-preference explanation, the economic-status explanation, the housing-discrimination explanation, and the historical and structural explanation have been suggested to account for residential segregation. The best explanation can be found by combining these existing theories. Current scholarship recognizes both negative and positive effects of residential segregation. School segregation is still significant today. School segregation decreased starting in the 1950s. However, recent evidence indicates that since the 1980s public schools have been resegregated to some extent, both across schools and within schools.

Ethnic conflict is at the heart of ethnic studies. Ethnic conflict includes both hostile actions (nonviolent and violent) and hostile verbal, written, and symbolic expressions. Cultural-clash theory, human ecology theory, competition theory, the ethnic inequality argument, and class theory are the main explanations for why ethnic conflict takes place. I have outlined a structural approach as a more comprehensive explanation of ethnic conflict, both majority-minority and interminority conflicts.

How ethnicity influences the political process and outcome is of critical concern in ethnic studies. Ethnicity affects political party affiliation, political ideology, voting behavior, and political representation in government. Many factors together account for differential power among ethnic groups.

The interrelationship of race, class, and gender has been a focus of new research among feminist scholars and ethnic studies scholars in recent decades. Contrary to the traditional approach that separates race, class, and gender in analysis and sees the effects of the three as additive, the new structural approach pinpoints the interlocking nature of race, class, and gender and the interactive effects of the triplicity. The three dimensions interlock to affect gender roles, work experience, societal and family power, and sexuality, and intersect with social institutions.

This book also discusses several current controversial issues in ethnic studies that demand social action, including affirmative action and Proposition 209, illegal immigration and Proposition 187, the legal immigration debate, bilingual education and Proposition 227, and the English-Only movement.

A central theme running through the entire book is that rather than a divisive force, ethnic studies is, and should be, a discipline that enhances our understanding of ethnic groups and their interrelations and strengthens interethnic and national unity based on ethnic diversity. If directed properly, ethnic studies will help reunite America, redefine "American," and rebuild a more inclusive, multicultural American society. Another recurring theme calls for an integrated, multidimensional approach, rather than a simplistic, unidimensional one, to achieving complete understanding of any ethnic issue. Comparativeness, comprehensiveness, conciseness, and thematic organization are some of the important characteristics that distinguish this volume from other books in the field.

CONTINUING INSTITUTIONALIZATION OF ETHNIC STUDIES

Since its inception in the late 1960s, ethnic studies has blossomed into a full-fledged academic discipline in higher education in the United States. Institutionalization has become a salient feature of the discipline.

In the late 1960s, the number of ethnic studies programs, centers, and departments was easily countable. Prominent among those few were the Ethnic Studies Department at UC Berkeley, and the School of Ethnic Studies at then San Francisco State College (now San Francisco State University). The next decade saw a marked expansion of ethnic studies programs. An inexhaustive survey conducted in academic year 1977–1978 by David Washburn (1979) identified 526 ethnic studies programs. After redesign, reorganization, and restructuring in the late 1970s and the 1980s, ethnic studies has gained further institutional ground in higher education. An earlier study by the National Association for Ethnic Studies counted more than eight hundred ethnic studies programs and departments in U.S. colleges and universities, including about six hundred ethnic-specific programs or departments (Bataille, Carranza, and Lisa 1996, xiii). Bataille, Carranza, and Lisa's research (1996) recorded almost seven hundred ethnic studies programs or departments with an emphasis on minority groups. They included 587 ethnic-specific programs or departments (including 359 programs on African Americans, 41 on Asian Americans, 127 on Chicano/Latinos, and 144 on Native Americans). There were also ninety-four multiethnic studies programs or departments, and six ethnic studies programs within traditional departments. If programs on European Americans are counted, the total number of ethnic studies programs or departments could be well above eight hundred. Many more are emerging, in response to student protests and demands.

Significant progress notwithstanding, success of ethnic studies programs in securing departmental status is still limited. Bataille, Carranza, and Lisa (1996) registered only 112 ethnic studies departments, among which twenty-five were comprehensive or multiethnic studies departments. Black studies or African American studies is by far the most successful in this regard. Forty-five black studies programs have become autonomous, degree-granting departments while only twenty-six Chicano/Latino studies programs, eleven Native American studies programs, and five Asian American studies programs have achieved such a measurable success.

Departmental status to a great extent ensures the survival and success of an ethnic studies program due to the structural and organizational position of departments in the business of colleges and universities. Resources are allotted by department; faculty are hired, retained, and promoted according to departmental criteria; the curriculum is primarily determined by department; courses are listed by department; and degrees are granted largely following requirements set up by department. Thus, to exist as a department puts ethnic studies on a par with other departments of traditional disciplines. On the other hand, a program has to rely on established departments for faculty, courses, and other resources. As a result, courses may not be offered due to an unfilled vacancy in a department; curriculum articulation can hardly be achieved; joint-appointment faculty have to fulfill their departmental responsibilities and ethnic studies program obligations; faculty in a program may be evaluated by criteria other than those of ethnic studies, increasing the difficulty of gaining tenure, and therefore competent faculty may opt for employment elsewhere in order to ensure job security.

Given all the advantages of a department over a program, ethnic studies programs should be encouraged to secure departmental status, if possible. Lessons and experiences of those programs successfully gaining departmental status should be examined and disseminated to programs that are seeking departmental status or may do so in the near future.

Another dimension of institutionalization concerns the further expansion of ethnic studies programs to campuses without such a program. So far, more than three-quarters of the 3,688 U.S. colleges and universities still have no ethnic studies programs. Although ethnic studies emerged at about the same time as women's studies and may claim parity with women's studies in terms of the number of programs, women's studies may have gained the upper hand. The majority of universities and colleges currently offer courses in women's studies (Chamberlain 1994). Feminist scholars are present in most schools, departments, and administrations, and their leverage has given women's studies programs a strong position in gaining status and resources (Hu-DeHart 1995). Compared to women's studies, ethnic studies needs a stronger voice in campus administration.

Changing demographics provide a vital source of continuing institutionalization for ethnic studies (Bataille, Carranza, and Lisa 1996). U.S. population is currently about 73 percent white, 12 percent black, 10.6 percent Latino, 3.6 percent Asian, and 0.8 percent Native American. According to the Census Bureau's projection, in the year 2050, U.S. population will be 52.8 percent white, 24.5 percent Latino, 13.6 percent black, 8.2 percent Asian, and 0.9 percent Indian. The shifting demographic composition means a more diverse student population on college campuses, which in turn increases the demand for ethnic studies programs as witnessed on some campuses in recent years. For example, student demands for an Asian American studies program at UC Irvine and for a Chicano program at UCLA are cases in point. Ethnic studies should capture this historical moment to expand its dominion and to universalize ethnic studies on college campuses.

Third, procurement of general education status for core ethnic studies courses and codification of ethnic studies courses into college graduation requirements can increase the audience for ethnic studies courses and solidify their status in higher education. Substantial and increasing demand for ethnic studies courses in turn sustains and augments demand for faculty and may lead to the growth of ethnic studies programs. Offering more general and ethnic-comparative courses rather than just ethnic-specific courses can also increase demand for ethnic studies courses.

Finally, successful institutionalization of an ethnic studies program requires strong leadership, especially in its founding stage. A strong department/program chair substantially increases the bargaining leverage of the program in terms of program status, resource allocation, and faculty stability. Familiarity with the administrative process is also essential in successful institutionalization. Strong leaders can be tapped within the discipline of ethnic studies or in traditional disciplines with a research orientation in ethnic studies.

ACADEMIZATION VERSUS POLITICIZATION OF ETHNIC STUDIES

Ethnic studies must weigh academization against politicization. The issue of academization is particularly pivotal and difficult because, unlike traditional disciplines, ethnic studies as a discipline grew out of student activism in the 1960s. To be sure, the mission of ethnic studies and the process of establishing and sustaining an ethnic studies program are political. Ethnic studies is a voice for progressive social change, humane treatment of ethnic groups, and improved intergroup relations. Each step forward entails hard-fought political battles. However, the discipline and the curriculum of ethnic studies should not be politicized. As a discipline, ethnic studies is a systematic study of ethnicity, ethnic groups, and intergroup relations using interdisciplinary, multidisciplinary, and comparative methodologies. It is by no means synonymous with political activism. Meanwhile, the ethnic studies curriculum should strive for scientificity and relative objectivity.

The academization of the discipline and curriculum of ethnic studies is important for several reasons.

1. Survival and advancement of the discipline. Although the past two to three decades have witnessed immense growth in ethnic studies in the United States, and its essential place in the academy has been widely endorsed, the scholarly merits of ethnic studies have largely been ignored (Hu-DeHart 1993). Without academization, ethnic studies will not be able to escape from its marginalized position and move into the academic mainstream. Without scholarship and intellectual rigor, ethnic studies programs will be doomed to elimination.

2. Changed social milieu. In the 1960s and early 1970s, political values were the litmus test for entry into the field; scholarly accomplishment meant little. Today, political rhetoric is no longer sufficient, and can actually breed distaste, enmity, and strife. Ethnic studies entails rigorous scholarship and intellectual credibility.

3. Shifting student composition of ethnic studies courses. While minority students still fill the majority seats of group-oriented courses, the composition of introductory, group-comparative, and thematic ethnic studies courses has changed drastically as ethnic studies courses have become included in general education and graduation requirements. These classes are either racially mixed or dominated by whites. Politicizing the ethnic studies curriculum could cause aversion, resentment, resistance, and antago-

nism among different groups of students. In fact, some white students who are required to take ethnic studies courses do have a mentality of resistance. The ethnic studies curriculum is not just a curriculum for minority students. Minorities are not the only ones ethnic studies needs to reach. It is important for everyone to be exposed to different cultures. One main purpose of the ethnic studies curriculum is to help students, especially *white* students, to understand the reality of ethnic stratification, to cherish the principle of ethnic equality, and to make ethnic equity a reality in the future. It is critical to present a plurality of perspectives, scientific empirical evidence, and the pros *and* cons of controversial issues in order to help students reach a consensus on these issues and nurture better interethnic group relations.

The academization of the ethnic studies discipline and curriculum is not only indispensable, but it is also attainable today. Calls for academization in the 1960s and 1970s would not have been realistic because of the paucity of expertise and scholarship in the field. The remarkable growth of the literature in the field during the 1980s and the 1990s has made the academization of the discipline viable.

The academization of ethnic studies invites endeavors in several areas. One such area is the continuing production of scholarship through scholarly books, academic journals, creative writings, etc. In addition to the in-depth analysis of particular ethnic groups, scholarship should be invited to focus on the construction of new theoretical approaches, the development of novel methodologies, and the comparative and integrative analysis of different ethnic groups and their experiences.

Textbooks constitute another area of undertaking. Textbooks play an important role in popularizing the discipline and increasing its acceptance by the larger society. Efforts are especially encouraged to develop texts that highlight important issues and approaches in the field, that engage in comparative analyses of different ethnic groups, and that utilize innovative perspectives and methodologies to portray group experience.

Another task is to depoliticize the ethnic studies curriculum. The infusion of an ethnically biased or self-serving political agenda into ethnic studies courses should be avoided. Setting a scientific and objective tone will help.

The academization of ethnic studies does not necessarily contradict the promotion of minorities' interests. Academization calls for further research on minorities and their communities. Via scientific study of the traditionally disadvantaged, ethnic studies scholars can better fathom their status, pinpoint their problems, needs, and solutions, and speak on their behalf.

MULTICULTURALISM AND ETHNIC STUDIES

A burgeoning literature on multiculturalism has emerged in the United States in the past two to three decades. Today, the popularity of the metaphor "multiculturalism" seems to overshadow those of "assimilation" and "melting pot." However, understanding and interpretation of multiculturalism vary greatly across disciplines. In the sociology of race and ethnic relations, multiculturalism is normally viewed as a synonym for or variant of cultural pluralism, which refers to cultural diversity or the co-existence of various cultures and ethnic/racial groups within the same national framework (see, for example, Farley 1995; Feagin and Feagin 1993). The multiculturalist approach stresses the importance of respecting different racial and ethnic groups and cultures and their collective contributions to the making of American culture. In history, multiculturalism is seen as an approach to understanding American culture via the study of all contributing cultures and their interactions (Levine 1996, 160). In education, multiculturalism often means the inclusion in the cirrculum of materials and perspectives that reflect diversity based on race, ethnicity, gender, class, religion, language, age, disability, and sexual orientation. Similar meanings of multiculturalism apply to the arenas of public life and public policy (La Belle and Ward 1994). Variation in scope notwithstanding, multiculturalism is a social movement toward openness and diversity.

A genuine drive toward multiculturalism in American universities and colleges has been evident since the 1980s. As multiculturalism expands its domain into the college curriculum and becomes an accepted curriculum-organizing principle, some concerns have been raised as to whether multiculturalism threatens the existence of ethnic studies.

According to the literature, multiculturalism imperils the existence of ethnic studies in at least two ways. First, multiculturalism could co-opt or ingest ethnic studies (Hu-DeHart 1993; La Belle and Ward 1994). Since traditional disciplines of social sciences and humanities and their departments increasingly recruit ethnically diverse faculty, integrate multicultural perspectives in their curricula, and/or offer multicultural courses themselves, ethnic studies will lose its necessity and vitality. In other words, the prevalence of multicultural education efforts in traditional disciplines could endanger the justification of autonomous ethnic studies programs. Second, in research universities the establishment of broad ethnic studies course requirements vies for the limited resources of ethnic studies programs, so that these programs will become teaching service stations for their campuses (Magner 1991).

In my opinion, the multiculturalism menace is exaggerated, for several reasons. First, the duplication of ethnic studies courses by traditional departments is limited and can be averted or mitigated through interdepartmental coordination and university orchestration if it occurs. Second, disciplinary approaches cannot substitute for the inter- and multidisciplinary and comparative approaches of ethnic studies. Third, although the creation of broad ethnic studies requirements may dilute the resources of ethnic studies programs in major research universities such as UC Berkeley, it is normally not a problem in teaching universities where expansion of ethnic studies course offerings into general education is desirable. However, the multiculturalism threat should alarm ethnic studies scholars to take preventive actions against this peril. Several measures may be considered by ethnic studies programs:

1. Strengthen ethnic studies programs by sharpening the uniqueness and advantages of the ethnic studies curriculum and making it irreplaceable.

2. Take an active leading role in coordinating the campus multicultural curriculum.

3. Prevent or lessen competition for resources and prioritize important areas of development.

4. Expand single-group-oriented ethnic studies into *multiethnic* studies by emphasizing the comparative approach.

By making assorted and precautionary efforts, the multiculturalism threat can become an impetus and advantage for the advancement of ethnic studies. The prevalence of multiculturalism per se is partly an outcome of ethnic studies, and it could, in turn, strengthen ethnic studies programs if steered properly. Ethnic studies and multiculturalism are in essence complementary rather than competitive. Multiculturalism is an ally of ethnic studies more than its rival.

THE STUDY OF WHITENESS AND ETHNIC STUDIES

Another critical issue that could have great potential impact on the future of ethnic studies is whether to incorporate whiteness in ethnic studies. The study of whiteness is a growing field of scholarship that examines whiteness as a social construct, as a system of power and privilege, as a group, as an identity, and as a social movement. Although the concept of whiteness is not new, this field has expanded rapidly over the last ten years or so partly as a result of suggestions by intellectuals, such as Nobel laureate Toni Morrison, who have long suggested that race studies must include a critical, self-reflexive body of work about whites. This antiracist and progressive body of scholarship gains momentum in the context of, and frequently in direct response to, a critique of racism and racial domination. A very diverse range of disciplines is represented by scholars of whiteness, including sociologists, historians, anthropologists, as well as specialists in ethnic, legal, cultural, and literary studies. They bring multidisciplinary and interdisciplinary methodologies and critical concerns to the study of whiteness. In addition, many antiracist activists have addressed issues regarding whiteness while involved in community organizing, coalition building, and other occasions.

There are risks attached to engaging in the discourse of whiteness. For one thing, intellectual work on whiteness may be construed as an affirmation of white privilege and domination (Chabram-Dernersesian 1997). For another, the study of whiteness may contribute to re-centering, rather than de-centering, it, as well as the reification of whiteness as a fixed category of experience and identity (Fine, Weis, Powell, and Wong 1997; Frankenberg 1997). Moreover, the invention of so-called "white studies" could eclipse important work done on "people of color," displace the study of traditionally neglected minority groups, and divert research funds to the new intellectual fetish (Fine, Weis, Powell, and Wong 1997). In addition, white writers may revel in a narrative of guilt, accusation, or denial, and therefore dispense with the real work of racial justice and antiracism pedagogy (Fine, Weis, Powell, and Wong 1997).

Nevertheless, scholars of whiteness argue that it is necessary to study whiteness for several reasons: First, while the voices of those historically excluded and marginalized have been heard and centered for the past three decades, little scholarly attention has been devoted to inquiry into whiteness; the asymmetric literature on whiteness and nonwhiteness hinders the comparative analysis of experiences and identities between minorities and whites. Second, the examination of whiteness enhances our understanding of racial formation (Frankenberg 1997). Like other racial identities, white is also a socially constructed identity. The meaning and boundaries of white are defined by society, especially the dominant group, and have evolved over time. For instance, Germans, Irish, Italians, and Jews were at one point or another excluded from white and later became part of white. Through comparative analysis of the construction of whiteness and other racial identities, we can better understand how whiteness is made and how it can be unmade. Third, the analysis of whiteness offers a ground for understanding racial positioning, racial domination, racism, and the role that whiteness plays in the perpetuation of ethnic inequality. Last, the study of whiteness also furthers our cognizance of white selves and how white identity affects both white people and people of color. In short, for comparative purposes, analysis of racial formation, critical studies of white domination, and self-reflection by whites, the study of whiteness has a place in the scholarship.

Recent work on whiteness has covered a range of issues. One main area focuses on the social construction of whiteness. Arguably, the best articulated work on the making of whiteness can be found in economic and social history. This body of scholarship includes, among others, the works of Reginald Horsman (1981), Alexander Saxton (1990), David Roediger (1991, 1994), Theodore Allen (1994), Tomas Almaguer (1994), and Noel Ignatiev (1995). It lays out the prominence of whiteness in the formation of race, class, and nation in the United States and Europe; it shows how whiteness was a cause and an outcome of the larger social and political processes; and it adds to the existing work on racism and the histories of colonized/racialized subjects. This body of scholarship also contains works on the legal construction of whiteness (Lopez 1996), the literary construction of whiteness (Aanerud 1997; Morrison 1992), and the construction of whiteness in daily experience (Frankenberg 1993).

Another major area of work, directed toward literature, films, and children's stories, examines how whiteness contributes to white privilege and white dominance, how white dominance is rationalized and legitimized, and how whiteness is associated with racism. Important works include Kimberle Crenshaw's (1988) analysis of how white race consciousness legitimizes racial coercion and racial hierarchy; Richard Dyer's discussion of whiteness in motion pictures, which portray whiteness as the norm and as an embodiment of such favorable attributes as power and safety; Harold Isaacs's (1963) classic depiction of blackness and whiteness as opposites;

David Milner's (1983) review of racism in children's literature that devalues dark people and celebrates light ones.

Other areas of whiteness studies include whites' self-perceptions and nonwhites' perceptions of whites; whiteness and Americanness/national identity; the White Power movement; and the intersection of whiteness, class, and gender. These areas of analysis should not be viewed as completely separated. In fact, they overlap thematically to no small extent.

Turning a blind eye to the existence of whiteness studies is ostrichism. The exclusion of the analysis of whiteness would not aid the cause of ethnic studies. A better strategy would be to incorporate the study of whiteness in ethnic studies. The incorporation of whiteness studies could have significant effects on the development of ethnic studies. First, the inclusion of whiteness studies as a focus of analysis would shift the emphasis of ethnic studies from the study of minority groups to a comprehensive and comparative analysis of all ethnic groups. This move would be consonant with the direction of ethnic studies toward comparativeness and academization.

Second, the study of whiteness would affect the ethnic studies curriculum. It would mean the addition and modification of ethnic studies courses that reflect this area of scholarship, and would also mean more comparative courses.

Third, the incorporation of whiteness studies might increase the acceptance of ethnic studies courses and boost ethnic studies programs. For instance, at UC Berkeley, the inclusion of comparative analysis of European Americans with other minority groups in the curriculum resulted in the passage of the American Culture Requirement for all undergraduate students. The development of a more inclusive ethnic studies discipline, together with the changing demographics of U.S. population and university campuses, could expand the territory of ethnic studies programs at American universities and colleges.

Finally and perhaps most controversially, the incorporation of whiteness studies could change the faculty composition of ethnic studies programs in the near future. The inclusion of whiteness in ethnic studies could give the green light to the entry of white scholars into ethnic studies programs, especially multiethnic studies programs. Currently, almost no ethnic studies program will hire a white scholar because of the emphasis on minority groups. The incorporation of whiteness and the move toward comparativeness could bring about a breakthrough in this arena. In fact, we have already seen some signals of change in one of the oldest ethnic studies departments in the nation. The inclusion of progressive white scholars in ethnic studies programs could strengthen them and might well change the image of ethnic studies programs from primarily minority programs to more inclusive ones.

Whether these potential changes are positive or negative depends on one's perspective, but there seem to be both opportunities and challenges.

ETHNIC STUDIES AND NATIONAL UNITY

Ethnic studies is often mistaken for ethnic particularism and even separatism. This misconception must be rectified. It is true that ethnic studies applauds ethnic diversity, but it is not true that ethnic studies has no concern for or even undermines national unity. In actuality, ethnic studies seeks to achieve solid national unity in diversity.

Before the 1960s, American society emphasized *unum* over *pluribus*, or the assimilation of all ethnic groups into the dominant White Anglo-Saxon Protestant culture—a homogenization process. Immigrant or ethnic groups were pressed to cast off their ethnic cultures and to become assimilated into the dominant culture. However, this kind of Anglo conformity has proven countereffective because of its implied cultural chauvinism. The Civil Rights movement and other social movements altered the societal emphasis toward a diversity of cultures, beginning a differentiation process. Today, diversity and cultural pluralism have become the new gospel of most Americans.

While the differentiation process is absolutely imperative, national unity should not be set aside. The republic, built on the canons of liberty, equality, and justice for all, must be held together. The nation and the system permit the celebration of ethnic diversity and therefore it must be given an honorable place.

However, national unity must not be grounded on the cultural superiority of one particular ethnic group over another. Unity must not be founded on ignorance of other groups. Peaceful coexistence and harmony of diverse ethnic groups must be based on equality and justice. Ethnic studies helps forge mutual understanding and respect for different ethnic groups. We can better understand the meaning of being American by learning about the experiences of other groups. Ethnic studies infuses and nurtures the notion of ethnic equality and justice. Through assorted channels, ethnic studies lays a solid foundation for a bona fide, sustainable national unity. Rejection and repression of cultural diversity breed hostility, not unity.

To be sure, ethnic studies does not champion separatism but calls for self-consciousness; it does not seek division but searches for accurate and mutual appreciation. Fragmentation of American society by race and ethnicity has always existed. However, to blame ethnic studies as the culprit for this fragmentation is to mistake effect for cause. The real causes of this fragmentation lie in ethnic inequity and inequality as reflected in the conquest of Indians, the slavery of blacks, the annexation of Mexican territories, the Chinese Exclusion and Asiatic barring, Japanese internment, and contemporary discrimination. Ethnic studies is not a force of fragmentation, Balkanization, and tribalization but a force that forges an eternal, unshakable national unity based on knowledge of and respect for diverse ethnic cultures. Ethnic studies seeks to "reunite America" on the basis of equality and equity and to redefine American identity (Takaki 1997). Ethnic studies prepares students for a common citizenship through understanding and appreciating cultures of different groups. Ethnic studies acclaims "out of many, one." Through ethnic studies research and teaching, we can be many and one at the same time.

Ethnicity is powerful. By itself, ethnicity does not create or destroy a nation. How to exercise it does construct or destruct our lives. False homogenization might destroy us, as would the misuse of a pluralistic system. The outcome will depend on how we nurture and enliven the strengths of our system. The challenge facing America in the next millennium is to shape a genuine common American culture that reflects both the traditional dominant culture and the long-silenced cultures of color. Each ethnic culture infuses blood to the common culture and contributes an ingredient to the American cauldron. In the effort to accomplish this goal, ethnic studies surely occupies a special place.

In sum, to broaden the societal basis of ethnic studies, we need to fine tune our direction. Ethnic studies needs to balance concerns about ethnic diversity and national unity. We must cherish diversity; we must maintain national unity; and we must build national unity in diversity.

FINAL REMARKS

Ethnic studies is a young and emerging discipline in America. Notwithstanding the giant strides made in three decades, many challenges still lie ahead. Ethnic studies stands at the crossroads. The next ten to twenty years may be crucial for the survival and advancement of the discipline. Ethnic studies ought to strengthen itself institutionally and academically, to fend off any attempts to co-opt or undermine the discipline, to extend its reach to most universities and colleges, to shift toward inclusiveness and comparativeness, and to gain wider societal support by celebrating ethnic diversity and preserving national unity. Ethnic studies will have a distinctive role to play in reuniting America, redefining "American," and rebuilding a more inclusive, multicultural American society.

REFERENCES

Aanerud, Rebecca. 1997. Fictions of Whiteness: Speaking the Names of Whiteness in U.S. Literature. In *Displacing Whiteness*, edited by Ruth Frankenberg. Durham, N.C. and London: Duke University Press.

Abelmann, Nancy, and John Lie. 1995. *Blue Dreams: Korean Americans and the Los Angeles Riots*. Cambridge: Harvard University Press.

Aboud, F. 1988. *Children and Prejudice*. New York: Basil Blackwell.

Acker, Joan. 1992. Gendered Institutions: From Sex Roles to Gendered Institutions. *Contemporary Sociology* 21: 565–69.

Adorno, Theodore et al. 1950. *The Authoritarian Personality*. New York: Harper and Row.

Aguirre International. 1991. Final Report: Longitudinal Study of Structural English Immersion Strategy, Early-Exit and Late-Exit Transitional Bilingual Education Programs for Language Minority Children. U.S. Department of Education. San Mateo, Calif: Aguirre International.

Alba, Richard. 1990. *Ethnic Identity: The Transformation of White America*. New Haven: Yale University Press.

Allen, Theodore. 1994. *The Invention of the White Race, Vol. 1: Racial Oppression and Social Control*. London: Verso.

Allport, Gordon. 1954. *The Nature of Prejudice*. Reading, Mass: Addison-Wesley.

Almaguer, Tomas. 1994. *Racial Faultlines: The Historical Origins of White Supremacy in California*. Berkeley: University of California Press.

Alvarez, Rodolfo. 1973. The Psycho-Historical and Socioeconomic Development of the Chicano Community in the United States. *Social Science Quarterly* 53:920–42.

Ambert, Alba, and Sarah Melendez. 1985. *Bilingual Education: A Sourcebook*. New York: Garland Publishing.

Amsterdam, Anthony. 1988. Race and the Death Penalty. *Criminal Justice Ethics* 7(1): 2, 84–86.

Andersen, Margaret, and Patricia Collins. 1995. *Race, Class, and Gender: An Anthology*, 2nd Ed. Belmont, Calif: Wadsworth Publishing.

AsianWeek. 1996. Asian Americans on the Issues: The Results of a National Survey of Asian American Voters, 23 August.

August, D., and E. E. Garcia. 1988. *Language Minority Education in the United States: Research, Policy, and Practice.* Springfield, Ill: Charles Thomas.

Austin, John L. 1962. *How to Do Things with Words.* Cambridge: Harvard University Press.

Ayres, I., and J. Waldfogel. 1994. A Market Test for Race Discrimination in Bail Setting. *Stanford Law Review* 46: 987–1048.

Babbie, Earl. 1995. *The Practice of Social Research*, 7th Ed. Belmont, Calif: Wadsworth Publishing.

Bailey, Kenneth. 1994. *Methods of Social Research*, 4th Ed. New York: The Free Press.

Bakalian, Anny. 1993. *Armenian-Americans: From Being to Feeling Armenian.* New Brunswick, N.J.: Transaction.

Baldwin, James. 1963. *The Fire Next Time.* New York: Dell.

Banton, Michael. 1983. *Racial and Ethnic Competition.* Cambridge, England: Cambridge University Press.

Barth, Frederick. 1956. Ecological Relationships of Ethnic Groups in Swat, North Pakistan. *American Anthropologist* 58: 1079–89.

———. 1969. *Ethnic Groups and Boundaries.* Boston: Little, Brown.

Bataille, Gretchen, Miguel Carranza, and Laurie Lisa. 1996. *Ethnic Studies in the United States: A Guide to Research.* New York and London: Garland Publishing.

Beck, Roy. 1996. *The Case against Immigration.* New York: W.W. Norton & Company.

Becker, Gary. 1957. *The Economics of Discrimination.* Chicago: University of Chicago Press.

Bell, Daniel. 1975. Ethnicity and Social Change. In *Ethnicity: Theory and Experience*, edited by Nathan Glazer and Daniel Moynihan, 141–74. Cambridge: Harvard University Press.

Berry, Wendell. 1970. *The Hidden Wound.* Boston: Houghton-Mifflin.

Bikel, Ofra. 1992. *Frontline.* PBS October 14.

Bing, Stephen, and S. Rosenfeld. 1970. *The Quality of Justice in the Lower Criminal Courts of Metropolitan Boston.* Mass.: Committee on Law Enforcement and Adminstration of Criminal Justice.

Blauner, Bob. 1994. Talking Past Each Other: Black and White Language of Race. In *Race and Ethnic Conflict: Contending Views on Prejudice, Discrimination, and Ethnoviolence*, edited by Fred Pincus and Howard Ehrlich. Boulder, Colo.: Westview Press.

Blauner, Robert. 1972. *Racial Oppression in America.* New York: Harper and Row.

Bogardus, Emory. 1933. A Social Distance Scale. *Sociology and Social Research* 22: 265–71.

Bohland, J. R. 1982. Indian Residential Segregation in the Urban Southwest, 1970 and 1980. *Social Science Quarterly* 63(4): 749–61.

Bohm, R. M., ed. 1994. *The Death Penalty in America: Current Research*. Cincinnati, Ohio: Anderson.

Bonacich, Edna. 1972. A Theory of Ethnic Antagonism: The Split Labor Market. *American Sociological Review* 37: 547–59.

Bouvier, Leon. 1992. *Peaceful Invasions: Immigration and Changing America*. Lanham, Md.: University Press of America.

Bowser, Benjamin, and Raymond Hunt. 1981. *Impacts of Racism on White Americans*. Beverly Hills, Calif.: Sage Publications.

———. 1996. *Impacts of Racism on White Americans*, 2nd Ed. Thousand Oaks, Calif.: Sage Publications.

Breton, Raymond. 1989. Canadian Ethnicity in the Year 2000. In *Multiculturalism and Intergroup Relations*, edited by James Frideres, 149–52. New York: Greenwood.

Brewer, Rose. 1993. Theorizing Race, Class, and Gender: The New Scholarship of Black Feminist Intellectuals and Black Women's Labor. In *Theorizing Black Feminisms: The Visionary Paradigm of Black Women*, edited by Stanlie James and Abena Busia. London and New York: Routledge.

Brimelow, Peter. 1996. *Alien Nation: Common Sense about America's Immigration Disaster*. New York: HarperPerennial.

Buchanan, Patrick. 1993. America Needs a "Time Out" on Immigration. *Conservative Chronicle*, 6 June.

Bullard, Robert. 1994. *Dumping in Dixie: Race, Class, and Environmental Quality*, 2nd Ed. Boulder, Colo.: Westview Press.

Bureau of Indian Affairs. 1987. *Indian Service Population and Labor Estimates*. Washington D.C.: Bureau of Indian Affairs.

Bureau of National Affairs. 1964. *The Civil Rights Act of 1964*. Washington D.C.: Bureau of National Affairs.

Burgest, David. 1973. The Racist Use of the English Language. *Black Scholar*, September.

Butler, Johnnella E. 1991. Ethnic Studies: A Matrix Model for the Major. *Liberal Education* 77: 26–32.

Cain, Bruce. 1988. Anti–Asian Electoral Power: Imminent or Illusory? *Election Politics* 9: 27–30.

Cain, Bruce, and Roderick Kiewiet. 1986. California's Coming Minority Majority. *Public Opinion* 9: 50–52.

Cain, Bruce, Roderick Kiewiet, and Carole Uhlander. 1991. The Acquisition of Partisanship by Latinos and Asian Americans. *American Journal of Political Science*: 35: 390–442.

Canner, Glenn, and Dolores Smith. 1991. Home Mortgage Disclosure Act: Expanded Data on Residential Lending. *Federal Reserve Bulletin* 77: 859–81.

————. 1992. Expanded HMDA Data on Residential Lending: One Year Later. *Federal Reserve Bulletin* 78: 801–24.

————. 1994. Residential Lending to Low-Income and Minority Families: Evidence from the 1992 HMDA Data. *Federal Reserve Bulletin* 80:79–108.

Caudill, W., and G. DeVos. 1956. Achievement, Culture, and Personality. *American Anthropologist* 58: 1102–26.

Chabram-Dernersesian, Angie. 1997. On the Social Construction of Whiteness within Selected Chicana/o Discourse. In *Displacing Whiteness*, edited by Ruth Frankenberg. Durham, N.C. and London: Duke University Press.

Chamberlain, Mariam. 1994. Multicultural Women's Studies in the United States. *Women's Studies Quarterly* 3&4: 215–25.

Chan, Sucheng. 1990. *Asian Americans: An Interpretive History*. New York: Twayne Publishers.

Cheng, Lucie, and Philip Q. Yang. 1996. Asians: The "Model Minority" Deconstructed. In *Ethnic Los Angeles*, edited by Roger Waldinger and Medhi Bozorgmehr. New York: Russell Sage Foundation.

Chow, Esther, Doris Wilkinson, and Maxine Baca Zinn. 1996. *Race, Class, and Gender: Bonds, Different Voices*. Thousand Oaks, Calif.: Sage Publications.

Chun, Ki–Taek. 1993. The Myth of Asian American Success and Its Educational Ramifications. In *American Mosaic*, edited by Young Song and Eugene Kim. Englewood Cliffs, N.J.: Prentice-Hall.

Clark, William. 1986. Residential Segregation in American Cities: A Review and Interpretation. *Population Research and Policy Review* 5: 95–127.

————. 1991. Residential Preferences and Neighborhood Racial Segregation: A Test of the Schelling Segregation Model. *Demography* 28: 1–19.

————. 1992. Residential Preferences and Residential Choices in a Multiethnic Context. *Demography* 29(3): 451–66.

Cohen, Abner. 1969. *Customs and Politics in Urban Africa*. Berkeley and Los Angeles: University of California Press.

Cole, David. 1994. The New Know-Nothingism: Five Myths about Immigration. *The Nation*, 17 October.

Collins, Patricia. 1990. *Black Feminist Thought: Knowledge, Consciousness, and the Politics of Empowerment*. New York: Routledge.

Cox, Olive. 1948. *Caste, Class, and Race*. Garden City, N.Y.: Doubleday.

Crawford, James. 1991. *Bilingual Education: History, Politics, Theory, and Practice*, 2nd, Updated Ed. Los Angeles: Bilingual Education Services.

Crenshaw, Kimberle. 1988. Race, Reform, and Retrenchment. *Harvard Law Review* 101(7): 1331–87.

————. 1989. Demarginalizing the Intersection of Race and Sex: A Black Feminine Critique of Antidiscrimination Doctrine, Feminist Theory, and Antiracist Politics. In *University of Chicago Legal Forum: Feminism in the Law: Theory, Practice, and Criticism*. Chicago: University of Chicago Press.

Cross, H. G., J. Mell, and W. Zimmerman. 1990. *Employer Hiring Practices: Differential Treatment of Hispanic and Anglo Job Seekers.* Washington, D.C.: Urban Institute.

Cummings, Scott. 1980. White Ethnics, Racial Prejudice, and Labor Market Segregation. *American Journal of Sociology* 85: 938–50.

Darden, J. T. 1987. Choosing Neighbors and Neighborhoods: The Role of Race in Housing Preference. In *Divided Neighborhoods*, edited by G. A. Tobin. Newbury Park, Calif.: Sage Publications.

Davis, Angela. 1981. *Women, Race, and Class.* New York: Random House.

Dedman, B. 1988. The Color of Money. *The Atlanta Journal and Constitution* 1 May: 4.

DeFleur, Melvin, and Frank Westie. 1958. Verbal Attitudes and Overt Acts. *American Sociological Review* 23: 667–73.

DeMarco, D. L., and G. C. Galster. 1993. Preintegrative Policy: Theory and Practice. *Journal of Urban Affairs* 15(2): 141–60.

Denton, Nancy, and Douglass Massey. 1988. Residential Segregation of Blacks, Hispanics, and Asians by Socioeconomic Status and Generation. *Social Science Quarterly* 69: 797–818.

Dill, Bonnie T. 1979. The Dialectics of Black Womanhood. *Signs: Journal of Women in Culture and Society* 4: 543–55.

Doherty, Steven. 1994. Native American Voting Behavior. Paper presented at the Midwest Political Science Association Annual Meeting, Chicago.

Dollard, John. 1937. *Caste and Class in a Southern Town.* New Haven: Yale University Press.

———. 1938. Hostility and Fear in Social Life. *Social Forces* 17: 15–26.

Dollard, John et al. 1939. *Frustration and Aggression.* New Haven: Yale University Press.

Dowdall, George. 1976. White Gains from Black Subordination in 1960 and 1970. *Social Problems* 22: 162–83.

DuBois, W. E. B. 1899. *The Philadelphia Negro.* Philadelphia: University of Pennsylvania Press.

Dugger, Karen. 1996. Social Location and Gender-Role Attitudes: A Comparison of Black and White Women. In *Race, Class, and Gender: Common Bonds, Different Voices*, edited by Esther Chow, Doris Wilkinson, and Maxine Baca Zinn. Thousand Oaks, Calif.: Sage Publications.

During, Simon, ed. 1993. Introduction to *The Cultural Studies Reader.* New York: Routledge.

Ehrlich, Howard. 1990. *Campus Ethnoviolence and the Policy Options.* National Institute Against Prejudice and Violence, Institute Report No. 4.

Ekland-Olson, Sheldon. 1988. Structural Discretion, Racial Bias, and the Death Penalty: The First Decade after *Furman* in Texas. *Social Science Quarterly* 69: 853–73.

El Paso (Texas) Independent School District, Office for Research and Evaluation. 1989. *Bilingual Education Evaluation: The Fifth Year in a Longitudinal Study.*

Espin, Oliva. 1984. Cultural and Historical Influences on Sexuality in Hispanic/Latin Women: Implications for Psychotherapy. In *Pleasure and Danger: Exploring Female Sexuality*, edited by Carole Vance. Boston and London: Routledge and Kegan Paul.

Espiritu, Yen. 1992. *Asian American Panethnicity.* Philadelphia: Temple University Press.

———. 1995. *Filipino American Lives.* Philadelphia: Temple University Press.

———. 1997. *Asian American Men and Women: Labor, Laws, and Love.* Thousand Oaks, Calif.: Sage Publications.

Essed, Philomena. 1991. *Understanding Everyday Racism.* Newbury Park, Calif.: Sage Publications.

Farley, John. 1995. *Majority-Minority Relations*, 3rd Ed. Englewood Cliffs, N.J.: Prentice-Hall.

Farley, Reynolds. 1984. *Blacks and Whites: Narrowing the Gap?* Cambridge: Harvard University Press.

Farley, Reynolds et al. 1978. Chocolate City, Vanilla Suburbs: Will the Trend toward Racially Separate Communities Continue? *Social Science Research* 7: 319–44.

Farley, Reynolds, Suzanne Bianchi, and Diane Colasanto. 1979. Barriers to the Racial Integration of Neighborhoods: The Detroit Case. *Annals of the American Academy of Political and Social Science* 441: 97–113.

Farley, Reynolds, and William Frey. 1994. Changes in the Segregation of Whites from Blacks during the 1980s: Small Steps toward a More Integrated Society. *American Sociological Review* 59: 23–45.

Farrell, John A. 1992. Open Doors, Closing Minds. *Boston Globe*, 23 February.

Feagin, Joe. 1991. The Continuing Significance of Race: Antiblack Discrimination in Public Places. *American Sociological Review* 56(1): 101–16.

Feagin, Joe, and Clairece Feagin. 1993. *Racial and Ethnic Relations*, 4th Ed. Englewood Cliffs, N.J.: Prentice-Hall.

Fine, Michelle, Lois Weis, Linda Powell, and L. Mun Wong, eds. 1997. *Off White: Readings on Race, Power, and Society.* New York and London: Routledge.

Firebaugh, G., and K. Davis. 1988. Trends in Antiblack Prejudice, 1972–1984: Region and Cohort Effects. *American Journal of Sociology* 94(2): 251–72.

Fischer, C. 1976. *The Urban Experience.* New York: Harcourt Brace Jovanovich.

Fitzpatrick, Joseph. 1987. *Puerto Ricans: The Meaning of Migration to the Mainland*, 2nd Ed. Englewood Cliffs, N.J.: Prentice-Hall.

Fordham, S., and J. Ogbu. 1986. Black Students' School Success: Coping with the "Burden of Acting White." *The Urban Review* 18(3): 176–206.

Frankenberg, Ruth. 1993. *White Women, Race Matters.* Minneapolis: University of Minnesota Press.

————, ed. 1997. *Displacing Whiteness*. Durham and London: Duke University Press.

Franklin, John. 1967. *From Slavery to Freedom: A History of Negro Americans*, 3rd Ed. New York: Knopf.

Frazier, Franklin. 1957. *The Negro in the United States*. Revised edition. New York: Macmillan.

Frey, William, and Reynolds Farley. 1996. Latino, Asian, and Black Segregation in U.S. Metropolitan Areas: Are Multiethnic Metros Different? *Demography* 33(1): 35–50.

Frey, William, and Alden Spear. 1988. *Regional and Metropolitan Growth and Decline in the United States*. New York: Russell Sage Foundation.

Fuchs, Lawrence. 1990. *The American Kaleidoscope: Race, Ethnicity, and the Civic Culture*. Hanover, N.H. and London: Wesleyan University Press.

Fukurai, H., E. W. Butler, and R. Krooth. 1993. *Race and the Jury: Racial Disenfranchisement and the Search for Justice*. New York: Plenum.

Furnivall, J. S. 1948. *Colonial Policy and Practice*. London: Cambridge University Press.

Gallup, George, Jr. 1982. *Religion in America, 1977–78*. Englewood Cliffs, N.J.: Prentice-Hall.

Galster, George. 1990. Racial Discrimination in Housing Markets During the 1980s: A Review of the Audit Evidence. *Journal of Planning Education and Research* 9(3): 165–75.

Galster, George, and W. M. Keeney. 1988. Race, Residence, Discrimination, and Economic Opportunities: Modelling the Nexus of Urban Racial Phenomena. *Urban Affairs Quarterly* 24(1): 87–117.

Gans, Herbert. 1962. *The Urban Villagers*. New York: The Free Press of Glencoe.

————. 1979. Symbolic Ethnicity: The Future of Ethnic Groups and Culture in America. *Ethnic and Racial Studies* 2(2): 1–20.

Garbarino, Merwyn. 1976. *American Indian Heritage*. Boston: Little, Brown.

Gatlin, Rochelle. 1987. *American Women Since 1945*. Jackson: University Press of Mississippi.

Gaylord, Clarice, and Elizabeth Bell. 1995. Environmental Justice: A National Priority. In *Faces of Environmental Racism*, edited by Laura Westra and Peter Wenz. Lanham, Md.: Rowman & Littlefield.

Geen, Russell. 1972. *Aggression*. Morristown, N.J.: General Learning Press.

Geertz, Clifford. 1973. *The Interpretation of Culture*. New York: Basic Books.

Getlin, Josh. 1998. Leaving an Imprint on American Culture. *Los Angeles Times*, 23 April.

Gilbert, G. 1951. Stereotype Persistence and Change among College Students. *Journal of Abnormal and Social Psychology* 46: 245–54.

Glazer, Nathan. 1958. American Jews and the Attainment of Middle Class Rank. In *The Jews: Patterns of an American Group*, edited by M. Sklare. Glencoe, Ill.: Free Press.

————. 1971. Blacks and Ethnic Groups: The Difference, and the Political Difference It Makes. *Social Problems* 18: 447.

————. 1975. *Affirmative Discrimination: Ethnic Inequality and Public Policy*. New York: Basic Books.

Glazer, Nathan, and Daniel Moynihan. 1963. *Beyond the Melting Pot: The Negros, Puerto Ricans, Jews, Italians, and Irish of New York City*. Cambridge, Mass.: Massachusetts Institute of Technology Press.

————. 1975. Introduction to *Ethnicity: Theory and Experience*, edited by Nathan Glazer and Daniel Moynihan. Cambridge: Harvard University Press.

Glenn, E. Makano. 1980. Dialectics of Wage Work: Japanese American Women and Domestic Service, 1905–1940. *Feminist Studies* 6: 432–71.

Glenn, Norval. 1966. White Gains from Negro Subordination. *Social Problems* 14: 159–78.

Golant, Stephen, and Christian Jacobson. 1978. Factors Underlying the Decentralized Residential Locations of Chicago's Ethnic Population. *Ethnicity* 5: 379–97.

Goodman, Mary. 1964. *Race Awareness in Young Children*. New York: Collier Books.

Gordon, Leonard. 1973. The Fragmentization of Literary Stereotypes of Jews and Negroes among College Students. *Pacific Sociological Review* 16: 411–25.

————. 1986. College Student Stereotypes on Blacks and Jews on Two Campuses: Four Studies Spanning 50 Years. *Sociology and Social Research* 70: 200–201.

Gordon, Milton. 1961. Assimilation in American Life: Theory and Reality. *Daedalus, Journal of the American Academy of Arts and Sciences*: 90(2): 263–85.

————. 1964. *Assimilation in American Life*. New York: Oxford University Press.

Grant, David, Melvin Oliver, and Angela James. 1996. African Americans: Social and Economic Bifurcation. In *Ethnic Los Angeles*, edited by Roger Waldinger and Medhi Bozorgmehr. New York: Russell Sage Foundation.

Greeley, Andrew. 1974. An Alternative Perspective for Studying American Ethnicity. In *Ethnicity in the United States: A Preliminary Reconnaissance*, 290–315. New York: John Wiley & Sons.

Green, James. 1972. Attitudinal and Situational Determinants of Intended Behavior toward Blacks. *Journal of Personality of Social Psychology* 22: 13–17.

Greenberg, Stanley. 1980. *Race and State in Capitalist Development*. New Haven: Yale University Press.

Guest, Avery, and John Weed. 1976. Ethnic Residential Segregation: Patterns of Changes. *American Journal of Sociology* 81: 1088–111.

Guillermo, Emil. 1998. "The Price of Racism." *AsianWeek*, 19 February.

Gump, Janice. 1980. Reality and Myth: Employment and Sex–Role Ideology in Black Women. In *Psychology of Women: Direction in Research*, edited by Julia Sherman and Florence Denmark. New York: Psychological Dimensions.

Guthrie, R. D., and M. L. Guthrie. 1980. On Mammoth's Dusty Trail. In *Mammals of the Mammoth Steppe as Paleoenvironmental Indicators*, edited by D. M. Hopkins. New York: Academic Press.

Gutierrez, Ramon. 1994. Ethnic Studies: Its Evolution in American Colleges and Universities. In *Multiculturalism: A Critical Reader*, edited by David T. Goldberg, 157–67. Cambridge, Mass.: Blackwell.

Haaland, Gunnar. 1969. Economic Determinants in Ethnic Processes. In *Ethnic Groups and Boundaries*, edited by Fredrik Barth, 58–73. Boston: Little, Brown.

Hacker, Andrew. 1988. Black Crime, White Racism. *New York Review of Books* 35: 36–41.

Hakuta, Kenji. 1986. *Mirror of Language: The Debate on Bilingualism*. New York: Basic Books.

Hamilton, David, ed. 1981. *Cognitive Processes in Stereotyping and Intergroup Behavior*. New York: Academic Press.

Hamilton, David, and R. Gifford. 1976. Illusory Correlation in Interpersonal Perception: A Cognitive Basis of Stereotypic Judgements. *Journal of Experimental Social Psychology* 12: 392–407.

Handlin, Oscar. 1957. *Race and Nationality in American Life*. Garden City, N.Y.: Doubleday.

Handlin, Oscar, and Mary Handlin. 1950. Origins of the Southern Labor System. *William and Mary Quarterly* 7: 199–222.

Harjo, Suzan. 1991. We Have No Reason to Celebrate an Invasion. In *Rethinking Columbus*. Milwaukee, Wisc.: Rethinking Schools.

Hawley, Amos. 1944. Dispersion versus Segregation: Apropos of a Solution of Race Problem. *Papers of the Michigan Academy of Science Arts and Letters* 30: 667–74.

Healey, Joseph. 1995. *Race, Ethnicity, Gender, and Class: The Sociology of Group Conflict and Change*. Thousand Oaks, Calif.: Pine Forge Press.

Hechter, Michael. 1975. *Internal Colonialism*. Berkeley: University of California Press.

———. 1986. Rational Choice and the Study of Race and Ethnic Relations. In *Theories of Race and Ethnic Relations*, edited by John Rex and David Mason, 264–79. Cambridge, England: Cambridge University Press.

———. 1987. *Principles of Group Solidarity*. Berkeley: University of California Press.

Hechter, Michael, Debra Friedman, and M. Appelbaum. 1982. A Theory of Ethnic Collective Action. *International Migration Review* 16: 412–34.

Heitzman, William. 1975. *American Jewish Voting Behavior*. San Francisco: R & E Research Associates.

Hero, Rodney. 1992. *Latinos and the U.S. Political System*. Philadelphia, Penn.: Temple University Press.

Herrnstein, Richard, and Charles Murray. 1994. *The Bell Curve: Intelligence and Class Structure in American Life*. New York: The Free Press.

Hershey, Marjorie R. 1978. Racial Differences in Sex-Role Identities and Sex Stereotyping: Evidence against a Common Assumption. *Social Science Quarterly* 56: 583–96.

Hill, M. S., and M. Ponza. 1983. Poverty and Welfare Dependence across Generations. *Economic Outlook USA* (Summer): 61–64.

Hill, R. C., and C. Negrey. 1985. Deindustrialization and Racial Minorities in the Great Lakes Region, U.S.A. In *The Reshaping of America*, edited by D. S. Eitzen and M. Baca Zinn. Englewood Cliffs, N.J.: Prentice-Hall.

Hirshman, Charles. 1983. America's Melting Pot Reconsidered. In *Annual Review of Sociology*, edited by Ralph Turner and James Short, Jr. Palo Alto, Calif.: Annual Reviews, 397–423.

Horsman, Reginald. 1981. *Race and Manifest Destiny: The Origins of American Racial Anglo-Saxonism*. Cambridge: Harvard University Press.

Hu-DeHart, Evelyn. 1993. The History, Development, and Future of Ethnic Studies. *Phi Delta Kappan*, September.

———. 1995. The Undermining of Ethnic Studies. *Chronicle of Higher Education*, 20 October.

Huizinga, David, and Delbert Elliott. 1987. Juvenile Offenders: Prevalence, Offender Incidence, and Arrest Rates by Race. *Crime and Delinquency* 33: 206–23.

INS (Immigration and Naturalization Service). 1997. *1995 Statistical Yearbook of the Immigration and Naturalization Service*. Washington, D.C.: U.S. Government Printing Office.

Isaacs, Harold R. 1963. Blackness and Whiteness. *Encounter* August: 8–21.

———. 1975. *Idols of the Tribe: Group Identity and Political Change*. New York: Harper and Row.

Isaacs, Stephen. 1974. *Jews and American Politics*. Garden City, N.Y.: Doubleday.

Jackson, Jesse. 1995. Affirming Affirmative Action. A press release from Rev. Jesse Jackson to the National Press Club, 1 March.

Jackson, Kenneth. 1985. *Crabgrass Frontier: The Suburbanization of the United States*. New York: Oxford University Press.

Jaffe, Abram. 1992. *The First Immigrants from Asia: A Population History of the North American Indians*. New York: Plenum Press.

Jaynes, Gerald, and Robin Williams Jr., eds. 1989. *A Common Destiny: Blacks and American Society*. Washington, D.C.: National Academy Press.

Jennings, Jerry. 1993. *Voting and Registration in the Election of November 1992*. U.S. Bureau of the Census, Current Population Reports, 20–466. Washington, D.C.: Government Printing Office.

Johnson, Charles. 1943. *Patterns of Negro Segregation*. New York: Harper and Bros.

Joint Center for Political Studies. 1985. *Black Elected Officials: A National Roster, 1985*. Washington D.C.: Joint Center for Political Studies.

Jones, James. 1997. *Prejudice and Racism*. New York: The McGraw-Hill Companies.

Jones, Jaqueline. 1985. *Labor of Love, Labor of Sorrow: Black Women, Work, and the Family from Slavery to the Present*. New York: Basic Books.

Jordan, Winthrop. 1968. *White Over Black: American Attitudes toward the Negro, 1550–1812*. Baltimore, Md.: Penguin.

Joseph, Gloria. 1981. Black Mothers and Daughters: Their Roles and Functions in American Society. In *Common Differences*, edited by Gloria Joseph and Jill Lewis. New York: Doubleday Anchor.

Kadetsky, Elizabeth. 1994. Anti-Illegal Immigration Measures Are Racist. In *Race Relations: Opposing Viewpoints*, edited by Paul Winters, 186–91. San Diego, Calif.: Greenhaven Press.

Kain, J. F. 1968. Housing Segregation, Negro Employment, and Metropolitan Decentralization. *Quarterly Journal of Economics* 82: 175–97.

Kane, Joseph. 1993. *Facts about the Presidents*. New York: The H.W. Wilson Company.

Kang, K. Connie. 1996. Filipinos Happy with Life in U.S., But Lack United Voice. *Los Angeles Times*, 26 January.

———. 1997. Chinese in the Southland: A Changing Picture. *Los Angeles Times*, 29 June.

Kasarda, John. 1989. Urban Industrial Transition and the Underclass. *Annals of the American Academy of Political and Social Science* 501: 26–47.

Katz, D., and K. Braly. 1933. Racial Stereotypes of 100 College Students. *Journal of Abnormal and Social Psychology* 28: 280–90.

Katz, P. A., ed. 1976. *Toward the Elimination of Racism*. Elmsford, N.Y.: Pergamon.

Keil, Thomas, and Gennaro Vito. 1989. Race, Homicide Severity, and Application of the Death Penalty: A Consideration Barnett Scale. *Criminology* 27: 511–31.

Kennedy, John. 1958. *A Nation of Immigrants*. New York: Harper and Row.

Kennedy, Rudy. 1944. Single or Triple Melting Pot? Intermarriage Trends in New Haven, 1870–1940. *American Journal of Sociology* 49: 331–39.

King, Deborah. 1988. Multiple Jeopardy, Multiple Consciousness: The Context of a Black Feminist Ideology. *Signs: Journal of Women in Culture and Society* 14: 42–72.

Kitagawa, Daisuke. 1967. *Issei and Nisei: The Internment Years*. New York: Seabury.

Kivisto, Peter, ed. 1989. *The Ethnic Enigma: The Salience of Ethnicity for European-Origin Groups*. Philadelphia, Penn.: Balch Institute Press.

Knowles, L., and K. Prewitt, eds. 1969. *Institutional Racism in America*. Englewood Cliffs, N.J.: Prentice-Hall.

Kosmin, Barry et al. 1991. *Highlights of the CJF 1990 National Jewish Population Survey*. New York: Council of Jewish Federations.

Kovel, J. 1970. *White Racism: A Psychohistory.* New York: Pantheon.

Kushnick, Louis. 1981. The Political Economy of White Racism in the United States. In *Impacts of Racism on White Americans*, edited by Benjamin Bowser and Raymond Hunt. Beverly Hills, Calif.: Sage Publications.

———. 1996. The Political Economy of White Racism in the United States. In *Impacts of Racism on White Americans*, 2nd Ed., edited by Benjamin Bowser and Raymond Hunt. Thousand Oaks, Calif.: Sage Publications.

Kutner, B., C. Wilkins, and P. R. Yarrow. 1952. "Verbal Attitudes and Overt Behavior." *Journal of Abnormal and Social Psychology* 47: 649–52.

Kwong, Peter. 1996. *The New Chinatown.* New York: Hill and Wang.

La Belle, Thomas, and Christopher Ward. 1994. *Multiculturalism and Education.* Albany: State University of New York Press.

Ladner, Joyce. 1971. *Tomorrow's Tomorrow.* Garden City, N.Y.: Doubleday.

La Gumina, Salvatore. 1973. *Wop!* San Francisco: Straight Arrow.

Laosa, L. M. 1984. Social Policies toward Children of Diverse, Ethnic, Racial, and Language Groups in the United States. In *Child Development Research and Social Policy*, edited by H. W. Stevenson and A. E. Siegel. Chicago: University of Chicago Press.

LaPiere, Richard. 1934. Attitudes vs. Actions. *Social Forces* 13: 230–37.

Lelyveld, Joseph. 1985. *Move Your Shadow: South Africa, Black and White.* New York: Penguin.

Lemann, Nicholas. 1986. The Origins of the Underclass. *The Atlantic Monthly* (June and July): 31–55, 54–68.

Levin, Jack, and William Levin. 1982. *The Functions of Discrimination and Prejudice*, 2nd Ed. New York: Harper and Row Publishers.

Levin, Jack, and Jack McDevitt. 1993. *Hate Crimes: The Rising of Bigotry and Bloodshed.* New York: Plenum Press.

Levine, Lawrence. 1996. *The Opening of the American Mind.* Boston: Beacon Press.

Lewis, Oscar. 1959. *Five Families: Mexican Case Studies in the Culture of Poverty.* New York: Basic Book.

———. 1965. *La Vida: A Puerto Rican Family in the Culture of Poverty.* New York: Random House.

Lieberson, Stanley. 1980. *A Piece of Pie: Blacks and White Immigrants Since 1880.* Berkeley: University of California Press.

———. 1985. *Making It Count: The Improvement of Social Research and Theory.* Berkeley: University of California Press.

Lindholm, Kathryn. 1990. Evaluation of an Elementary School Bilingual Immersion Program. In *Bilingual Education: Issues and Strategies*, edited by Amado Padilla, Halford Fairchild, and Concepcion Valadez. Newbury Park, Calif.: Sage Publications.

Linn, Lawrence. 1965. Verbal Attitudes and Overt Behavior: A Study of Racial Discrimination. *Social Forces* 43: 353–64.

Lopez, David, and Yen Espiritu. 1990. Panethnicity in the United States: A Theoretical Framework. *Ethnic and Racial Studies* 13(2): 198–224.

Lopez, Haney. 1996. *White by Law: The Legal Construction of Race.* New York and London: New York University Press.

Lurie, Nancy. 1991. The American Indians: Historical Background. In *Majority and Minority: The Dynamics of Race and Ethnicity in American Life*, 5th Ed., edited by Norman Yetman, 132–45. Boston: Allyn and Bacon.

Macionis, John. 1995. *Sociology*, 5th Ed. Englewood Cliffs, N.J.: Prentice-Hall.

Madhubuti, S. L. 1977. *The Story of Kwanzaa*. Chicago: Third World.

Magner, D. 1991. Push for Diversity in Traditional Departments Raises Questions about the Future of Ethnic Studies. *Chronicle of Higher Education*, A11–A13, 1 May.

Maharaj, Davan. 1997a. E-Mail Threat Case Tests Free Speech Limit. *Los Angeles Times*, 8 July.

———. 1997b. UC Irvine Internet Hate Crime Case Ends in Mistrial. *Los Angeles Times*, 22 November.

———. 1998. Man Guilty in E-mail Hate Crime. *Los Angeles Times*, 11 February.

Malakoff, Marguerite, and Kenji Hakuta. 1991. History of Language Minority Education in the United States. In *Bilingual Education: Issues and Strategies*, edited by Amado Padilla, Halford Fairchild, and Concepcion Valadez. Newbury Park, Calif.: Sage Publications.

Malson, Micheline, Elisabeth Mudimbe-Boyi, Jean O'Barr, and Mary Wyer, eds. 1990. *Black Women in America: Social Science Perspectives*. Chicago: University of Chicago Press.

Mason, Patrick. 1996. Race and Egalitarian Democracy: The Distributional Consequences of Racial Conflict. In *Impacts of Racism on White Americans*, edited by B. P. Bowser and R. G. Hunt. Thousand Oaks, Calif.: Sage Publications.

Massey, Douglas S., and Nancy A. Denton. 1987. Trends in the Residential Segregation of Blacks, Hispanics, and Asians, 1970–1980. *American Sociological Review* 52: 802–25.

———. 1988. The Dimensions of Residential Segregation. *Social Forces* 67(2): 281–315.

———. 1993. *American Apartheid: Segregation and the Making of the Underclass.* Cambridge: Harvard University Press.

McCool, Daniel. 1982. Voting Patterns of American Indians in Arizona. *Social Science Journal* 19: 101–13.

McDonnell, Patrick. 1997. Illegal Immigrant Population in U.S. Now Tops 5 Million. *Los Angeles Times*, 8 February.

McIntosh, Peggy. 1995. White Privilege and Male Privilege: A Personal Account of Coming to See Correspondences through Work in Women's Studies. In *Race, Class, and Gender: An Anthology*, 2nd Ed., edited by Margaret Andersen and Patricia Collins. Belmont, Calif.: Wadsworth Publishing.

Meier, Kenneth, and Joseph Stewart. 1991. *The Politics of Hispanic Education.* Albany: State University of New York Press.

Meier, Matt, and Feliciano Rivera. 1972. *The Chicanos: A History of Mexican Americans.* New York: Hill and Wang.

Merton, Robert. 1949. Discrimination and the American Creed. In *Discrimination and National Welfare,* edited by Robert MacIver, 99–126. New York: Harper and Row.

Miles, Robert. 1989. *Racism.* New York and London: Routledge.

Milner, David. 1983. *Children and Race: Ten Years On.* Beverly Hills, Calif.: Sage Publications.

Min, Pyong Gap. 1996. *Caught in the Middle: Korean Communities in New York and Los Angeles.* Berkeley: University of California Press.

Mirande, Alfredo. 1987. *Gringo Justice.* Notre Dame, Ind.: University of Notre Dame Press.

Mirande, Alfredo, and Evangelina Enriquez. 1979. *La Chicana: The Mexican-American Women.* Chicago: University of Chicago Press.

Moore, Robert. 1976. *Racism in the English Language.* New York: Council on Interracial Books for Children.

Morgan, P. R., and J. M. McPartland. 1981. The Extent of Classroom Resegregation within Desegregated Schools. Report No. 314. Baltimore, Md.: Johns Hopkins University, Center for Social Organizations of Schools.

Morrison, Toni. 1992. *Playing in the Dark: Whiteness and Literary Imagination.* Cambridge: Harvard University Press.

———, ed. 1992. *Race-ing Justice, En-gendering Power: Essays on Anita Hill, Clarence Thomas, and the Construction of Social Reality.* New York: Pantheon.

Mullings, Leith. 1997. *On Our Own Terms: Race, Class, and Gender in the Lives of African American Women.* New York: Routledge.

Murray, Charles. 1984. *Losing Ground: American Social Policy, 1950–1980.* New York: Basic Books.

Myrdal, Gunnar. [1944] 1962. *An American Dilemma: The Negro Problem and Modern Democracy,* 20th Anniversary Edition. New York: Harper and Row.

Nagel, Joane. 1994. Constructing Ethnicity: Creating and Recreating Ethnic Identity and Culture. *Social Problems* 41(1): 152–68.

———. 1996. *American Indian Ethnic Renewal: Red Power and the Resurgence of Identity and Culture.* New York: Oxford University Press.

Nakanishi, Donald. 1991. The Next Swing Vote: Asian Pacific Americans and California Politics. In *Racial and Ethnic Politics in California,* edited by Bryan Jackson and Michael Preston. Berkeley, Calif.: Institute of Governmental Studies.

Nayar, Baldev Raj. 1966. *Minority Politics in the Punjab.* Princeton: Princeton University Press.

Neuhaus, Richard. 1993. Immigration and the Aliens among Us. *First Things*, August/September.

Noel, Donald. 1968. A Theory of the Origin of Ethnic Stratification. *Social Problems* 16(2): 157–72.

Novak, Michael. 1973. *The Rise of the Unmeltable Ethnics: Politics and Culture in the 1970s*. New York: Collier.

Ogbu, John. 1978. *Minority Education and Caste: The American System in Cross-Cultural Perspective*. New York: Academic Press.

Olzak, Susan. 1986. A Competition Model of Ethnic Collective Action in American Cities, 1877–1889. In *Competitive Ethnic Relations*, edited by Susan Olzak and Joane Nagel, 17–46. New York: Academic Press.

———. 1992. *The Dynamics of Ethnic Competition and Conflict*. Stanford, Calif.: Stanford University Press.

Omi, Michael, and Howard Winant. 1994. *Racial Formation in the United States*, 2nd Ed. New York and London: Routledge.

Orfield, Gary. 1980. School Segregation and Residential Segregation. In *School Desegregation*, edited by Walter Stephen and Joe Feagin, 227–47. New York: Plenum Press.

———. 1993. *The Growth of Segregation in American Schools: Changing Patterns of Separation and Poverty Since 1968*. Cambridge, Mass.: Harvard University Graduate School of Education.

———. 1996. Turning Back to Segregation. In *Dismantling Desegregation: The Quiet Reversal of Brown v. Board of Education*, edited by Gary Orfield, Susan Eaton, and the Harvard Project on School Desegregation, 1–22. New York: The New Press.

———. 1996. The Growth of Segregation. In *Dismantling Desegregation: The Quiet Reversal of Brown v. Board of Education*, edited by Gary Orfield, Susan Eaton, and the Harvard Project on School Desegregation, 53–71. New York: The New Press.

Owen, Carolyn, Howard Eisner, and Thomas McFaul. 1981. A Half-Century of Social Distance Research: National Replication of the Bogardus Studies. *Sociology and Social Research* 66: 80–97.

Park, Robert. 1937. The Race Relations Cycle in Hawaii. In *Race and Culture*, vol. 1(1950), edited by E. C. Hughes et. al., 188–95. Glencoe, Ill.: Free Press.

Park, Robert, and Ernest Burgess. 1921. *Introduction to the Science of Sociology*. Chicago: University of Chicago Press.

Passel, Jeffrey. 1994. *Immigrants and Taxes: A Reappraisal of Huddle's "The Cost of Immigrants."* Washington, D.C.: Urban Institute.

Patterson, Orlando. 1975. Context and Choice in Ethnic Allegiance. In *Ethnicity: Theory and Experience*, edited by Nathan Glazer and Daniel Moynihan, 305–49. Cambridge: Harvard University Press.

Pearce, D. M. 1979. Gatekeepers and Homeseekers: Institutional Patterns in Racial Steering. *Social Problems* 26(3): 325–42.

Perry, Robert, and Susan Pauly. 1988. Crossroads to the 21st Century: The Evolution of Ethnic Studies at Bowling Green State University. *Explorations in Ethnic Studies* 11(1): 13–22.

Phillips, Richard. 1995. Evanston Community and Environmental Racism: A Case Study in Social Philosophy. In *Faces of Environmental Racism*, edited by Laura Westra and Peter Wenz, 93–112. Lanham, Md.: Rowman & Littlefield.

Pinkow, L. C., H. J. Ehrlich, and R. D. Purvis. 1990. Group Tensions on American College Campuses, 1989. *Institute Working Papers, No. 1.* Baltimore, Md.: National Institute against Prejudice and Violence.

Pittigrew, Thomas F. 1971. *Racially Separate or Together?* New York: McGraw-Hill.

———. 1973. Racism and the Mental Health of White Americans: A Social Psychological View. In *Racism and Mental Health*, edited by C. V. Willie, B. M. Kramer, and B. S. Brown. Pittsburgh, Penn.: University of Pittsburgh Press.

———. 1981. The Mental Health Impact. In *Impacts of Racism on White Americans*, edited by B. P. Bowser and R. G. Hunt. Beverly Hills, Calif.: Sage Publications.

Pitts, J. P. 1982. The Afro-American Experience: Changing Modes of Integration and Race Consciousness. In *Minority Report*, 2nd Ed., edited by A. G. Dworkin and R. J. Dworkin, 141–67. New York: Holt, Rinehart Winston.

Portes, Alejandro, and Robert Bach. 1985. *Latin Journey: Cuban and Mexican Immigrants in the United States*. Berkeley: University of California Press.

Portes, Alejandro, and Robert Manning. 1986. The Immigrant Enclave: Theory and Empirical Examples. In *Comparative Ethnic Relations*, edited by Susan Olzak and Joane Nagel, 47–68. New York: Academic Press.

Portes, Alejandro, and Ruben G. Rumbaut. 1996. *Immigrant America: A Portrait*, 2nd Ed. Berkeley: University of California Press.

Portes, Alejandro, and A. Stepick. 1985. Unwelcome Immigrants: The Labor Market Experiences of 1980 (Mariel) Cuban and Haitian Refugees in South Florida. *American Sociological Review* 50(4): 493–514.

Puddington, Arch. 1995. What to Do about Affirmative Action. *Commentary*, June.

Ragin, Charles. 1987. *The Comparative Method: Moving Beyond Qualitative and Quantitative Strategies*. Berkeley: University of California Press.

Ragin, Charles, and Jeremy Hein. 1993. The Comparative Study of Ethnicity: Methodological and Conceptual Issues. In *Race and Ethnicity in Research Methods*, edited by John Stanfield II and Rutledge Dennis. Thousand Oaks, Calif.: Sage Publications.

Reynolds, M. D. 1973. *Economic Theory and Racial Wage Differentials*. Madison: University of Wisconsin, Institute of Research on Poverty.

Ritt, Leonard. 1979. Some Social and Political Views of American Indians. *Ethnicity* 6: 45–72.

Robertson, Ian. 1989. *Society: A Brief Introduction*. New York: Worth Publishers.

Rodriguez, Clara. 1975. A Cost-Benefit Analysis of Subjective Factors Affecting Assimilation: Puerto Ricans. *Ethnicity* 2: 66–80.

Roediger, David. 1991. *The Wages of Whiteness: Race and the Making of the American Working Class*. London: Verso.

———. 1994. *Towards the Abolition of Whiteness: Essays on Race, Politics, and Working Class History*. London: Verso.

Roof, W. C. 1972. Residential Segregation of Blacks and Racial Inequality in Southern Cities: Toward a Causal Model. *Social Problems* 19: 393–407.

Rose, Peter. 1990. *They and We: Racial and Ethnic Relations in the United States*, 4th Ed. New York: McGraw-Hill.

Rudolph, Lloyd, and Susanne Rudolph. 1967. *The Modernity of Tradition: Political Development in India*. Chicago: University of Chicago Press.

Saenger, G. 1965. *The Social Psychology of Prejudice*. New York: Harper and Row.

Saltman, Juliet. 1979. Housing Discrimination: Policy Research, Methods, and Results. *Annals of the American Academy of Political and Social Science* 441: 186–96.

Sanders, Jimy, and Victor Nee. 1987. Limits of Ethnic Solidarity in the Ethnic Economy. *American Sociological Review* 52: 745–73.

San Francisco Chronicle, 14 Sept. 1882, 19 May 1983, and 23 June 1983.

Sarna, Jonathan. 1978. From Immigrants to Ethnics: A New Theory of Ethnicization. *Ethnicity* 5: 370–78.

Sassen, Saskia. 1988. *The Mobility of Labor and Capital*. Cambridge, Mass.: Cambridge University Press.

Saxton, Alexander. 1990. *The Rise and Fall of the White Republic: Class Politics and Mass Culture in Nineteenth Century America*. London: Verso.

Schneider, William. 1985. The Jewish Vote in 1984. *Public Opinion* 7: 58.

Schnore, Leo. 1965. *The Urban Scare*. Glencoe, Ill.: Free Press.

Schuman, Howard, Charlotte Steeh, and Lawrence Bobo. 1985. *Racial Attitudes in America: Trends and Interpretations*. Cambridge: Harvard University Press.

Schwab, W. A. 1982. *Urban Sociology: A Human Ecological Perspective*. Reading, Mass.: Addison-Wesley.

See, Katherine, and William J. Wilson. 1988. Race and Ethnicity. In *Handbook of Sociology*, edited by Neil Smelser. Newbury Park, Calif.: Sage Publications.

Seifer, Nancy. 1973. *Absent from the Majority: Working Class Women in America*. New York: American Jewish Committee.

Sheth, Manju. 1995. Asian Indian Americans. In *Asian Americans: Contemporary Trends and Issues*, edited by Pyong Gap Min. Thousand Oaks, Calif.: Sage Publications.

Simms, Margaret, and Julianne Malveaux. 1986. *Slipping through the Cracks: The Status of Black Women*. New Brunswick, N.J.: Transaction Publishers.

Simpson, George, and J. Milton Yinger. 1965. *Racial and Cultural Minorities: An Analysis of Prejudice and Discrimination*, 3rd Ed. New York: Harper and Row.

————. 1985. *Racial and Cultural Minorities: An Analysis of Prejudice and Discrimination*, 5th Ed. New York: Plenum Press.

Smelser, Neil. 1976. *Comparative Methods in the Social Sciences*. Englewood Cliffs, N.J.: Prentice-Hall.

Smith, Abbot E. [1947] 1965. *Colonists in Bondage: White Servitude and Convict Labor in America, 1607–1776*. Massachusetts: Gloucester.

Smith, James, and Barry Edmonston, eds. 1997. *The New Americans: Economic, Demographic, and Fiscal Effects of Immigration*. Washington, D.C.: National Academy Press.

Smith, James, and Finis Welch. 1984. Affirmative Action and Labor Markets. *Journal of Labor Economics* 2: 269–99.

Smith, M. G. 1965. *The Pluralist Society in the British West Indies*. Berkeley: University of California Press.

Smith, Tom. 1991. *What Do Americans Think about Jews?* New York: The American Jewish Committee.

Snow, Catherine. 1990. Rationales for Native Language Instruction: Evidence from Research. In *Bilingual Education: Issues and Strategies*, edited by Amado Padilla, Halford Fairchild, and Concepcion Valadez. Newbury Park, Calif.: Sage Publications.

Sollars, Werner, ed. 1989. *The Invention of Ethnicity*. New York: Oxford University Press.

Sowell, Thomas. 1981. *Ethnic America*. New York: Basic Books.

————. 1984. Black Progress Can't Be Legislated. *Washington Post Outlook*, Section B, p. 4.

Spencer, Robert, Jesse Jennings et al., eds. 1977. *The Native Americans*, 2nd Ed. New York: Harper & Row.

Steeh, Charlotte, and Howard Schuman. 1992. Young White Adults: Did Racial Attitudes Change in the 1980s? *American Journal of Sociology* 98: 340–67.

Steele, Shelby. 1990. *The Content of Our Character: A New Vision of Race in America*. New York: St. Martin's Press.

Stein, Dan. 1992. Why America Needs a Moratorium on Immigration. *The Social Contact*, Fall.

Steinberg, Stephen. 1974. *The Academic Melting Pot*. New York: McGraw-Hill.

————. 1981. *The Ethnic Myth: Race, Ethnicity, and Class in America*. Boston: Beacon Press.

Stone, Philip, and Robert Weber. 1992. Content Analysis. In *Encyclopedia of Sociology*, vol. 2, edited by Edgar Borgatta and Marie Borgatta, 290–95. New York: Macmillan.

Strodtbeck, Fred. 1958. Family Interaction, Values, and Achievement. In *The Jews: Patterns of an American Group*, edited by M. Sklare, 147–64. New York: Free Press.

Strodtbeck, Fred, M. McDonald, and B. Rosen. 1957. Evaluation of Occupations:

A Reflection of Jewish and Italian Mobility Differences. *American Sociological Review* 22: 546–53.

Stubbs, Michael. 1987. *Discourse Analysis*. England: Basil Blackwell Publisher.

Szymanski, A. 1976. Racial Discrimination and White Gain. *American Sociological Review* 41: 403–14.

Taeuber, Karl, and Alma Taeuber. 1965. *Negroes in Cities*. Chicago: Aldine.

Taggart, T. 1974. Red-Lining. *Planning* 40(11): 14–16.

Takagi, D. Y. 1990. From Discrimination to Affirmative Action: Facts in the Asian American Admissions Controversy. *Social Problems* 37: 578–92.

Takaki, Ronald. 1993. *A Different Mirror*. Boston: Little, Brown and Company.

———. 1997. Reuniting America. Keynote speech delivered at the Silver Anniversary Conference of the National Association for Ethnic Studies, La Crosse, Wisconsin.

Tate, Katherine. 1993. *From Protest to Politics: The New Black Voters in American Elections*. Cambridge: Harvard University Press and Russell Sage Foundation.

Tienda, Marta. 1990. Race, Ethnicity, and the Portrait of Inequality: Approaching the 1990s. In *U.S. Race Relations in the 1980s and 1990s*, edited by G. E. Thomas, 137–59. New York: Hemisphere.

Tinker, George, and Loring Bush. 1991. Native American Unemployment: Statistical Games and Coverups. In *Racism and the Underclass: State Policy and Discrimination against Minorities*, edited by George Shepherd Jr. and David Penna. Westport, Conn.: Greenwood Press.

Tsukashima, Ronald. 1986. A Test of Competing Contact Hypotheses in the Study of Black Anti-Semitic Beliefs. *Contemporary Jewry* 7: 1–17.

Turner, C. G. II. 1983. Dental Evidence for the Peopling of the Americas. In *Early Man in the New World*, edited by R. Shutler. Beverly Hills, Calif.: Sage Publications.

———. 1987. Telltale Teeth. *Natural History* 1: 6–11.

Turner, Margery, Michael Fix, and Raymond Struyk. 1991. *Opportunities Denied, Opportunities Diminished in Hiring*. Washington, D.C.: The Urban Institute.

Urban Institute. 1991. *The Housing Discrimination Study: Synthesis*. Washington, D.C.: The Department of Housing and Urban Development.

U.S. Bureau of the Census. 1979. *Twenty Censuses: Population and Housing Questions, 1790–1980*. Washington, D.C.: U.S. Government Printing Office.

U.S. Commission on Civil Rights. 1961. *1961 Report, VI, Housing*. Washington, D.C.: U.S. Government Printing Office.

———. 1976. *Fulfilling the Letter and Spirit of the Law: Desegregation of the Nation's Schools*. Washington, D.C.: U.S. Government Printing Office.

———. 1986. *Recent Activities against Citizens and Residents of Asian Descent*. Washington, D.C.: U.S. Government Printing Office.

———. 1992. *Civil Rights Issues Facing Asian Americans in the 1990s*. Washington, D.C.: U.S. Government Printing Office.

U.S. Commission on Race and Housing. 1958. *Where Shall We Live?* Berkeley: University of California Press.

U.S. Department of Labor. 1965. *The Negro Family: The Case for National Action.* Washington, D.C.: U.S. Government Printing Office.

———. 1991. *Preliminary Report on Discrimination in the Workplace and the Existence of the "Glass Ceiling."* Washington, D.C.: U.S. Government Printing Office.

van den Berghe, Pierre. 1981. *The Ethnic Phenomenon.* New York: Elsevier.

van Dijk, Teun. 1993. Analyzing Racism through Discourse Analysis: Some Methodological Reflections. In *Race and Ethnicity in Research Methods,* edited by John Stanfield II and Rutledge Dennis. Thousand Oaks, Calif.: Sage Publications.

Vigil, Maurilio. 1987. *Hispanics in American Politics: The Search for Political Power.* Lanham, Md.: University Press of America.

Wagley, Charles. 1971. *An Introduction to Brazil,* Revised Ed. New York: Columbia University Press.

Waldinger, Roger. 1986–87. Changing Ladders and Musical Chairs: Ethnicity and Opportunity in Post-Industrial New York. *Politics and Society* 15(4): 369–401.

Walker, Samuel, Cassia Spohn, and Miriam DeLone. 1996. *The Color of Justice: Race, Ethnicity, and Crime in America.* Belmont, Calif.: Wadsworth Publishing Company.

Washburn, David. 1979. *Ethnic Studies: Bilingual/Bicultural Education and Multicultural Teacher Education in the United States.* Miami, Fla.: Inquiry International.

Washington Post. 1993. Race Plays a Decisive Role in Home Loans, Study Shows. 6 June.

Waters, Mary. 1990. *Ethnic Options: Choosing Identities in America.* Berkeley: University of California Press.

Weaver, R. 1948. *The Negro Ghetto.* New York: Harcourt, Brace.

Weber, Max. 1961. Ethnic Groups. In *Theories of Society,* edited by Talcott Parsons et al. Glencoe, Ill.: Free Press.

Wei, William. 1993. *The Asian American Movement.* Philadelphia, Penn.: Temple University Press.

Weinberg, Meyer. 1977. *A Chance to Learn: The History of Race and Education in the United States.* New York: Cambridge University Press.

Weiss, Kenneth. 1997. Plans Seek More UC Pupils from Poorer Schools. *Los Angeles Times,* 12 May.

Weiss, Robert. 1997. *We Want Jobs: A History of Affirmative Action.* New York and London: Garland Publishing.

Welch, Susan, and Lee Sigelman. 1992. A Gender Gap among Hispanics? A Comparison with Blacks and Anglos. *Western Political Quarterly* 36: 660–73.

Westra, Laura. 1995. The Faces of Environmental Racism: Titusville, Alabama, and FBI. In *Faces of Environmental Racism,* edited by Laura Westra and Peter Wenz, 113–34. Lanham, Md.: Rowman & Littlefield.

Wienk, Ronald, C. E. Reid, J. C. Simonson, and F. C. Eggers. 1979. *Measuring Racial Discrimination in American Housing Markets: The Housing Market Practices Survey.* Washington, D.C.: U.S. Department of Housing and Urban Development.

Wigley, Daniel, and Kristin Shrader-Frechette. 1995. Consent, Equity, and Environmental Justice: A Louisiana Case Study. In *Faces of Environmental Racism,* edited by Laura Westra and Peter Wenz, 135–59. Lanham, Md.: Rowman & Littlefield.

Wilhelm, Sidney. 1980. Can Marxism Explain America's Racism? *Social Problems* 28: 98–112.

Williams, Linda. 1987. Black Political Process in the 1980s: The Electoral Arena. In *The New Black Politics: The Search for Political Power,* 2nd Ed., edited by Michael Preston, Lenneal Henderson, and Paul Puryear. New York: Longman.

Williams, R. M. Jr. 1964. *Strangers Next Door.* Englewood Cliffs, N.J.: Prentice-Hall.

Willig, A. 1985. A Meta-analysis of Selected Studies on the Effectiveness of Bilingual Education. *Review of Educational Research* 55: 269–317.

Wilson, John. 1978. *Religion in American Society: The Effective Presence.* Englewood Cliffs, N.J.: Prentice-Hall.

Wilson, K., and A. Portes. 1980. Immigrant Enclaves: An Analysis of the Labor Market Experiences of Cubans in Miami. *American Journal of Sociology* 86(2): 295–319.

Wilson, Pete. 1994. Anti-Illegal Immigration Measures Are Not Racist. In *Race Relations: Opposing Viewpoints,* edited by Paul Winters, 192–96. San Diego, Calif.: Greenhaven Press.

Wilson, William J. 1981. The Black Community in the 1980s: Questions of Race, Class, and Public Policy. *Annals of the American Academy of Political and Social Science* 454.

———. 1987. *The Truly Disadvantaged: The Inner City, the Underclass, and Public Policy.* Chicago: University of Chicago Press.

Woo, Elaine. 1997. Boalt Hall Law School Kills Its Grade-Weighting Policy. *Los Angeles Times,* 27 November.

Wrobel, P. 1979. *Our Ways: Family, Parish, and Neighborhood in a Polish-American Community.* Notre Dame, Ind.: University of Notre Dame Press.

Yancey, William, Eugene Erikson, and Richard Juliani. 1976. Emergent Ethnicity: A Review and Reformulation. *American Sociological Review* 41(3): 391–403.

Yetman, Norman, ed. 1991. *Majority and Minority: The Dynamics of Race and Ethnicity in American Life,* 5th Ed. Boston: Allyn and Bacon.

Yinger, J. Milton. 1961. The Assimilation Thesis. *Daedalus* 90(2): 247–62.

Yinger, John. 1995. *Closed Doors, Opportunities Lost: The Continuing Costs of Housing Discrimination*. New York: Russell Sage Foundation.

Yip, Alethea. 1996. Making Babies: New Findings on Birthrates Confirm Ethnic Differences. *AsianWeek*, 8 November.

Zelder, R. E. 1970. Racial Segregation in Urban Housing Markets. *Journal of Regional Science* 10: 93–105.

Zhou, Min. 1992. *Chinatown*. Philadelphia, Penn.: Temple University Press.

INDEX

Adorno, Theodore, 122–124

Affirmative action: defined, 236; origins of, 237–238; pros and cons of, 239–241, 267; solutions to controversy of, 243–245, 267–268

African Americans: as an ethnic group, 11; citizenship rights of, 150; congressional representation of, 211–212; discrimination against, 108, 149–150, 152–154, 156–159, 177–178; in the criminal justice system, 158; party affiliation of, 203–204; political ideology of, 207; representation of, in the administration, 216; socioeconomic status of, 29, 96–97, 107, 113; stereotypes of, 117–118; voting behavior of, 209–210

Allport, Gordon, 116, 122, 144, 159

American Indian Studies Association, 6, 12

American Indians. *See* Native Americans

Anderson, Margaret, 220, 222–223

Anglo conformity. *See* assimilation

Aryans, 10

Asian Americans: citizenship rights of, 151; congressional representation of, 211–212; identity formation of, 51; determinants of identity formation of, 51; discrimination against, 109, 151–153, 156–159; party affiliation of, 204–205; panethnic identity of, 51, 54; political ideology of, 208; representation of, in the administration, 216; socioeconomic status of, 96–97, 99, 106; stereotypes of, 116; voting behavior of, 209–210

Asian Indians: citizenship rights of, 151; immigration of, 80; racial identity of, 10; reclassification of, 10, 54; socioeconomic status of, 99

Asiatic barred zone, 80

Assimilation: as a societal emphasis, 4; evidence on, 84; meaning of, 82; process of, 82–84; theory, 82–85, 94

Association for Asian American Studies, 6, 12

Association of Indians in America, 10

Banton, Michael, 47, 137

Barth, Frederick, 193

Bilingual education: effectiveness of, 262–263; meaning of, 258; origin of national policy on, 258–259; pros and cons of, 261–263; types of programs of, 260–261, 268

Bilingual Education Act of 1968, 259